What We Fear Most

What We Fear Most

Reflections on a life in forensic psychiatry

Dr Ben Cave

SEVEN DIALS

First published in Great Britain in 2022 by Seven Dials
an imprint of The Orion Publishing Group Ltd
Carmelite House, 50 Victoria Embankment
London EC4Y 0DZ

An Hachette UK Company

1 3 5 7 9 10 8 6 4 2

A CIP catalogue record for this book is
available from the British Library.

ISBN (Hardback) 978 1 8418 8554 4
ISBN (Export Trade Paperback) 978 1 8418 8555 1
ISBN (eBook) 978 1 8418 8557 5
ISBN (Audio) 978 1 8418 8558 2

Typeset by Born Group
Printed and bound in Great Britain by Clays Ltd, Elcograf S.p.A.

MIX
Paper from
responsible sources
FSC
www.fsc.org
FSC® C104740

www.orionbooks.co.uk

This is for my patients and the brilliant nurses, health care assistants and other professional colleagues I have had the good fortune to know, and from whom I have learnt so much

Deciding to be a doctor, part I

I was walking along a coastal path in Anglesey with my father. As we approached the RNLI station in Moelfre, he asked me what I wanted to do when I got older.

'Business?'

'No,' I said.

'The law?'

'Not really.'

'Accountancy?'

I almost laughed. 'No way.'

'Military?'

'Don't think so.'

'Medicine?'

'Yes.'

It just clicked – completely and irrevocably. In that moment I knew exactly what I wanted to do with my life.

'Orthopaedic surgery?' he asked hopefully. He liked woodwork.

I snorted. 'I'll be a psychiatrist.'

He paused for a moment and looked a little pained. 'Well, there's plenty of time to think about it . . .'

I was only fourteen, but I'd already thought about it as much as I needed to. The decision was made. Even if I didn't have a clue what psychiatry was all about.

The writing on the wall

The interview room was a small one, beside the prison health care centre. There was a table and two chairs, and not much else. Frank, the man charged with murder, told me how he had gone to his mother's home.

'She realised I was angry. I was pacing up and down all the time.'

'What did you say to her?'

'I asked why she was working for MI5.'

'Was she?'

'It was the only explanation I could come up with. She was trying to kill me.'

'How do you know she was trying to kill you?'

'She denied it, of course. But I knew she was lying. And then she asked me if I'd stopped taking the medication.'

'Had you?'

'Yes. It was slowing me down. I needed my mind clear to stop the thoughts coming in.'

'What do you mean?'

'I could hear what she was planning. It wasn't just her, loads of people were involved. There was a big conspiracy going on.'

Frank had been diagnosed with schizophrenia when he was in his early twenties. In all that time, and despite several admissions to acute psychiatry units, he'd never been violent to her or anyone else.

'What was different this time? It's not the first time you've had these thoughts . . .?'

He hesitated. 'I started to use cocaine.'

'When?'

'About a month before I hit her. I hit her, that's all. I didn't mean to kill her.'

He'd gone round to celebrate her sixtieth birthday.

'How many times did you hit her?'

The post-mortem showed multiple skull fractures. She made it to the hospital but died the next day from bleeding into the brain.

Frank looked down at the table and his fingers traced some of the graffiti carved into it. He looked a bit like me, thinner, but he was tall, and we had the same brown hair and eye colour. I glanced at the file on the desk. We were born two months apart.

'What did you say?' He looked up at me. 'I'm sorry, my concentration is all over the place.'

'How many times did you hit her?'

He shrugged. 'Don't know exactly. Three, maybe four times.'

'Why?'

'She could see what I was thinking. She had some . . . I don't know what it is. It's what MI5 use to monitor my thoughts.'

I noticed his hands shake a little and wondered if it was anxiety or a withdrawal state – he'd been in prison for less than a week. He must have noticed it himself because he clasped his hands together.

'It was so confusing. I thought that she was interrogating me, like she was in my head. I still hear her. I know she's dead, but I still hear her.'

'What does she say?'

'It doesn't make sense. She says she'll get me sent to prison.' He put his hands up, as if to remind us where we were, and then he put his head in his hands. 'I'm not a violent man.'

He was right and he was wrong. He had been violent on one occasion, and it had destroyed two lives, probably more.

Frank put his face on the table in front of me and beat his fists against the back of his head. He howled in anguish. A prison officer looked through the window to see what was going on and I nodded back to reassure him.

I sat quietly, watching Frank. It took several minutes for him to calm down. 'When did you start to use the cocaine?'

'I met this person in the pub. I went there every night. He said the cocaine might take away the voices. Can you give me something for the dreams, Doc? I wake up every night and I can't breathe. I just curl up into a ball and cry myself back to sleep.'

I had seen the newspaper headline.

Woman killed in frenzied attack.

His neighbour said he'd always been weird. I thought about the headline I would write.

Sad schizophrenic self-medicates, commits a serious offence and gets PTSD.

I realised it wasn't as snappy, but I wasn't there to sell papers. Maybe both were true. I told Frank that we'd finish the meeting the next day.

'Will the voices go, Doctor?' he asked as he stood up.

'I'll look at the medication. I'll write you up for some sedation at night.'

He nodded his thanks and went out into the corridor. I watched as he was let back into the six-bedded ward. I realised I'd been talking to him for almost two hours. I had lost all sense of time.

I was writing up some of my early observations about his mental state when one of the prison officers appeared at the open door. 'Knock, knock,' he said. Officer Chopin had a massive moustache and tiny bright, black eyes. Other

4

than that, I have no idea what he looked like – those two features seemed to take over his whole face and define him. 'You really need to see this.' Chop beckoned me to follow him. He seemed quite insistent.

We talked as we walked. 'I'm going to get a section 48 transfer for Frank. He needs to have a work-up in medium security.' I was referring him to Lakeview Medium Secure Unit, the secure psychiatry service at St Jude's Hospital.

Chop nodded. 'Sounds good. He's been responding to voices all through the night.'

As we passed one of the cells on the right of the corridor, Billy, a man with learning disability, had his nose pressed to the bars. 'Is Mummy coming to see me later?'

'Don't think so,' I replied, not breaking my stride. I had said the same thing ten times that morning. Billy's mother was still in hospital after he had fractured her skull a week earlier. He thought she had been taken over by an evil force.

'I had to get it out of her,' he called after me.

I stopped and turned back to him. 'You need to take your medication, Billy.' I realised that both men had attacked their mothers.

Chop stopped at the end of the corridor and unlocked the door. He stood there waiting for me like an estate agent taking a viewing.

Yes, it's compact. But with a bit of imagination and a lick of paint . . . and it's very convenient for work.

I walked past him, into the cell. 'It needs a good clean,' I said, half holding my breath. There was a low-wattage bulb in the ceiling, set behind some dirty Plexiglas, and it took a while for my eyes to accustom to the gloom.

It was about nine feet long and six feet wide, with a bed bolted down on one side. I knew what cells looked like. I also knew the person who had been in here. He had convictions for rape and the police intelligence report linked him to drugs importation and murder. He wasn't a nice man, and after I had interviewed him for about six hours, it was quite clear that psychopathy was only part of the problem – he was actually psychotic.

He thought he was on a divine mission and that a Masonic society was testing his faith. Neither of these facts alone would normally lead me to diagnosing psychosis. The clincher was watching him perch on his faeces-soiled mattress, his arms outstretched as if trying to propel himself into flight and reciting biblical verses he had learnt as a God-fearing youngster.

It had taken me a month to send him to a high security hospital and he had been transferred there an hour earlier.

'What is it, Chop?' I asked, a little irritated my ward round was being delayed.

He gestured to the walls as if it were self-evident. 'It's all around you, Doc.'

The walls were scuffed, and bits of plaster were missing. There was some graffiti, and a neat pattern around the wall, at about chest height.

'He was up all night doing it.'

I walked to the end of the cell, where a little light percolated in through the barred window.

Dr Ben Cave

I didn't really notice it at first, not consciously, it was so small, barely even the size of newspaper print. It was neat and regular, and when my eyes were only six inches from it, the penny dropped.

Dr Ben Cave Dr Ben Cave . . .

I counted eight rows, top to bottom.

Dr Ben Cave Dr Ben Cave Dr Ben Cave . . .

'That's my name,' I said, involuntarily. Chop was nodding slowly. My name drew me towards him and as I walked, my eyes were fixed to the wall.

Dr Ben Cave Dr Ben Cave Dr Ben Cave Dr Ben Cave . . .

It went on and on. I reached him and brushed him aside. I went past the door and turned the corner and got to the bed.

*Dr Ben Cave Dr Ben Cave Dr Ben Cave Dr Ben Cave Dr
Ben Cave . . .*

'Fuck,' I said, when I had done a complete circuit.

Chop winced as I sat down and I realised my mistake
immediately. 'Fuck,' I said again, but just sat there on the
filthy sheet. It seemed pointless getting up.

He had written my name, never changing and never
varying, in eight continuous loops.

'You OK, Doc?' Chop was a good man, and he could see
how affected I was. 'I just thought you should see it. Sorry.'

'Thanks,' I said weakly, wondering if I had a spare pair
of trousers in my car.

I walked around the cell again, hypnotised by my once
familiar name, now alien and weaponised against me.

I could see where he had started, but there was no end,
no denouement, no threat, no sting in the tail. He'd simply
stopped, leaving nothing on which to hang any emotion.

I've told the story to friends, some of them psychiatrists,
and mostly they assume that I was frightened. They're right,
in part, I was. But there was something else.

I went home that evening in tracksuit trousers and told
my wife, Jo, what had happened. 'I'm going to train in
forensic psychiatry when I finish my research,' I announced.

She didn't seem that surprised. 'We'll need an alarm for
the house.' She looked me up and down. 'Have you been
to the gym?'

When I have talked to people who've lost the ability to
set limits on their spending, people who've lost their houses
and their families because of their gambling habit, many of
them tell me that they got addicted when they had their
first big win. If I'm honest, reading my name around the
cell walls was my first big win. I had been blooded, but the
excitement far outweighed the fear. I was hooked.

★

What about Frank?

He went to Lakeview three weeks later. He was convicted of manslaughter on the grounds of diminished responsibility, and was being discharged when I started work there as a consultant several years later.

The man who was writing on the wall?

He's doing life now. I'll tell you more about him later. I'll tell you about the last twenty-five years working in prison and secure hospitals, diagnosing and treating people with mental disorders in the criminal justice system and working as an expert witness – in short, a career in forensic psychiatry, behind locked doors.

It's about my patients, and it's about me. It's about what we have taught each other and how it has changed me.

It's about all of us, and what we fear most.

Lakeview House,
twenty-five years later

My office isn't large, but it's where I spend most of my time when I'm not seeing patients on the ward, and it's where I find myself now, surrounded by a lifetime of notes.

The unit is where mentally disordered offenders are treated, people who used to be called 'the criminally insane'. It's surrounded by a 5.2-metre fence which help-fully reminds everyone what it does. If you're wondering what 5.2 metres looks like, it's almost a metre higher than a double-decker bus.

When it was built, there was a lot of opposition in the local community. I was having a haircut and a shave in the local barbershop at the time the planning application was going through. 'Disgusting, if you ask me,' said my barber. 'We don't need that sort here. It's a respectable neighbourhood.'

He foamed up my stubble. 'So, what's your line of work?'

I would have said something, but for the cut-throat razor at my neck.

In fact, the secure unit has always been there, smaller than it is now, but still doing the same job, and largely forgotten by the local residents.

My cubby hole is grey, a dull, dreary 'office' grey, with a desk down one side, a bookcase on the other and two large filing cabinets framing the window which overlooks the tennis court.

Accountants will know the colour I'm talking about. It's the same shade their clients go when they receive an unexpectedly large tax bill. Doctors in A & E know it from the ashen countenance of heart attack victims, when they've just been transported by ambulance from their accountant.

Even the vertical blinds obscuring the tennis court are grey – a slightly darker shade than the filing cabinets; 'cardiac grey', but still grey. I last used them six or seven years ago when one of the vertical blinds fell off. It now looks like a gap where a tooth should be and I have always promised myself that I would put it back up, but I never have. There's always been something more interesting to do.

The chair I use is like most secretaries' chairs. The back and the seat can be adjusted up, down, forwards and backwards and it's perched on five little wheels. Well, it was, but one of them kept turning the wrong way whenever I pushed myself from desk to filing cabinet, like a recalcitrant supermarket trolley, so I pulled it off.

I think I'm a bit like my chair. It still wobbles a bit, but it's more predictable now, and I know how to balance it properly. The chair isn't grey, it's maroon. I don't know why, but it's a little bit unsettling.

The view of the tennis court is not what you might imagine. It was last used twenty years ago, and has been in a state of genteel decline ever since. Some quiet evenings when I'm working late, I imagine I can hear the ghosts of earlier generations of players, the patient warming up with his therapist and exchanging gentle banter across the net . . .

So, Doctor, do you think my Oedipal complex will get better once my father dies? Nice return by the way.

It's an overflow car park now, rutted with potholes and puddles. And it's not a gentle summer evening fifty years ago, it's a cold morning, barely light, and tomorrow is my last day at Lakeview.

I hear Anthony's familiar footsteps outside my window and then I glimpse him through the gap-tooth blind, walking in with his junior doctor. I don't think I'd be here at St Jude's were it not for Anthony. He's been the best of colleagues and the best of friends, and it's only this that allows me to say he is larger than life, a rather theatrical character. He'd have been much better as an old-fashioned judge. 'The court were very impressed with my evidence,' I hear him say. 'It's not often you get a successful insanity defence. He's very paranoid. Let's increase the olanzapine to 20mg and try him on some clonazepam – 2mg tds should do it.'

My gaze returns to the rusty, decaying fence around the tennis court. It's in stark contrast to the close-mesh affair that seals the unit, reminding everyone that this place is different and special in some way – a place where doctors detain their patients and restrict their freedoms. Apart from controlling infectious disease, there is no other branch of medicine where patients are detained by their doctors. Besides providing a custodial function, the fence also sends the reassuring message to the public that they are protected from the people inside. If you didn't know better, you'd think it was a prison in a hospital.

On any given day, I have fifteen inpatients. Ten of them will have schizophrenia, two of them bipolar, and the remainder will have a mixed bag of learning disability, autistic spectrum conditions, brain injury, or small-print neurological conditions that even I have to look up.

Many will have a history of substance abuse – alcohol, cocaine, crack, amphetamines or heroin – and most a personality disorder of some sort. By and large, they're young, and they're all detained under the Mental Health Act (the MHA).

More footsteps, this time in the corridor. I know them all and I wait for Elaine's face to appear around the door. She's my ward manager and my favourite nurse in the whole world. She's five foot nothing, a matchstick body, cornrow braids, and in a dangerous situation there is no one I'd rather have at my side. I once saw her talk down a psychotic man armed with a knife. He was a professional boxer, sweating with anger and up for a fight, and she outclassed him in every round.

She peers at me. 'How are you doing, Ben?'

I try for a dismissive shrug. 'All good. You?'

She doesn't answer. She never does. 'Have you been to the ward yet?'

'No. I came in early to pack up the notes.'

'Last day then?'

'Tomorrow,' I correct her. 'I'll be saying my goodbyes tomorrow.'

She stands there for a moment, probably wondering what to say. She looks around my office taking in the half-packed boxes and her eyes land on my pin board. In the top left corner, next to some photographs, there's an old yellow envelope addressed to *Dr Ben Cave, Consultant Forensic Psychiatrist,* in faded blue ink. There are ten or more pinholes randomly arranged around my name, each one made when my office moved. It is the only thing that has travelled with me over the years – that and my growing collection of medico-legal reports and my own case notes and summaries.

'That's my handwriting . . .' Elaine, puzzled, points to the envelope.

'You wrote me a welcome note when I first started. It was the first letter I got as a new consultant.'

'And you kept it. How long ago was that?'

'Too long. Seventeen years or so.'

I don't tell her that it was one of the most passive-aggressive welcome notes in history.

'I just want you to know that your predecessor was the best psychiatrist I've ever worked with. I do hope you will live up to his reputation. I look forward to working with you, Elaine.'

Still, it was a welcome, and, more importantly, it had my new title on it. My nice, new, shiny title: *Consultant Forensic Psychiatrist.*

At St Jude's. I'd bloody made it.

My predecessor had been everybody's favourite, mine included. He was bright, generous with his time, pioneering, and then he had taken a patient off his depot medication and the patient had relapsed and then stabbed a person to death.

'Listen, the ward's pretty quiet,' Elaine says. 'I've sent some of my team to help with the new admission. He was kicking off last night. Why don't you get the ward doctor to do the round?' She looks at the piles of notes on the floor and on the desk. 'Looks like you need to sort your stuff.'

'Thanks.' I nod and point to her shoulder and arm. 'Is it getting better? I'm sorry, I forgot to ask.'

In the clinic-room on the ward, where patients are examined, the privacy curtains were tensioned with metal rods, each about 40cm long with a diameter of 3mm. They were hidden from view by the material wrapped around them. But the patient who assaulted Elaine had removed one. And that's what he'd used.

She takes her arm out of the sling and raises it. 'It hurts when I do this.'

She smiles, waiting for my punchline.

'Then don't do it.' I give her a weak grin. 'Seriously, are you OK?'

She nods as she walks off, but she doesn't answer. I close the door, sit down and unconsciously push the *Oxford Textbook of Psychiatry* under my chair in place of the missing wheel. It doesn't have a section on what happens when it all goes wrong. There is no chapter headed 'Homicide enquiries and how to retire gracefully'. After the inquiry found criticism of his actions, my predecessor had left work one day and got pancreatic cancer the next. Well, not exactly, but he was dead six months later.

Despite its shortcomings, the *Oxford Textbook of Psychiatry* is just the right thickness for my missing wheel. *Principles and Practice of Forensic Psychiatry* is a little large and my latest textbook on criminology is a little small. Freud's slimmer volumes are completely useless and Jones' *Mental Health Act Manual* is in constant use.

I spin myself on the chair and decide that if I end up facing the filing cabinets, I'll sort out my notes, and if I face any other way, I'll have a cup of tea. It's like Luke Rhinehart's *The Dice Man,* but without the unpleasantness. Anyway, I don't feel like making any decisions, not today. I end up facing away from the cabinets, and find myself looking at my desk again, and the yellow envelope above it. Next to it is a picture of me, aged ten, when I was leaving primary school. I am holding a clutch of sporting trophies. I take a look at myself, lean over and put the kettle on. Was that really the father of the man?

That's when I see an envelope being pushed under my door. It is yellow but it doesn't have any pinholes in it. It is addressed to *Dr Ben Cave, Medical Director.* My new title. I am leaving the NHS and going to manage a chain of psychiatry hospitals. I read the note inside.

I remember what I wrote to you all those years ago. You may be interested to know that I will send the same message to your successor as I did to you.

There is a postscript. She says she isn't thinking about retiring because of what has happened. But I know she is lying, and I am probably the only person who does.

I sit down and open iTunes on my phone. I scroll down past Schubert. Schubert isn't going to cut it, not today. I keep going until I get to Talking Heads. 'Once in a Lifetime' seems to fit the bill.

I smile, push the door closed, take a sip of tea, turn the volume up and put the next bundle of notes in front of me.

Tea and loud music. No decisions, not today. It feels like I am playing truant.

Today is for reflection. Tomorrow is for goodbyes.

The need to reflect

Working in psychiatry, I know that things can go wrong. I know I've made mistakes, but I also know that I have always had high standards. The obsessional part of me demands that I get it right and I berate myself if I don't. I want it to be perfect, though sadly, it never is.

In all the time I have worked in psychiatry, I've learnt that my particular stress comes from the mismatch between my ideal and the reality. Coming up short, not being able to tweak the medication just right, not being able to persuade an insightless patient to take it. I suspect others are the same, and it takes its toll.

Three of my colleagues have ended their lives due to mental illness. Many others have had their lives shaped and affected by their own experiences of illness, or the challenges of dealing with it, day after day. Divorce, depression and dependency are common in my profession. It's a stressful job and the demands are high.

General and forensic psychiatry, my specialisms, tend not to be gentle or contemplative endeavours. People are brought into hospital, often against their wishes, quite literally screaming and shouting. Patients hurt themselves, and sometimes they hurt others, including the staff looking after them. I'd go as far as saying that most of us get assaulted by a patient at some point in our careers. There isn't a couch in sight, unless it's for the nurse taking their well-earned break.

I see nursing and medical colleagues who 'burn out'. It's the point you reach when you know you've had enough. You lose interest and there's nothing left in the tank, a bit like the long-distance runner hitting the wall.

If I'm entirely honest, after so many years as a consultant forensic psychiatrist, I had recently been feeling the wall getting closer. I'd lost my sparkle. Some days I just didn't want to go into work. I spoke to one friend who listened dutifully and then told me that he had 426 days left before he could retire. Another suggested antidepressants. 'They helped me,' he confided.

But it isn't retirement or antidepressants I want. It is the sense of purpose and fulfilment that I have enjoyed for most of my career.

I want it back.

I have had time to reflect. And that is why, I think, that when it came to my most recent appraisal, the message given to me reached a receptive audience. It was a pivotal moment for me. The appraisal was the last one before my five-year revalidation.[1] I didn't know Claire, the appraiser, who is a psychiatrist and psychoanalyst.

Analysis, or psychoanalysis, is an increasingly marginalised branch of psychiatry as budgets are squeezed. It examines our unconscious drives; it examines why we do things and why we act in the way we do. In that sense, it is the ultimate form of reflective practice, and if there is anywhere you'd find a couch still being used in modern practice, it would be here.

'Where are your case reports and self-reflection?' Claire asked. She had been through the bundle I'd submitted before we met.

---

1 Every five years, doctors undergo a process of revalidation. This examines their yearly appraisals and ensures they are up to date and fit to practise.

'I've got the case reports here. I haven't really done much of the self-reflection,' I said. 'Let me show you my 360-degree appraisal.'

Every so often, we ask our colleagues what they think about us: people in charge of us, people whom we manage, our peers, our patients and anyone else important in our roles. It's a 360 appraisal because it records the opinion from those around us.

I'd scored very highly in almost all the domains. I was approachable, I was clear in my decisions, I was empathic, I was a good manager and my patients liked me and felt listened to. The only sour note was that I wasn't very good at taking criticism.

She smiled. 'They're very impressive scores.'

I felt a warm glow of satisfaction.

'You must work very hard to get these scores.'

I nodded eagerly. She was so right.

'Do you feel the need for others' approval?'

Yes. 'No, that's not it. I just thought you'd like to see it.'

'It's very revealing.'

'How so?'

'It must be a lot of work, to be so many things to so many people.'

I could feel myself flushing.

'You don't like criticism.'

'Does anyone?'

I sat there and thought about how she had turned the thing I was proud of into a criticism. I know it wasn't really, but it's how it felt at the time and she sat there being all 'psychoanalytic' about it.

I just sat there.

I listened to the clock ticking. I looked out of the window. I looked at my fingernails for a bit, and I thought about all the work that I needed to be doing.

And then I reflected.

'I think I need to be in control,' I said eventually. 'I don't like it when I'm not in control of the situation, when things aren't right. The feedback's about satisfying the needs in others, often contradictory needs; it's managing their anxiety. The ward needs to have rules, but the patient needs autonomy. The patient needs autonomy, but they also need to be contained.'

I tried to look for other examples of how I had managed complex situations, but I found my thoughts wandering. 'It's like the adult who becomes a child in a relationship and the child who becomes a father figure. That's all I do, I control things. I'm good at it. I don't know why, but I am.'

Claire looked at me. 'When we booked this meeting, you said that your mother was ill, possibly dying.'

I felt a lump in my throat. 'She is. I'm going to see her tomorrow.'

'What is she like?'

'She's got dementia now. For years, ever since I was young, I needed to support her emotionally. She was always anxious and often depressed.' I found myself unable to speak any more.

Let me reflect.

I am no more in control of things than anyone else. I realise that now. It was a comforting delusion I had created for myself. It is time for me to overcome my concerns about reflective practice and it is time to be open about what I do and what I think.

This is my antidepressant. I want to make up for lost time.

To protect anonymity, I have changed names, dates, chronologies and key details. If anyone recognises themselves, they must be mistaken. Some stories are conflated, male can morph to female, and old can become young.

There are some exceptions where cases are in the public domain and could not be anonymised without losing meaning, and I discuss a colleague's suicide, but only with permission from her husband.

I have worked in many prisons and more than twenty hospitals. The hospitals collectively become St Jude's, the prisons become HMP Campsmoor, and the high secure hospitals become Bramworth.

Any similarity to real people is coincidental. Other than that, it's all true. It all actually happened. Enjoy the moments of light, because much of it is very dark; very dark indeed.

Finding my vocation:
Glorious and terrible powers

I haven't always wanted to be a doctor. There was a time as a youngster when I looked up at the planes passing over-head, on their way to Ringway, now Manchester Airport, and yearned to be on them. I'd never been on a plane, so the only logical conclusion was to become a pilot. That's what I was going to be all through primary school, right up to the point I discovered I was colour-blind.

There was an older boy at school who had his hopes of joining the RAF dashed at the age of eighteen when he discovered he couldn't tell red from green. Knowing my career choice, I was marched off to the optician in the centre of Stockport. I think he was another Rotarian – my mother seemed to know him. He got out the Ishihara plates and put them in front of me. Professor Ishihara designed the test in 1917 in Tokyo. In essence, they're coloured blobs that show a number to those with colour vision but look like a Jackson Pollock dust sheet if you don't.

First, they warm you up with easy pictures but then it gets harder and harder. It was like doing my maths eleven plus again. It's very sneaky. Professor Ishihara gives you a plate that reads '74' to those with normal eyes, but to the colour-challenged like me, looks like a bunch of green dots against a forest of red – something like a blurry '21', and even then you're not sure. I imagine that a person able to discriminate their colours would find it quite preposterous that the person sitting next to them would not be able to read out the number 74, but that was the situation I was about to find myself in.

The start was easy. '14,' I said confidently.

My mother smiled and the optician turned to the next plate.

'68,' I said hesitantly, and looked up at my mother.

'Just read the number, Ben.'

Then the optician turned to the sneaky one and no doubt he and my mother were looking at '74', as clear as a neon sign on a dark night.

'Mmm, not sure, it's a bit like—'

'Ben, just read the number,' my mother said, quite insistently.

'I'm not sure. I think the first number is a two—'

'Ben, don't mess around.'

'Mum, I'm not.'

I looked at the plate again. '21,' I said, almost apologetically.

That's when I felt my mother clip the back of my head with her hand. 'Ben, don't be so stupid.' She apologised to the optician and picked up her handbag as if to leave.

'Mrs Cave,' said the optician, 'Ben is colour-blind. He can't see the numbers properly.'

My mother sat down, visibly shaken. 'Is that why he bought green trousers for school? He said he thought they were grey.'

The optician nodded, and I looked at him with new-found respect. He was wearing a white coat.

'I'm sorry, Ben,' said my mother. I think it was for hitting me, which she never did again, but part of it – probably about 20 per cent – was because we both knew I was not going to be a pilot.

★

Whilst the link might not be immediately apparent, my choice of career was also influenced by an early interest in golf, or more specifically, a golf-related injury the like of which I have never seen written up in the medical literature.

My brother and I grew up in a house that backed on to a school playing field and we decided it was big enough to be used as our own golf course. It was odd really because Dad didn't play golf – he'd grown up in relative poverty in Birmingham during World War II and seemed to have spent most of it in an Anderson shelter craving bananas. In fact, no one we knew played golf; it just wasn't part of our lives.

Lacking the necessary equipment, we went with our Christmas money to the local sports shop and bought a five-iron each and some Penfold balls. We practised endlessly and eventually could hit them a reasonable distance. Whilst big brother could mostly hit them straight, in my case, anyone within forty-five degrees of my intended target was putting themselves in mortal danger.

As summer arrived and our expertise grew, we competed against each other, still entirely on the field at the back of our house, pretending to be Jack Nicklaus or Tom Watson or some other golfing great. We were both entirely satisfied with our football and rugby pitches and I never hankered to go to a real golf course. Entire games, entire tournaments were played out with just two clubs and a flowerpot for a hole. We competed on level terms. We had no concept of handicaps and my brother made no allowance for my age, nor would I have wanted him to do so.

On this particular long-shadowed August evening, Tom Watson (my brother Phil) had won a closely contested shoot-out by birdying the rugby pitch, and although Jack Nicklaus had complained that Tom had kicked his ball forwards on the football field, this had been overruled by the referee (my brother Phil), because he was bigger than me.

I conceded defeat, was angry for a while and then we fell into a comfortable torpor, which, as we all know, can allow 'great' ideas to emerge.

'I wonder what's in the middle of a golf ball,' I said, idly, probably sounding a bit like Piglet to my brother's Pooh.

'I don't know,' said he, sitting up. 'Shall we find out?'

Suddenly, the day had a new intensity. It was filled with the excitement of investigation, the science of discovery and the thrill of a project. We went into the garage and scanned Dad's workbench, where he spent many of his evenings.

We started by attacking the ball with a large metal file, but this didn't prove very successful, and every time Phil tried to push the file across the ball's leathery skin, he simply shaved some of mine off the back of my knuckles.

Two decisions then combined to cause the subsequent injury. I know this now, because of my root cause analysis training, which I use to examine medical mishaps and try to work out how to stop them happening again. My brother, who went on to do a PhD in risk management would, no doubt, come to the same conclusion.

The first root cause was Phil putting the golf ball into the vice on the side of the workbench. The next was me looking up at Dad's tools, neatly arranged on the wall. My eyes fell on what I subsequently learnt was a rasp planer. It is a vicious looking implement, something like a cheese grater designed by a carpenter. Every home should have one.

I took the rasp planer, pushed away my brother's attempts to snatch it off me and attacked the ball with it.

It worked a treat, but after about three or four 'rasps', the ball began to move in the vice. We should have stopped at that point, but instead we took it out, examined the coiled rubber bands now exposed and constituting its mantle, and decided that our experiment was both interesting and incomplete.

We needed to reach the core and the fabled ball of latex that we suspected lurked within. We fed it back into the jaws of the vice and tightened it as hard as we could. We pulled and pushed the lever with all our might and then we got a hammer and bashed at the handle to make it even tighter. I can only imagine all those little rubber bands desperately trying to find a way out of the unbearable pressure on them, fighting the forced incursion against their neighbours. It was a recipe for disaster.

Then my brother relieved me of the rasp and carried on the job I'd started. I tried to get it off him, but he employed his superior strength to repel me. At first I was indignant, and then I got angry. I could feel it welling up inside me. It was a familiar feeling though I am not sure that back then I would have been able to give it a name.

I tried again to grab back the rasp, but I was swatted away like a fly, and so reduced to impotent rage, I stood behind him and stared malevolently at his back.

Every fibre of my body hated him.

The stage was set. The ball was in the vice held at pressures only known in a black hole, Phil's face was just inches above it and my hidden powers to cause destruction knew no bounds.

Even back then I was a rational little child. I wanted to have superhuman or telekinetic powers, and whilst I often pretended I did, deep down I knew it was just make-believe. But just for a second or two after it happened, such was my anger, I did wonder if I had made it so.

When I divorced many years later, the only message to my two daughters was that they were not responsible. I kept telling them, over and over again, 'It's not your fault,' until one of them took me aside and said, 'Dad, we get it.' It was a bit like that. I just needed someone to tell me that telekinetic powers were not necessary to make golf balls leave a vice at the speed of a bullet – that, they do all by themselves.

The first thing I heard was a fizzing noise, as if something had just depressurised very rapidly, and then, almost immediately, a soft thud like a sledgehammer being slammed into wet soil. There are times when you just know something bad has happened, and this was one of them. Phil seemed to freeze and then turn slowly away from the workbench and arc in slow motion to the floor. The golf ball, or what remained of the golf ball, then continued its upward trajectory like, well, like a golf ball hit by Jack Nicklaus getting his own back on Tom Watson, before hitting the tin roof with a resounding crack. Then, apart from our projectile bouncing back to the ground, nothing else seemed to happen for a while. The images were slow, so slow you could almost count the frames of existence.

But then, same as it always does, the frozen tableau thawed, reality moved on, and my brother continued his arc to the floor like a Messerschmitt crashing into a Kentish field.

Silence.

I had killed him.

He deserved it. I had glorious and terrible powers, powers that I had to learn how to use responsibly.

Then Phil started to scream. Not having heard him scream before, it took me a while to process this new sensory input, decide that he was still alive, conclude that I didn't have superhuman powers after all, and resolve that things had reached a point when it was necessary to go and get Christopher Robin – in this story, the role being played by my father.

I looked at Phil's bloody maroon face and took in the swelling, the asymmetry and the curious way he appeared to be looking both at me and the other side of the garage at the same time. It was all very disconcerting.

'Dad,' I shouted, then I found my voice. 'DAAAAD—'

Fortunately, I didn't need to run to get Dad. Hearing the 'gunshot' of ball hitting roof, and knowing his two boys were playing outside, he came running into the garage and there he found us, Phil sitting on the floor covered in blood, me pointing at him and saying, 'The golf ball hit him in the eye,' and a layer of dust dislodged from the roof falling like dirty snow and gently covering us both and turning us ashen grey.

There are many positive things I could say about my father, but this was his first masterclass in how to keep calm in times of crisis. He debriefed me quickly and efficiently whilst examining my brother's face and checking for other injuries. The first time I dealt with a major incident in A & E, I channelled the memory of Dad examining my brother.

He told me to get Mum, tell her what had happened and that we were driving to hospital. If he wondered how exactly a golf ball could almost remove my brother's eye in the confines of a garage, it was not discussed at this point.

It was discussed later, frequently in fact, and I still remember being confined to my bedroom for long periods in August that summer and frequently being invited to consider the folly of putting a golf ball in a vice. It's good advice. Do not try to dissect golf balls with a rasp planer in a vice. Or if you do, wear protective goggles.

The trip to A & E remains a blur, but I remember being allowed to watch the doctor scrutinise my brother's injury. 'We'll need the ophthalmic surgeon,' he pronounced at length. Dad just nodded, and Mum, well, I have to hand it to her, when she was really up against it, she held it together. But I knew she was desperately worried.

I can't imagine a child being allowed to watch a doctor's examination these days. Things have changed, and I wonder if it is for the better.

The first time I flew on a plane, I remember going into the cockpit with the pilot and being allowed to look around. When I was seventeen, I did a work placement in A & E in anticipation of trying to get into medical school. I was watching the registrar do a skin graft on the ulcerated leg of a homeless man. The registrar was a friend of my brother, in the army and no doubt familiar with battlefield techniques. He then instructed the house officer on how to use a dermatome to harvest some skin from the patient's thigh. He made a right hash of it, even I could see that, and I could hear the registrar say, 'For fuck's sake,' several times under his breath. The tool looked a lot like a small plane that my father used for fine work and he had taught me how to use it.

'I could do that,' I heard myself say.

The army doctor looked at me and gestured to the patient. 'Fine, then do it. Go and glove up.'

That's when I did my first surgery, aged seventeen, in a hospital in north Manchester. I did quite a good job too, certainly better than the house officer.

Watching my brother being examined was the first time I saw how medicine worked. I was shooed away eventually, but it was a real eye-opener.

Sometime later, I was with my mother and father when his bandages came off and the consultant ophthalmic surgeon came to talk to us. Mum and Dad were hanging on his every word.

'He's OK. He'll keep his vision. It's not as bad as we feared.'

I watched my parents process the information, look for any hidden message, examine his words for any doubt and then show their relief. The consultant was brilliant. The news he gave them was clear, unambiguous and instilled confidence. It was pitch perfect. He smiled with Mum and Dad, accepted their thanks on behalf of his team, and then walked off, his white coat trailing behind him like Superman's cape. The whole thing took less than a minute.

I wasn't going to be a pilot any more. I didn't realise it at the time, but I had just found my vocation.

★

Many years after my ill-fated experimentation with a golf ball, I found myself back on an ophthalmology ward and walking past the patients lying in bed, their faces bandaged after surgery, their relatives sitting next to them holding their hands.

One of the staff nurses greeted me. 'Thanks for coming,' she said.

I was there to see a young man called Sam. 'Will he keep his vision?' I asked. It sounded so familiar.

'They think so.' She led me to the end of the ward where he was waiting to see me with his parents. 'They operated yesterday. He's still bandaged up at the moment.'

'What's he like to nurse?'

'Seems distracted, like he's away with it.'

'His injuries, were they self-inflicted?'

She nodded emphatically and I followed her over to the nursing station and watched as she reached into the ward-round files. 'There's a photograph his father took. You need to see it.'

I found myself looking at a picture of a piece of wood like a small floorboard ripped up from the rafter with the nail still in place.

'That's what he used. He held the wood and used it to hit the nail into his eye. There were some wounds around the orbit, but one of them penetrated the eyeball itself. The police brought him in, well, they came with him in the ambulance. Then he tried to leave, and he started to quote the Bible at us. He went straight to surgery and we called you guys.'

I nodded. 'Good. Why was there police involvement?'

'Before he injured himself, he attacked his neighbours. He thought they were trying to kill him.'

The nurse opened the door to the relatives' room. 'I've got the psychiatrist to see you. This is Dr Cave.'

Sam's parents were sitting either side of him and Mrs Nelson had a girl on her lap. I guess she was about six.

'Is he going to go blind?' the girl asked the moment I sat down, and I saw her mother gently tap her leg in admonishment. I imagine she'd been told not to say anything and especially not to ask if her big brother was going to go blind.

'I don't know,' I answered. 'I'm here to find out how and why it happened. The surgeons will be able to answer your question.'

She nodded thoughtfully. She was an intelligent little girl. 'Is he mad?'

It was remarkable. It would take her parents weeks to ask that same question, and yet they had obviously been discussing it. Her mother didn't admonish her, she just leaned forward a fraction, and then I saw Mr Nelson look up at me too. They looked like my parents, hanging on every word of the consultant, but I had no words of comfort for them, not yet.

What's a psychiatrist?

Can we trust you?

Will Sam be safe?

Is our son mad?

Will you make him better?

What's to become of him?

Will he be prosecuted?

Even Sam turned to me momentarily but then his attention wandered, and I saw he was muttering under his breath.

Where did I put my cape?

I looked at the girl and felt three pairs of eyes boring into me. Is he mad? That was the question.

'It depends what you mean by mad,' I addressed the girl. 'When I was about your age, I tried to cut a golf ball in half. I wanted to know what was in the middle. But we squashed it so hard it squirted out of the vice and right into my brother's eye. My dad said we were mad, but it wasn't madness, it was just a silly thing to do.'

I looked to Sam's parents. 'The question is, why did he hurt himself, does he have an illness, and how can we help him?'

I turned back to the girl. 'We still need to find out why Sam hurt his eye.'

'Did your brother lose his eye?' she asked immediately.

'No, he was OK.'

She digested my answer, turned back to her mother and nestled her head against her.

'Would you like me to take her out?' asked Mrs Nelson, cradling her daughter.

'I don't mind. I'm happy if she rests here with you but remind her that she's not responsible for any of this. Children get the strangest ideas.'

I'd been watching Sam through this exchange. He was actively hallucinating. He was responding to his voices. He was so distracted by them that he was barely able to focus on what was going on around him. He was occasionally reaching out and plucking at something in front of him, so he might have visual hallucinations too. He had damaged his eye so severely he could be blinded, and he probably had some religious delusions.

Sam didn't want his parents to leave, so I spoke to him with them still by his side, his little sister now sleeping on her mother's bosom.

'How are you feeling, Sam?'

'I . . . I . . . I don't know. It's in me. The sin is in me. It's in my eye. I can see it, seething. I see things.' He broke off and made a fist and hit his head a few times. 'I can't think. It makes me do things. What have they done to my eye?'

Mrs Nelson was still but the tears flowed down her cheek. I tried to ask Sam some more questions but even getting that far seemed to have taxed him and he went back to his mutterings.

I turned to his parents. 'When was he last completely himself?'

They looked at each other, and Mr Nelson answered. 'About a year ago. When he turned eighteen, just after his A levels. I know he used some cannabis, but I wasn't worried. Then he got religious. I thought it was just a phase he was going through. I mean we believe in God, but eventually he just spent all day in his room going over the Bible. Then, a month ago, he just stopped looking after himself.'

'He wouldn't talk to us,' said Mrs Nelson.

'Has he had any unusual symptoms, like hearing voices or feeling paranoid.'

Again, they looked at each other, perhaps wondering if they should have done something sooner.

'I heard him talking in his bedroom,' said Mrs Nelson. 'He'd say he was on the phone, but I knew he wasn't. And sometimes he would come down at night and eat by himself. He wouldn't eat with us. He said the food tasted funny.' She put her hand to her mouth to stifle her emotion. 'He thought I was trying to poison him.'

'And has he been using any drugs since the cannabis you mentioned?'

'He's not been out. No one sees him. He thinks people come in and move his things around at night. We had the community psychiatry team out a couple of times, but he said he was OK. He said he didn't want to see them, and he was good at pretending to be well.'

'Listen,' I said, turning to my patient. 'Sam, I think you need to come on to my ward over in the psychiatry wing. I'm worried about you and I want to make sure you're safe.'

'Thank God,' I heard Mr Nelson sigh.

'I need to make sure he doesn't hurt himself again. I'm going to get a nurse from my ward to sit with him whilst he's recovering from the surgery.' Frankly I needed to be sure he didn't run amok again. Sam had a psychotic illness and I'd seen enough acute presentations to know that it was likely to be schizophrenia.

I knew I had to admit him and given the history, his risks and his inability to consent to admission, I knew that he needed to be detained under the Mental Health Act.

At some point, we'd find out if the police were going to pursue the matter, and he might face criminal charges – perhaps even grievous bodily harm. The courts would want to know if he was fit to stand trial and fit to plead, and if he was, they'd want to know if he was legally insane at the time of the offence, or if it fell short of that, whether he needed further treatment under section 37 of the Mental Health Act.

And more importantly, I knew that at some point there would be another discussion with Mr and Mrs Nelson, and they would ask me if Sam had schizophrenia, and I would look at them and say, 'Yes, Sam has schizophrenia.' Then they would nod grimly and tell me that it confirmed their suspicions, their worst fears, but they couldn't bring themselves to believe it until they heard it from me.

Your son has schizophrenia. Clear, unambiguous, bad news. That's what doctors do.

Your son has lost his hearing. Your son has cancer. Your son has leukaemia. Your son has a brain tumour. Your son has diabetes. Your son is dying.

What the consultant told my parents all those years ago was probably the only good thing he'd been able to say all day. He'd probably just come from telling another patient that they were going blind and there was nothing that could be done about it. It all takes its toll.

My meeting with Sam and his parents finished twenty minutes later, and I said I'd be back the next day. As I left, both his parents thanked me. I hadn't done anything really, but I suppose from their perspective, Sam was out of the burning building, and whilst not cause for celebration, it was at least grounds to give them hope.

If I gave them reassurance, it was three weeks later with Sam being given intramuscular antipsychotic drugs on a low secure ward at St Jude's. His bandages were off, and he had kept the vision in his eye. The nursing staff were still keeping a very close watch on him because of his ongoing psychotic symptoms. He was convinced that he needed to blind himself and occasionally he would try to poke his injured eye. It wasn't that he wanted to hurt himself, he felt it was his duty, even his responsibility. There was an altruism to his illness that demanded self-sacrifice for the sake of others – on occasions he likened himself to Jesus. Though he was far from well, he was able to talk about his symptoms more coherently. One day, he told me he was hearing a voice in his head. 'It's me, it's my voice,' he told me. 'But it seems to know what I'm thinking and I hear it out loud, like I'm hearing you.'

It's a clear description of something called a first rank symptom of schizophrenia and couldn't have been more 'textbook'. The Germans call it *gedankenlautwerden* and it's a type of hallucination, one of a group of symptoms that psychiatrist Kurt Schneider thought was characteristic of schizophrenia. He wrote about it in 1939 and it reached a receptive British audience in the 1950s. Now we know the symptoms can occur in other conditions, but it still influences one's clinical judgement.

Sam continued to refuse oral medication.

'There's nothing wrong with me,' he said, repeatedly, so that eventually I had to prescribe him a long-acting injection of an antipsychotic drug. He'd need this depot every month or so, possibly for the rest of his life. His parents visited him the same evening, just as I was leaving. They wanted to catch up on how he was doing, so I took them to the coffee shop and we sat on the benches outside. It was a warm, pleasant evening, a little like the time I sat with my brother and we decided to dissect the golf ball.

'Doctor, thanks for everything you've done for Sam. He sounds a lot better than he was.'

'It's a team effort.' In fact, not counting the team dealing with his eye, there were six nurses, twenty health care assistants, a psychologist, a psychology assistant, an occupational therapist, two other doctors and a social worker who had all played a part in his treatment.

'We were wondering if you could . . . well, you know . . . explain what's going on,' they said, almost sharing the question.

Even now, they found it almost impossible to ask.

'May I tell you what I think has happened?' I asked, and they both nodded.

'Sam has schizophrenia. He's still getting hallucinations and he still has some religious beliefs, which are part of his illness. I'm going to keep him in hospital until it's safe for him to leave. That'll mean keeping him on a section for now. I'm giving him medication by injection – I hope to see a big improvement over the next few weeks.'

I don't know how long we sat there. I saw an old man walk past us to one of the benches nearby, pushing his IV drip stand as he went. He sat down and took out a packet of cigarettes, lit one and inhaled deeply. He looked at me and I realised I was staring. I turned back to Mr Nelson.

'Was it the cannabis?' he asked.

'No,' I said, not entirely correctly, but it was true enough for now. It might have made it a bit more likely, but it wasn't the root cause – it would be like blaming the golf ball for my brother's injury.

'Was it something we did?' said Mrs Nelson. 'Was it something we didn't do?'

'No. It wasn't you. He's got a mental illness. It's just like when other parts of the body go wrong, but it's the brain. There are all sorts of theories why people get schizophrenia, but no one knows for sure. You wouldn't blame yourselves if he had developed diabetes.'

They shook their heads. 'Will he get better?'

'He'll improve. I'm optimistic he'll make a good recovery, but it's a long process. It's going to be medication and psychology. And when he is better, he'll need medication, probably for quite a while.'

'So there's no cure?'

'No. But in truth doctors don't cure conditions. We treat the illness, whether it's rheumatoid arthritis, or high blood pressure, or asthma, but we don't cure it – the patient still needs medication, often for the rest of their lives. Psychiatric conditions are no different. How's his sister by the way?'

I looked over to the man with his drip stand and noticed his sunken eyes and his prominent cheekbones. He was cachectic – his illness was eating him up.

'She's OK, thanks. She's getting a lot of time and support from us, and she did wonder if her brother's illness was her fault. Actually, she misses him at the moment. Thank you, Doctor. I think we knew what you were going to tell us.'

I nodded. 'People often do.'

Sam's parents walked off together, slowly, and I sat there listening to the sounds of the hospital. Some of the medical students were sitting out, telling each other about their day on the wards. I heard the low rumble of a plane on its way to Heathrow and I looked at the birds in the trees above me and remembered the endless summer evenings of childhood.

'I heard what you said to them,' said the man with the cheekbones, his drip stand advancing towards me.

'It was difficult news for them.'

'My son had schizophrenia.' He pulled out another cigarette and offered me one.

'I quit.'

'Too late for me.'

I looked at the man's thoracotomy scar. 'Cancer?'

He nodded. 'My own fault. Smoked these things since I was a boy on the docks. Should have listened to you lot.'

We fell into a comfortable silence. It was that sort of evening.

'What you said back there . . .' he said at length. 'You were wrong.'

I looked up and saw a twinkle in his eye. 'You said that people know what you're going to tell them. No one told me about my son and his illness. I blamed myself for it and I blamed him for it.'

'Did he recover?' I asked.

'For a while,' said the man wearily. 'But then he just seemed to give up. He's been in and out of hospital for years.' He rubbed his face. 'Nah,' he said, throwing down his cigarette and crushing it under his slipper. 'Gotta give 'em hope. What's life without hope?'

He left soon enough – a nurse from his ward came to find him and scold him. 'You know what I've said about smoking,' and then I was just left with the gentle sounds of evening.

*

I pick up Sam's discharge summary from my desk and put it in the box 'to keep'. It's a good case to discuss with students and junior doctors. Anyway, I was proud of how he did. He stayed in hospital for about four months. His symptoms resolved with medication and he engaged well with the psychologists. We discharged him to a community psychiatry team.

I learnt a couple of years later that he was taking accountancy examinations. He was never charged with an offence. I did a full report for his lawyers, and the CPS decided that it wasn't in the public interest to prosecute him. No further action, they said. Fortunately, the person who was injured also agreed. How would it help if he was punished?

He was ill, he was psychotic, but he wasn't bad.

Quality Street

I like visiting other people's homes. I always have. I like to see how they live, what furniture they surround themselves with and generally the sort of nest they create for themselves. Being a psychiatrist has meant that I have been into hundreds of my patients' homes, and it's better than being an estate agent, because you get to interview them too.

I was in my early teens when the family firm, an iron foundry, went under. After that, I don't think that my parents were very happy. They held it together, but they put our home up for sale. I think it was about saving money and moving to a smaller house. I still had four years left at school, and although I didn't understand it at the time, there were still fees to pay. Don't get the wrong idea. We only had three bedrooms to begin with – it wasn't a palace. And if I am being brutally honest, whilst I think my parents tried hard, it was a little neglected.

True, my father had put in a new kitchen, a perfectly good kitchen. In some places it could almost be described as 'fitted', but in others there were gaps and mysterious crevices between the units, that over time had become filled with kitchen grease, dog hair (a golden Labrador called Buffalo) and an annual deposit of Quality Street wrappers, which we devoured every Christmas.

The layers were like a geology field trip of the mind.

I was fourteen, with an obsessive–compulsive disorder, and an anxiety disorder. My mother was depressed, my father was out of work, and by this point, my brother, having got into university, was failing his exams there too. It's no exaggeration to say that we had lost pretty much everything, so it's hardly surprising that our place of residence wasn't going to be featured in *Homes & Gardens*.

I remember noticing a bulge on the ceiling of the upstairs landing. The Anaglypta wallpaper, which hung on every internal wall and ceiling, had started to sag. It was quite subtle to begin with, then grew steadily. I told Dad about it every week for a month, but he just ignored me, perhaps for the same reason people ignore their own lumps and bumps until it's too late.

Well, if it's not doing any harm . . .

Eventually, I'd had enough and decided to investigate the matter; it was time to do what all aspiring doctors must do – examine the growth.

It was by now about two feet across. I fetched a stepladder from the garage and tapped gingerly at its edge, to be rewarded by a slight ripple. It was how I imagined a breast might feel if I ever got to touch one, and at the age of fourteen, I was imagining this a lot.

If I were examining a patient now, I would press down gently with my palm to see if they winced or gasped in pain. But then, as most students do, I simply poked at it. Instead of seeing the patient wince, my finger went straight in, swallowed whole. And as I withdrew it, a gallon or so of cold, dirt-brown water erupted from the inverted Anaglypta volcano.

To my distress, it took me some years to learn my lesson. When I was examining a patient with explosive diarrhoea on Martha Ward at St Jude's, I should have remembered what can happen when you take your finger out and fail to move to one side.

That is all I am saying.

For the next month, a bucket caught the slow drip from the leaking pipe in the loft. Eventually, Dad went up there and fixed it. But the volcano, now extinct, became an enduring feature in our lives.

In fact, I don't think I really knew what a painter and decorator was until I visited a school friend's home a year later. I assumed that dads patched stuff up or replaced missing roof tiles or put in a new radiator, or sometimes didn't when they were feeling down.

My friend's home had a swimming pool. I had never seen such luxury in a house. They had two TVs and one of the bedrooms had a bathroom all to itself. On the way in I naturally assumed the man on a ladder painting the upstairs windows was my mate's father. I called up and introduced myself. 'Hi, nice to meet you. My name's Ben.'

He looked down and nodded without expression, and my friend pulled me through the front door. 'What are you doing?' he rasped, making it clear that I had embarrassed him.

We got changed and went for a swim and not wishing to make the same mistake again, I studiously ignored the rather fat middle-aged man lying by the side of the pool. He tried to make some conversation with me, but I had no idea who he was or what he was doing there, and I really didn't want to cause further embarrassment, so didn't say a word. This man wasn't 'doing' anything, nothing at all, and that made no sense to me.

On the way out I said goodbye and thanks to the man on the ladder. He had moved on to the next window by this point, and just looked at me again.

My friend gave a snort and was nowhere to be seen when I turned to wave goodbye. I looked at the house. The paint was all the same colour. It didn't just protect the wood, it looked nice too. The guttering was horizontal, and the downpipes were vertical. It looked solid and neat and there was no Anaglypta anywhere.

I got home and took a brush from under the sink and spent the rest of the day cleaning the kitchen and then I hoovered and wrapped some PTFE tape around a leaking joint on the radiator where the carpet was rotten. I think Mum was having a rest in bed upstairs and Dad was in the garage, over-engineering his next not-quite-finished project. We were going to a nearby village later on, to check out a house my parents had seen advertised. 'We don't think it's right for us,' they had said. 'But perhaps it's worth a look.'

Memories can be funny things. The trip to my friend's swimming pool had been floating around, homeless and unfiled, for close to twenty years when there it suddenly was, top of the pile one Christmas Day.

The social worker, Dawn, was behind me, and the GP nowhere to be seen. We'd waited for him outside the terraced house and watched a couple of boys ride past on their new bikes. The places on either side looked well tended, their front gardens neat and tidy. The one in the middle, where we were heading, had dirty windows and black bin bags lying by the front door, half eaten by foxes. A couple of roof tiles were missing.

'Her father left keys with the neighbours,' Dawn said.

I nodded. 'What's the story?'

She told me that Veronica was forty-two and had a history of schizophrenia. She'd stopped her medication and her family had become worried about her in mid-December. She was under the care of the community forensic psychiatry services because she had set fire to her hostel some years earlier. It was initially unclear whether it was intentional, which is what the professional evidence suggested, or as a result of a carelessly discarded cigarette, which she continued to assert, right through the trial at which she was convicted of arson. In fact, she continued to claim it was an accident right

40

through her hospitalisation, through her time in a specialist hostel, and then here, in the first home she'd ever had.

'So how come we're out on Christmas Day?' I asked rather tetchily.

Dawn looked at Veronica's file. 'Her parents came yesterday to deliver her presents, but she wouldn't answer the door. They went home and got their own set of keys. She was lying in bed not doing anything. She wasn't responding, and that's when they called her GP.'

'Can I have a look?'

Dawn passed me her medical records. If we admitted her, and it sounded like we were going to, this would be her fifth admission.

The Mental Health Act allows us to detain people if they have a mental disorder bad enough for them to need to be in hospital for the sake of their own health and safety, or for the protection of others.

There are always more people waiting for admission than there are beds, so the earlier we discharge a patient, the sooner one becomes available. In general, this suits psychiatric patients just fine, even if it's not in their best interests. They don't want to be there, partly because they don't think it's necessary, and partly because they know what the wards can be like. So most don't protest over the delay in admission, and very few protest about a premature discharge.

This is the only reason why the chronic underfunding of psychiatry is not front-page news every day of the week. Hardly anyone complains, and if they do, they often lack the capacity to influence opinion. It's not psychiatric conditions that make the headlines, it's children with leukaemia.

Veronica had schizophrenia, and it sounded like she ticked all the hospital care boxes. Her relatives had largely disowned her because mental illness was something of a curse within their cultural landscape. Even Veronica herself believed her problems were caused by demonic possession. There were plenty of notes detailing the attempts to get her to have her next dose of depot medication. One of the community nurses wrote, 'Spoke to Veronica for over an hour and she understood why I felt it so important that she continues with medication, but she has lost faith in pharmaceutical treatments and has decided to put her faith in the power of prayer.'

Dawn and I knocked on the well-kept door to the left of Veronica's home and two little girls ran to open the door, screaming, 'It's Father Christmas.'

I smiled at them. Mine, about the same ages, were with their mother at the local hospital, both dressed as little green elves and helping the 'real' Father Christmas deliver presents to the children on the paediatric wards, the children too ill to go home.

The bright-eyed girls looked up at us, lost interest, and shouted to their mother to come to the door.

'I'm pleased you're here,' she said, handing the keys to Dawn. 'She's not been out for days. I went in yesterday, and it's . . . well . . . I've been so worried all night.'

We let ourselves in and I called out, 'Veronica, it's the doctor and social worker.' The house remained silent. It was cold and smelt damp and dirty. I opened the door to what I took to be the bedroom and saw a neat pile of still-wrapped presents by the wall, no doubt left there by her relatives. I confess I felt a little angry.

She was lying on the bed, staring at the ceiling. 'Veronica,' I said, 'it's Dr Cave. I'm a psychiatrist, and I've got Dawn with me. She's a social worker.'

I walked across the bedroom to stand by her, only pausing to bend and pick up a discarded sweet wrapper. It was bright green and had Quality Street written on it in silver white. A Noisette Triangle, which in combination with a Toffee Penny was my absolute favourite. I played with it for a moment between my finger and thumb and then filed it away in my pocket.

Mum, are you OK? I wanted to say.

'Veronica,' I said again, 'are you OK?'

Her skin was dry, and she wasn't speaking. 'Are these presents from your family? They look lovely. Do you want to open one?'

She didn't respond and I looked at the cold cup of tea by her bed. The milk had risen to the top and formed a mottled skin that matched her own. The smell became stronger as I approached her, and I realised she was lying in her faeces.

I spent a few minutes trying to talk to her, but she didn't respond. I felt her pulse and it was rapid and shallow. I lifted her hand, told her she could relax her arm and then let it go. It stayed raised. I told her that I was going to look round her home.

Dawn and I swapped places and she tried to engage Veronica in conversation. I could hear her asking about which church she went to, but I didn't hear any reply. There was a mouldy piece of cheese in the fridge, half a can of Guinness, and nothing else. Her mail had been scooped up by her relatives and left on the hallway table. They all looked like bills and offers of interest-free credit. I looked at the dripping tap in the bathroom and fiddled with the sweet wrapper in my pocket. I had made up my mind and strode back into the bedroom. Veronica's arm was still raised and I eased it back down again. I'd never seen a case of catatonic schizophrenia before. She had something called waxy flexibility, which was why her arm had stayed upright. She was stuporose and mute.

'She needs to come in,' I said.

Dawn nodded and got out her mobile. 'I'll call an ambulance.'

There are all sorts of theories about how catatonia comes about, but in essence, Veronica's schizophrenia was affecting the motor centre of her brain – the part that controls her muscles and consequently her movement.

We got her into hospital and then gave her large doses of benzodiazepines (like Valium) and antipsychotic drugs.

I resisted her father's call to allow them to exorcise her on the ward. I was pretty firm with him. 'That would not be appropriate,' I said, thinking about the still-wrapped presents by her bed.

The treatment was remarkable and after two weeks she was walking around, conversing, and perhaps most importantly, drinking and using the bathroom again.

I gave her leave with her family a short while later, and they went to their church and she was exorcised. She didn't seem to mind, and it didn't seem to do her any harm. Her family were delighted. 'It's driven out the demons,' they said, and were looking forward to a belated Christmas celebration.

Veronica told me that she had been surprised to see her family on Christmas Eve and even more surprised to see the social worker and me on Christmas Day, because she thought she was dead.

I met her parents on the ward before they took her home and they asked me about the exorcism. 'Why did it not work before, but it does now?' They sounded so earnest.

Sometimes, memories can be unreliable things, malleable and yielding, and this was one of those moments. 'I think I remember reading some research,' I began, somewhat tentatively, 'which said that exorcism is more effective in her particular condition if it is combined with monthly injections.'

Veronica's father looked up and smiled slowly, and I think we both realised that here was a solution for our diametrically opposed opinions.

'So, the injections and exorcism together, that would be good for her?'

He was pushing me further than I wanted to go, but I wasn't sure I had a choice. I hesitated fractionally before answering. 'Yes. Definitely.'

I got home in time for our late lunch on Christmas Day. The girls, still in their elf costumes, showed me photographs of them on the ward and said that one of the children's parents had given them some sweets. They took out a large tub of Quality Street and I made a grab for the green triangle and the toffee coin, stuck them together and threw them in my mouth.

'Euww, you can't do that,' they said. 'You can't mix them.'

'It's a well-known fact that this is the best combination in the world,' I mumbled through stuck together toffee-teeth.

'Mum said that we were given them because Tommy was too ill to eat them.'

'Tommy?' I asked.

'Tommy. The boy on the ward. He's got leukaemia. His mum gave them to us. Where did you go this morning?'

I looked at their mother and she nodded.

'Well, I saw a person a bit like Tommy – a grown-up. She was too ill to eat or drink anything.'

'Did she have leukaemia?' asked Big Elf.

'No,' I said. 'She had schizophrenia.'

'Will she get better?'

'I hope so. I think so. Will Tommy get better?'

'I hope so.' Big Elf looked uneasy and looked up at her mum.

'I think so,' Jo said.

My eyes met hers. 'Happy Christmas,' I ventured. Things had been difficult between us for a year or more.

'Happy Christmas,' she said.

I threw her one of the purple ones.

Well, no one else liked them.

45

B stream:

Black is not a colour

'Ben, it's Mike,' says the voice on the phone.

I've just put another batch of notes from the grey filing cabinet on to my desk and my mind is elsewhere. 'Mike?'

'Your friend, Mike.'

'Ah, that one. How are you?'

'Sorry to call you at work, but I've got this new patient with manic depression and they're just on an antidepressant. Don't they need to be on a mood stabiliser too?'

'Yeah, the risk is that they might flip into mania. Best to have them on a mood stabilising antipsychotic, or a mood stabiliser. They might not actually need the antidepressant.'

'Thanks, Ben. Last day isn't it?'

'Tomorrow,' I said. 'I'm packing things up today, but I keep getting distracted by the notes. You know, all the cases I've done.'

'Well, enjoy it. Are you looking forward to finishing?'

'You know very well I'm not finishing – I'm just moving away from forensics – I'm going to be a bloody manager.'

Finishing, I thought. Mike and I started together. Anyway, I wasn't finishing, not really.

Mike and I had announced our decision to study medicine to our biology teacher, Mr Tomkins, when we were both about fifteen. It was the time we had to decide which A levels to study.

46

I had thrown myself into my studies and was reading anything I could find about psychiatry, which was very little, and psychology, which was a little bit more. This might be unfair, but I think that Mike had made his decision to be a doctor with considerably less conviction than me. He had reasoned himself into his decision, he had considered the matter carefully and he had even spoken to real doctors about the work they did, all of which was admirable, but in my opinion, quite inferior to my technique, which I charitably termed *a vocation*. In fact, I know now that my decision was due to a state of mind that I would describe as a firm belief, held with conviction that was not going to be altered by anything or anyone. It wasn't an obsession, it was more than an *idée fixe*; it was, as I now realise, delusional in nature.

By the time that I told Mr Tomkins about my vocation, I had spent over four years in the B stream of my school. I started in 1B when I was eleven (which is now Year 7), and I was by now in 5B and shaving at least twice a week.

There were three classes I could have been in at school, and although it was officially denied, pretty much everyone who had been in the junior school went into the A stream and everyone else was divided by the first-year exams into either the B stream, which might sound a little prejudicial by today's standards, or the X stream.

Really, the X stream.

That was what happened, and parents paid good money for it. If the A stream marked you out as a future professional, then being placed in the B stream predicted a career in local government or sewage disposal, and being placed in the X stream marked you out for a life of petty larceny or perhaps estate agency if you were of sufficient intelligence to attain basic literacy skills.

I had always maintained my dignity after being placed in the B stream, by reminding myself that I had turned up to school one day approaching my twelfth birthday and been told that the *'exams start today'*. I had entirely forgotten about them, not done my homework, and come twenty-sixth in a class of thirty. I know this because I found my early school reports in my mother's home when I was clearing it out with my brother. Funny what you find in shoeboxes at the back of wardrobes.

Whilst I don't entirely blame the school for their lack of faith in me, I do remember being called back after class one day.

'Richardson and Cave, I need to have a chat with you,' Mr Tomkins said, after imparting his wisdom about fungal life cycles, which whilst not even on the curriculum was, in fairness, taught better than it was at medical school.

Everyone looked round at us and wondered what we had done wrong. We wondered what we had done wrong. Mike and I looked at him as he sauntered down to us, at the end of the lesson, past Beatrice the hamster and past our wallchart examining the flora and fauna of a rock pool in Trearddur Bay. It must be serious if he was coming to us; he never came to this side of the lab – this was our domain.

'Look, lads . . .' He seemed ill at ease and I looked past him at Beatrice who was looking back at me and listening carefully through the bars. 'I know you say you want to be doctors, but . . . do you think you're really cut out for it?'

Mike and I looked at each other and then back at Mr Tomkins.

'There are some very good biology degrees you might be interested in.'

I am sure he meant well and was managing our expectations, but once we got out of earshot, one of us said, 'Fuck him,' and the other said, 'Fuck him,' too. I forget now who spoke first.

Then I heard Mike's voice again on the phone. 'So you are looking forward to finishing!'

'Mike,' I said, 'I'm not retiring. It feels like I've only just started.' And then I looked at the pile of notes still to go through, and the as yet unopened cabinet to the right of the window and realised I had come a long way since learning to examine lumps.

I don't think I've ever really analysed how I felt as I approached my A levels. My mother was more depressed than ever, my father was just about holding it together and had found a new job working for a friend, and my brother had just left university without a degree and joined the army.

The only certainty I had was my ambition and to be told that this exceeded my ability made me angry. It felt as if I was being discriminated against because of my scholastic record rather than being judged by my potential.

I don't mean to liken my experience of discrimination to the terrible injustices we see in other walks of life, but discrimination can happen just because your eyes are a particular colour. I had just read about it at school.

Martin Luther King was assassinated on 4 April 1968, in Memphis, Tennessee. The next day, almost 700 miles north in Riceville, Iowa, a schoolteacher called Jane Elliott discriminated against some of the children in her class, and she did so on the basis of their eye colour.

Without context, most people would be outraged by her actions, but Jane Elliott was deeply saddened by the death of Martin Luther King, appalled by racism and determined to teach her entirely white Christian pupils a lesson about discrimination they wouldn't forget. The first day she told her class that children with brown eyes were not as clever as the blue-eyed children, not as gifted and she stopped them from using the drinks fountain and told the brown-eyed children they could no longer play with their blue-eyed classmates.

She created a pattern of positive and negative reinforcement solely dependent on the children's eye colour and kept reinforcing the false stereotype. The blue-eyed children were the first to go to lunch and only they got second helpings.

'We'll spend a long time waiting for the brown-eyed people.'

By the afternoon, 'brown eyes' had become a term of abuse and everyone knew that it meant *stupid*. Fights broke out between children who had been best friends the day before.

'They always call us that,' complained a brown-eyed girl, and the boy said, 'Well, she does have brown eyes,' as if that meant something.

When she was interviewed later, Jane Elliott described how her marvellous, wonderful and cooperative third graders quickly became nasty, vicious and discriminatory.

The next day, with a veritable tour de force, she simply reversed the rules and the children accepted it, as readily as they accept all 'received wisdom'. As the rules changed, so did the children. The downtrodden flourished, the new taunt became 'blue eyes', and the favoured group worked faster and more accurately in their lessons.

When the children were interviewed years later, they spoke eloquently about their experience and recalled their sense of helplessness, demoralisation and humiliation caused by a physical characteristic over which they had no control.

I imagine that her school was not dissimilar to mine. There were no Black children and there were no Black teachers. When I went to medical school, there were no Black students in my year, there were no Black lecturers or professors. In fact, I don't remember being taught by a single Black doctor until my house jobs, and this was in South London in the 1980s.

And then suddenly I was walking on to my ward as a young psychiatry trainee and twelve of the sixteen patients were Black. Stephen Lawrence was still alive, institutional racism was yet to be acknowledged and if Black lives mattered, there didn't seem much evidence of it.

'You won't understand me,' said the first patient I saw, a thirty-year-old man called Leo. He had a striking appearance.

'You may be right,' I answered.

He looked at me suspiciously. 'What's the point? We never saw the last doctor on the ward. He just came and told us to stay on the same drugs.'

'Doesn't sound right,' I agreed. 'Why are you here?'

'A misunderstanding. There's nothing wrong with me.'

'Can you tell me why you were sectioned?' That much I knew about him.

'The police picked me up. I was just out. They notice me. They always stop me.'

'You must be six foot five. You stand out.'

Leo looked at me and laughed. 'You know that's not it. It's the colour of my skin.'

'I see a Black man.'

Leo nodded, as if I'd passed a test of some sort.

'When do you go out?' I asked.

'Night-time, mostly.'

'Have you been admitted before?'

'Three, four times. All on section when I'm high.'

'Drugs?'

'Mania,' he corrected me.

I noticed my own prejudice. 'When did you first get bipolar?'

'College. It was the stress of doing my college work. I was finding it hard to cope. I was bullied.'

It's difficult to think of a big man like Leo being a victim of bullying, but it happens more than we think. I've seen more than one 'big man' on the wards who is attacked by his smaller peer. It's all about being 'top dog'.

'Not only bullied,' he continued, 'but I never knew where I fitted in. You know, coming from a Black family, and me being like this.'

He pulled up the sleeves of his shirt to expose pale forearms. They had deep old scars.

'I used to do this because I couldn't cope – it was stupid really, but I pretended I got the scars from a fight. But I wasn't like that.'

'Did your family reject you?'

'There was a nice teacher who told me stuff, you know, about life. He took me under his wing. But then he left. Mum had alcohol problems and Dad, he wasn't there. See, I told you that you wouldn't understand me.'

'I had a teacher once who told me that I wasn't bright enough to be a doctor,' I said. 'I think it made me work harder, but I can see it might have destroyed my dream. What did you want to be?'

'I liked building things. Art, DT, that sort of thing.'

'Builder? Architect?'

'Nah, I wasn't academic. I did building work but I got laid off because I got ill – they didn't want me back, and to be honest, it wasn't good for me being out like that.'

'What happens when you get high?'

'I strip off. I run around. I talk a lot. I feel great. I'm energised. It's like being on speed.'

'When the police see you, are they checking your welfare?'

Leo winced. 'You could say that, but I hit a couple of them when I was first arrested. I was ill – public disorder – they haven't forgotten that.'

'Tell me about your albinism. How does that affect you?'

People with albinism lack an enzyme, tyrosinase, that the body needs to make melanin, the pigment that colours our skin, eyes and hair. Leo's skin was pale, his eyes were blue and his hair was an orange-blond.

'When I was growing up, people used to ask my mum if I was hers. Once or twice, when I was a bit older, some white kids asked what I was doing with, well, my mum.'

Leo censored the word they had clearly used about his mother. He pulled down the blind of the day room and came to sit down again. 'I never really knew what I was, but then I realised that I *had* to be Black, more Black than anyone else.'

'What does that mean?'

'I read about Black Consciousness, Black Power, Malcolm X, the Nation of Islam, Black Panthers.'

'Would you rather have a Black psychiatrist?'

'Do you know one?' said Leo, gently mocking. 'How did you get into psychiatry?'

I told him. I told him about my brother injuring his eye, and about Mr Tomkins taking Mike and me aside.

He laughed. 'That sort of thing happened to me all the time.'

'There was another teacher though,' I told him. 'It sounds trivial now, but he gave me a form prize before I went into sixth form. He helped me believe in myself again.'

'My teacher . . .' Leo hesitated. 'The one I mentioned, he gave me a certificate for Design Technology.'

'You seem better from the last manic state. How are you feeling now?'

He looked thoughtful. 'I'm 80 per cent. Will you tell me about lithium? It's what the consultant wants me on. I want you to tell me everything you know about it.'

'OK,' I said. 'How about a deal? I'll tell you about mood stabilisers and you tell me about race and your experiences. You have a unique perspective.'

I didn't need to wait. Leo gave me a one-hour master-class from slavery to Mandela and beyond. 'There is so much racism,' he concluded. 'It's everywhere. I got in a lift the other day at John Lewis and this mother dragged her little girl out. I knew it wasn't their floor — they got out at menswear.'

It was a week later when I went out for dinner with my friend Faisal. I told him about Leo's experiences.

'I get pulled over once a month,' Faisal said.

'What sort of car do you have?'

'BMW 7 series.'

'Serves you right,' I said. My Fiat was off the road.

Last week, two decades later, my Nigerian ward doctor, a wonderful, bright, kind woman, was sitting with her husband on a bench outside their village church.

'Go home,' said the nice-looking white couple walking past. The next day her son was followed by a car with tinted windows whilst he was out jogging – for four miles.

I think I've always underestimated the malignant power of racism. I knew the theory, but I confess I was reluctant to admit to being part of an institutionally racist society. Then, while studying criminology, I looked at the arrest statistics for young Black men, and then I worked in a prison, and then I worked on the general wards in London, and then I worked in forensic psychiatry services in London, and to be truthful, I have seen far more Black people in the process than I should have.

I don't mean that I have consciously diagnosed people wrongly, it's just that in some areas of psychiatry you don't need a statistician to tell you that there is a clear excess of patients from Black ethnic groups. We need to ask difficult questions about inequality of opportunity, about education and housing and policing. And then we need to work out why people become unwell.

The issue of whether you have blue eyes or brown eyes has never been so important.

I checked Leo's bloods and he started on lithium the following week. I saw him again in outpatients and he was in touch with his old teacher again and told me he was in a new relationship.

'She's nothing at all like me,' he said excitedly.

Black, bipolar, social activist. 'What do you mean?' I asked.

'She's only five foot two.'

I've not seen my teachers since I got my A level results. I went back home and walked down the drive. Dad was standing in front of the garage, Mum was by the back door, and they both looked worried.

'Well . . .?' Dad said. Mum had her hands over her mouth.

I could simply have told him that I'd got the grades, but I gave him the slip of paper.

I never saw him so still. 'You're going to be a doctor,' he said, finally.

It was then that he put out his arms. I didn't know what he was doing to begin with, then it dawned on me that he was inviting me to hug him. I moved forwards and he embraced me. It was the first time I had hugged my father, and it was that one, and the last one that I will always remember.

Getting into medical school and hugging Dad were the best things that had happened to me, except perhaps the thing that happened behind the biology labs soon after girls were admitted to my sixth form.

But what happens behind the biology labs, stays behind the biology labs.

Mum put her arm over my shoulder, and I could see she was crying but I didn't mind this time. She was happy.

I left home shortly after my A level results. Now I could start learning about psychiatry for real, not just from the vicissitudes of family life. It took me a while to realise that everyone had a messed-up family like mine. 'Normality', whatever that is, is a very rare thing indeed.

The only other person who might not realise their effect on me was one Peter D Thomas. He taught me English, which was, without doubt, my worst subject. Thank you, Mr Thomas, for your many timely behavioural nudges.

Medical school:
Lup-de-dooooh

I don't think I was a very good medical student.

I liked the theory well enough, but it didn't take me long to realise that there were people much brighter than me who would become leading professors and drive forward the science.

I liked the surgery in the post-operative period, when the management of the patient was more medical in nature, but I didn't really like the surgery itself. One of my first experiences was helping the surgical registrar open the abdomen of an elderly woman with peritonitis.[1] It was pretty clear what had caused it once we inspected the duodenum, the bowel immediately beyond the stomach. She had a large hole in the wall of her gut, which had once been an ulcer, and I watched a pea fall out of it, closely followed by a diced carrot.

In fact, we found most of the remains of her Sunday lunch floating around in her abdomen. We got out the suction machine, a bit like the thing the dental nurse uses when you're being given a filling, and hoovered out her insides.

She was only a little old lady, but my goodness, she really enjoyed her food.

---

1 Peritonitis is inflammation of the tissues lining the inside of the abdomen.

'Anyone feeling peckish?' the surgeon asked. 'Or have you eaten already?'

I think she was enjoying my discomfiture. I went outside, pulled down my mask, vomited, then scrubbed up and helped her close.

Quite a few of my friends liked nothing better than scrubbing up and spending the day in theatre, helping the surgeons, but I was quite happy to chat with the patients before and after.

I didn't like paediatrics and I positively hated obstetrics and gynaecology. Quite how I managed to deliver twelve healthy babies into this world during my attachment at St Jude's is beyond me.

What I did like was my stethoscope and, as a result, I found myself quite interested in chest medicine. It's nice clear physiology, there is a wonderful pump mechanism to play with, and best of all, it's entirely devoid of bowel, or, more specifically, the contents of the bowel. I had been cured of any interest in the abdominal region by my experience of explosive diarrhoea on Martha Ward, and the 'meat and two veg' where it shouldn't be. Admittedly, the bowel does occasionally make an unwanted foray into the chest cavity in the form of a hiatus hernia,[2] but mostly it is safe territory, pleasantly confined by ribs and diaphragm. And, as any good patient knows, the chest is examined with a stethoscope. That's what the GP does when we are children . . .

Deep breaths . . .

. . . so, we rather take it for granted. Actually, examining the chest with a stethoscope is a skill doctors have to learn. First you inspect it, watching the patient breathe, looking for the rate and the rhythm, any asymmetry or intercostal

---

2 A hiatus hernia is where part of the stomach goes through the diaphragm into the chest cavity.

recession.[3] Then you palpate — you feel the pulse, check the blood pressure, feel the carotid arteries in the neck and check that the trachea is where it should be, or displaced by a collapsed lung or a tension pneumothorax.[4]

It all takes a while to assimilate. I recall my first chest examination on an elderly man. I followed the consultant's advice assiduously — to observe his respiratory pattern from the end of the bed for a full minute. I probably overdid it a bit, because the patient eventually turned to the consultant and said, 'So is he going to fucking listen to my murmur, or what?'

The consultant didn't even meet his gaze. He just raised a finger in admonishment. 'Mr Higgins, you are a patient at St Jude's. St Jude's is a teaching hospital, and I am teaching. Please do not interrupt.'

I expect that this would now lead to a complaint from the patient about the paternalistic nature of medicine, emotional trauma and no doubt financial loss incurred by the needless extra minute I spent examining him. But back then, Mr Higgins looked suitably chastened and remained resolutely quiet for the duration of my examination.

How could we not love Dr Scott? He was enjoying teaching us, and what's more, he cared about it.

After thorough inspection, you are allowed to percuss the lungs. This is the bit where the doctor presses their hand against your chest and taps the back of their finger with their other hand. If the lung is healthy and full of air, you hear a pleasingly resonant note like tapping a small drum.

---

3 Intercostal recession is where the tissues between the ribs are sucked inwards when you inspire. It can be caused by a blocked upper airway.

4 In a tension pneumothorax, air is trapped in the chest cavity between the ribs and the lung. It can push the heart and lung to the other side, causing problems breathing and cardiovascular collapse.

If the lung is full of fluid, or solid with infection, it can sound like a dull thud. Finally, you are allowed to get out your stethoscope, and I was itching to do so.

By this point in my training, I had just about accustomed my ears to the 'lub-dup' of the two heart sounds, and had read up on valvular heart disease and what type of murmur it causes.

But I'd never actually heard them in real life. I knew some heart murmurs go *PSHHH* as the blood flows back into the top chamber, and I knew some go *lup-de-dooooh* as the knackered old mitral valve snaps to attention under external pressure. But it remained theoretical to me, till now.

There I was, listening to Mr Higgins' heart with my almost-new Littmann stethoscope, under the close scrutiny of my consultant, the Grand-Old Chest Physician.

'Cave, can you hear the opening snap?'

Grand-Old Chest Physician had seen it all. He exuded confidence and practised his art with poise and grace. I didn't want to disappoint him. Nobody wanted to disappoint him, even the patients. They probably got better for fear of doing so. I looked up at him and felt awful because all I'd heard was a wet, gloopy sort of noise, which was more likely to have originated in the patient's intestine than their heart.

'Well, can you hear it?' He raised his voice a little, as if talking to a foreign waiter.

I couldn't hear a damned thing. I decided, on the spur of the moment, to try to reach for a way of saying 'yes' that wasn't exactly a lie. So, with his question still ringing in my ears, I said, 'Definitely.' Quite why, I have no idea. I guess I felt 'definitely' conveyed conviction without actually saying anything at all.

There was a brief, wonderful moment when I thought I had got away with it. But then I looked up. His habitually bright though wrinkled face seemed to have drooped. He looked hurt, and, worse still, disappointed.

I felt awful.

'Cave, have I told you my second law?'

I shook my head, uncertain to this day what his first law was, and most certainly too frightened to ask.

'People who say *definitely* rarely are.'

I ran it through my mind a bit, trying to make sense of it, and then it kind of clicked. He was right, of course. If you are sure of something, you don't need to say you're definitely sure. A simple *yes* suffices.

I was rumbled.

Try it for yourself.

Spot the lie in response to the question that I have often asked my patients in the drug dependency clinic:

'Are you still using heroin?'

Generally, there are two possible responses. Either, 'No,' or, 'No, I've *definitely* stopped using heroin.'

You will have spotted that the second answer is the lie and can actually be translated as: 'Hurry up and write the bloody methadone prescription because otherwise I'll miss my dealer and I might actually have to take this green shit.'

Methadone, for those who have avoided it, is used to treat heroin dependency. It comes as a thick green liquid and every year is tragically ingested by a number of children who find it too enticing to leave alone in their parents' fridge.

Grand-Old Chest Physician took pity on me. He motioned me back to the patient and asked me to listen again. 'You need to anticipate what you are listening for,' he said, in a grand, old and infinitely wise sort of a way.

He got me to say lup-de-dooooh quietly, to rehearse it in my mind. 'What we hear is a projection of what we expect to hear.'

It was like listening to a Shaolin master. The man should have been a psychiatrist. He was right on every count. After you've taken a history from the patient and done a good examination, by the time you listen to his chest, you should know what you're going to hear.

The same is true in psychiatry. It's all about the history.

So, I listened again to Mr Higgins' heart and once again heard nothing. And then Grand-Old Chest Physician leaned forward and put his hand over my hand, cupping the stethoscope and pushing it gently but firmly against the patient's chest wall. And I listened, and I listened for what seemed like an eternity, and the sounds slowly resolved and clarified themselves.

'There it is!' I was ecstatic. The gloopy noises had receded and I could hear the unmistakable and rather wonderful sound of *lup-de-dooooh*. 'I can hear it,' I said, probably too loudly. I stood and removed my earpieces.

So much of the way that we understand our world is a projection from within us, and it turned out that listening to heart sounds with a stethoscope was no different from listening to my psychiatric patients.

And psychiatry was my next attachment at medical school.

Despite my brief flirtation with the stethoscope, I always knew deep down that I was going to be faithful to my first love. By this point in my life, my near delusional desire to be a doctor was matched only by my desire to be a psychiatrist, and a good one at that.

Unfortunately, it did not kick off that way. In fact, it was a pretty ropey start, and whatever false memories I have created for myself are immediately dispelled by the faded pages I now look at, sitting at my grey desk on my maroon chair.

I am in the habit of writing up case notes to act as an aide memoire, for revision or teaching purposes, and I am holding the notes from Mrs Campbell, the first psychiatry patient I had ever clerked in as a student – that's the process of interviewing them, examining them and initiating treatment.

The only choice now is whether to put it in the *keep* box or the *shred* pile. It's not a forensic case, even though it was the police who brought her in – I must have misfiled it, but it reminds me how even psychiatrists need to learn how to use their 'stethoscope'.

Mrs Campbell, a large Cockney woman of a certain age, had been brought into St Jude's A & E screaming and shouting. The on-call psychiatry senior house officer (SHO), a doctor who had survived his house jobs, told me to go and clerk her in. He sent me with one of the more experienced night nurses, a Ghanaian chap whom I was meeting for the first time.

'Look after him,' he called after us, but it was me who looked back and nodded. We went to A & E and followed the shouting.

'He's in the 'ouse next door. Never bleedin' been the same since I came south of the river. He's the one who needs arrestin.'

I introduced myself to her as did my nurse colleague, Moses.

'You're 'avin' a laugh, you're not old enough,' she said. She had a strong Cockney accent and being from 'up north', I was still getting used to it. 'Go get the real doctor. He'll send me 'ome.'

'Mrs Campbell, I need to find out why you're here and then the *real doctor* can come and see you.' It hurt to say that, *real doctor*, but she was probably right. I was a very young-looking twenty-one-year-old. I'd even grown a moustache to look older.

She kissed her teeth and tutted a bit, from which I inferred she was irritated with me. 'It is not me, Doc, it's me neighbour. He's buggin' me.'

Being bugged is a fairly non-specific symptom in psychiatry and by itself could mean anything, but it does make you wonder if the patient has a persecutory delusion. I needed to know more.

'Where do you live?' I asked.

'Bermondsey. '

'And the person you've got a problem with, he lives next door?'

'Bleedin' right he does.'

'How long has he been bugging you for?'

'He not buggin' me, he's bleedin' buggin' me.' She tutted a bit more.

I confess I was starting to get a bit irritated. 'Yes,' I said, raising my voice ever so slightly to match hers. 'I heard you. So, for how long has been he been doing *that thing that you just said*?'

'Weeks. Bleedin' weeks it's been.'

Soon enough I noticed that every time I mentioned her being bugged, she got angry with me. Simple, I thought. Respond to her evident distress and don't use the word.

I was good.

By the end, I had interviewed her almost entirely without using the word 'bugged'. *Quite an achievement,* I thought to myself.

In summary, what I learnt was that her male neighbour was bugging her. It had started some weeks earlier, occurred through the wall, although she wasn't entirely certain about this, and it occurred mostly at night and when she was asleep.

'I feel it in me, see,' she tried to elaborate, and just occasionally, I couldn't help but feel I was missing something.

'How do you know you're being bugged, if you're asleep,' I asked, trying to maintain my caring and empathic demeanour.

She seemed to be more confused than me by this point. 'Well, Doctor, I bleedin' feel it. It wakes me up.'

'But how can you *feel* you're being bugged?' I persisted.

She pointed over to Moses, who I noticed was wearing a small cross. She looked me in the eyes and articulated her words more clearly than previously.

'Doctor, if that bleedin' nurse there *buggered* you all night, you'd 'ave something to say about it.'

Then she seemed to make that tutting noise again, but this time it was to emphasise her point and draw a line under the conversation. It wasn't necessary. I was beetroot red and Moses was trying not to laugh at me.

I had been so intent on trying to get my history about a persecutory delusion, I had quite missed the salient feature of her presentation. She might have been deluded too, but it was due to her feeling that she was being buggered at night, which she falsely ascribed to her neighbour. She was in fact describing a type of somatic hallucination – a hallucination affecting the body. You can hallucinate in any of your senses; this one involved touch.

Feeling that you have been sexually interfered with when you haven't is not uncommon – it's enshrined in folklore. If the assailant is male, the demon is called an incubus, if it is female, it's a succubus.

Even I have been accused of being an incubus. I was treating a patient in Lakeview House, medium secure accommodation, who complained about me buggering him senseless most nights of the week.

Quite aside from the register showing that I was not on the unit at the time, he also asserted that the abuse was commissioned by the Queen and presided over by several MI5 officers, but I do remember a very odd meeting with my line manager the day after he first complained.

'Ben, I just want to check, you didn't come into work last night, did you?'

Fortunately for me, I had not come on to the ward, but unfortunately for the patient, my innocence proved that he was hallucinating, and ultimately confirmed his diagnosis of schizophrenia.

Over the years I have practised, it is worth mentioning that I have been accused of raping my patients, and conspiring with any number of secret organisations to subjugate and control them. Several have accused me of killing their relatives, and in one case, the patient said I had murdered him. He even phoned the police – I would love to have been a fly on the wall when the constable took the call.

So, Mr Smith, if I've got this right, you're dead, and your doctor killed you. Hmmm . . . this sounds like one for the sergeant.

It is, sadly, an occupational hazard and each one has been reported, considered and investigated. It could be worse. Dr Jan Falkowski, a colleague, was arrested and charged with rape before it was discovered that the complainant was a stalker who had made it all up, going as far as taking a used condom out of his rubbish bin and putting his semen on her knickers. She was sent to prison.

Meanwhile, Mrs Campbell now had a very different type of symptom. I explained my confusion, apologised and started again. She seemed to warm to me after that, and I even became a 'lovely young man' when we parted company.

I went into the medical records office and pulled out her notes. She'd had four previous admissions, and in each case she had said that one of her neighbours was sexually assaulting her. Her diagnosis was schizophrenia.

She was admitted, treated with antipsychotic medication and we sent her home about three weeks later, denying she had an illness but no longer concerned about her neighbour's nocturnal pursuits.

My first case. My first lesson.

Listen. People don't always say what they mean, but it's a good starting point.

Lup-de-dooooh.

Delusions:

Don't believe everything you think

'When did you cut your penis off?' I asked.

It occurred to me that this was an unusual conversation to have over a game of draughts, even for a medical student.

We had been talking for about an hour and seemed to be getting on well enough, perhaps because Graham was winning. He was a patient on the general psychiatry ward at St Jude's. I often stayed behind to see what the ward was like after the doctors went home.

It was more relaxed, the patients were more 'alive' – most are more owl than lark – and I had become a fixture, like the noticeboard displaying the next trip to the gym.

All of which was as I wanted it.

I ate with them, and when there was a spare bed I slept there. After a while, despite my badge proclaiming my name and student status, I think I'd become an honorary patient.

'About two years ago,' Graham said in answer to my penis question. 'I was in a bad way back then. I can tell you about it if you want. I still see them read about it in my notes, and then they look at me, but they don't ask about it any more.'

I nodded and moved my piece, which he immediately took.

'I was about twenty when it first started. I'd just separated from my girlfriend, about a month before. Then I thought

66

I'd got VD. I don't know why, but I did. So I went to the local clinic, and they couldn't find anything wrong, but gave me some penicillin anyway and told me to come back if I was worried. Well, I was worried. That's why I went back the next day and told them that I was worried that they'd missed something. They were nice enough that time, but they couldn't find anything.'

'What were you worried about?'

'Syphilis,' Graham said. 'It wasn't so much that I was worried I had it, I just kind of knew I had it. It's hard to explain. It's what they say I'm deluded about now.'

'Did you have any symptoms?'

'No. I'd looked it all up. I think I might have had a little pain when I peed, but nothing serious.'

'What did you do?'

'I went back. And I kept going back. Eventually they told me that they weren't prepared to see me.'

'Did you go somewhere else?'

Graham seemed to hold himself still for a moment, then made another move.

'Go somewhere else?' he repeated, as if this had never occurred to him. 'No, I didn't.' He laughed it off but sounded uneasy. 'I suppose I should have. They might have found it.'

'The syphilis?'

'Yes. They never found anything. I was writing to them and complaining, but they were useless. Eventually I decided to disinfect myself.'

'Disinfect?'

'I got some bleach, I thought that would kill the infection. Crazy, really.'

'Yes,' I said, finding comfort in his insight.

'But I should have known better. I mean, the bleach was never going to get rid of it.'

'Oh. What did you do next?'

'That's when I decided to take matters into my own hands.'

67

He paused. 'Ben, are you OK?' I think I must have looked a little green. 'Do you want some tea?'

'No, thanks. I'm fine. What did you do, Graham?'

'Well, the clinic said that I couldn't go back there.'

'Why?'

'They said it was because I had threatened the consultant, but it was really because they weren't treating me properly. They were covering it up.'

'And then what?'

'You know the rest. I went into the garage and I found a chisel.'

'Yes.'

'And I put my penis on the workbench.'

'Mmm.'

'And I amputated the end of my penis. The part that had the infection.' He looked at me intently. 'Are you sure you don't want some tea?'

'Thanks. Maybe I will.' I examined the board as he went to the kitchen. Black and white. Rules and order. Clarity.

He came back and I put some sugar into my tea and stirred it carefully. 'Why are you here now?'

'My consultant. I went to see him in clinic last week, and he said that it'd be good to come in to sort out my medication.'

'Why?'

'Don't know. He said he was worried about me.'

'What did you tell him?'

'I told him I was worried that the syphilis had spread. It can go anywhere in the body, you know.' He pointed to his temple. 'Even the brain.'

'Ah. Do you have a mental illness?'

'No, not really. The consultant says I do. It started off as depression, but now it's a delusional disorder. Sort of like schizophrenia but without the voices. We're all a little bit mad, aren't we, Ben?'

We fell into silence for a while as we concentrated on the next game. It was a lot closer than the first, but he still won.

He then told me about the restraining order at the genito-urinary clinic that banned him from going anywhere near it.

'Why did they do that?' I asked.

'I went there one night when everyone had gone home. I put some matches through the letter box.'

'Why?'

He shrugged. 'Dunno really. Teach them a lesson.' He looked tired and I thanked him for talking to me. I went back to my on-call room and reflected on the conversation whilst reading his notes. It turns out his relationship had ended because of his refusal to have sex with his girlfriend. He didn't want to give her syphilis, he told a doctor during the first admission. Then he had become so preoccupied with this belief that he had threatened people, tried to commit arson, got a restraining order, dipped his penis in neat bleach, and then cut it off. He cut off his own penis. And now he thought he had neurosyphilis, for which there was not a shred of evidence.

His was a hypochondriacal delusion, and it made me realise that there is clear daylight between 'normal' hypo-chondriacs and people like Graham. His beliefs were not only real, they were consuming him, and had come close to consuming those around him.

Sometimes I meet people who don't think that mental illness really exists. 'It's just that we live in a mad world,' they tell me over starters. Then they tell me, usually now with my eyes glazing over, that any psychiatric diagnosis is subjective . . .

Gosh is that the time?

. . . and that the patient has no power in the relationship and that any form of coercive treatment is wrong.

Taxi!

I came to the opposite conclusion. It seemed pretty clear to me, as a young man, that dipping your dick in Domestos and then cutting it off was a pretty psychotic thing to do, never mind trying to burn down the GU clinic.

I formed my beliefs that night. Mental illness is not a social construct, and no, we're not all a little bit 'mad' – whatever that means – any more than Graham had syphilis or someone with normal blood sugar is a little bit diabetic. I decided that mental illness, more specifically psychosis, is a disease, like syphilis and like diabetes.

I went back to see Graham the next week. He'd gone. The nurses told me that he'd been transferred to the newly opened medium secure unit, where I would later work. The day after I saw him, he had threatened a nurse who questioned his beliefs. He'd said a medical student had agreed that he had syphilis and needed treatment for it.

That's delusion for you.

What we believe is not always true and it's probably as much as the average medical student needs to know.

Hallucinations:

Don't believe everything you hear

Besides delusions, the other 'big thing' that medical students need to get to grips with is hallucinations. Mostly, it's about hearing voices, but not invariably so. I trained with a psychiatrist who had musical hallucinations – 'La Marseillaise'.

Let me bring you up to speed. Before psychiatrist Emil Kraepelin came along at the end of the nineteenth century, the classification of mental disorders was a bit of a mess. His genius was to simplify the whole thing. He said there were two types of psychosis. First there was manic depressive illness (which includes what we now think of as depression) and the second was something called dementia praecox, what we now call schizophrenia. So, basically, he made the vital distinction between schizophrenia and the affective (or mood) disorders, which is how we still look at things.

That's it really; when I talk about psychosis, I am talking about delusions, hallucinations and thought disorder, and between them they can cause some really bizarre behaviour, not least taking a chisel to your penis.

If you know this much as a student you're doing well. If you've also heard of David Rosenhan's paper in *Science* from 1973, you'd be doing very well indeed. I mention this paper simply because it is still trotted out by well-meaning but ultimately vacuous anti-psychiatrists. I admit I was initially quite taken with the experiment, but having met Graham, I was starting to question its findings.

Rosenhan was examining how psychiatry services responded to normal behaviour on the wards, where everyone was expecting to see abnormal behaviour. In his experiment, Rosenhan got normal people admitted to places like St Jude's on the grounds they were hearing voices. He wanted to know how the psychiatrists dealt with them. They were fabricating their symptoms, making them up, faking it – nothing terrible, they were just saying they were hearing words like 'empty' or 'hollow' when there was no one around, in effect inviting the doctor interviewing them to conclude they were hallucinating.

Nowadays, the doctors in A & E would listen to your concerns and send you back to your GP, or your community mental health team (CMHT). Back then, in 1970s America, they were admitted into hospital. Once admitted, they never complained again about hearing voices. They behaved normally, they were friendly and cooperative – their normal good selves.

Whilst serious questions have recently been asked about the veracity of the research, guess what? It took an average of nineteen days for Rosenhan's 'patients' to be discharged.

The Oscar-winning film *One Flew Over the Cuckoo's Nest* was released in 1975, just two years after this research, so you might have expected these experimental volunteers to have been incarcerated for many years and eventually lobotomised. But they weren't.

It's also interesting to note that the next film to win the big five Academy Awards also perpetuated a negative stereotype of psychiatry. *The Silence of the Lambs* in 1991 not only gives us Hannibal Lecter, a flesh-eating, serial-killing forensic psychiatrist, but also Dr Frederick Chilton, the lecherous, jealous and vindictive shrink looking after Lecter, and in this situation, the face of institutional psychiatry. It's curious that in many ways, the portrayal of the evil patient is more sympathetic than the inadequate doctor caring for him.

And what's wrong with a nice Chianti?

So being discharged after only nineteen days with the experts saying you are in remission because you are no longer hallucinating isn't as bad as I would have predicted in 1973. In fact, I'd say it's pretty good.

As critics of the paper at the time pointed out, if you went into A & E and lied to the surgeon that you'd just vomited a pint of blood, you'd also be admitted. Most likely you'd be in the operating theatre quicker than you could count down from five, and they'd be scratching their heads when they couldn't find any evidence of a bleeding ulcer. You wouldn't criticise them for this – they're just being good doctors.

We are taught to believe what our patients tell us and not start from a position of disbelief. So, if a patient says they're hearing voices, it needs to be taken seriously. There is no X-ray, there is no test for mental illness, and we can't operate to sort out the problem. We do take it seriously, have a look at them, see if there are any other signs of mental illness, check they don't have an unhealthy interest in bleach or chisels and then discharge them. And, in my experience, that takes about nineteen days.

Having laid Rosenhan's research to rest, back to St Jude's and a patient called Rachel. She said she was hearing voices. It was real for her, terribly real, every bit as real as the accountant telling you to pay your tax bill, and often just as unpleasant.

She'd had them for years, and by the time I first met her, they had literally become part of her. Rachel had become unwell in her early twenties, which is a pretty typical age for schizophrenia to start, but even at that point, she told me, she had been experiencing symptoms for about two years. It's a common story, often referred to as the *prodrome,* before symptoms become more intrusive or florid.

She did reasonably well in her A levels and went to university. By this time, she was having more and more problems concentrating on her studies.

'It's like my mind wasn't working right; I had no focus. Actually, I'd stopped caring about what I was doing, and I'd stopped caring about me.'

She fell out of her chemistry degree and fell out with her family. 'Pull yourself together,' they told her, which is pretty typical too, but she couldn't. Her illness made her paranoid. She got suspicious of people around her and saw people looking at her on the streets.

'They think I'm no good.'

Gradually the paranoid thoughts followed her home and she thought that her mother was listening in on her private conversations.

'I could hear the clicks on the phone. It was obvious what she was doing, but then it got worse.'

The suspicions became a reality to her. The overvalued idea became a delusion.

'I just *knew* Mum was trying to kill me,' she said. 'People were following me in the street, and that's when I started to hear them talking about me.'

She looked wistful. 'It's never stopped after that.'

Whilst she was talking, she occasionally became distracted and looked over to her left. She saw me follow her gaze.

'It's them. They're talking about you now.'

She said it with such conviction, even I felt that her voices were talking about me.

What were they saying?

They had become more and more derogatory over the years, she told me. 'Useless bitch, you're pathetic,' they would say. They were commanding, 'Wear the blue skirt,' and sometimes supportive, 'You'll be OK in the exams.' Sometimes they spoke to each other about her and sometimes they commented on what she was doing. 'She's reading the book.'

74

It was as typical a description of schizophrenic hallucinations as you could hope to put in front of a medical student. She was like the perfect patient for a medical final examination.

Yes, she's got auditory hallucinations, derogatory in nature, command hallucinations and third person commentary. She's used cannabis to see if it would help, but it didn't. She's got secondary delusions about her mother and a reasonable degree of insight. Generally she is compliant with medication.

Sadly, most patients' illnesses have not read the textbooks, but hers had, right down to the slow dimming of her creative spark and the cannabis making her paranoid beliefs worse. There were two principal voices she experienced, with a host of minor characters. Most of the time, she knew they weren't real and even used the word 'hallucination' to describe them to me, but despite this, she had given them names, Tweedledum and Tweedledee, which she abbreviated to Dum and Dee.

Her life had become a solitary one, but she helped out in a charity shop when she was feeling up to it. She told me that there had been a bit of an improvement recently, and now in her early thirties, she had seen her mother socially for the first time in years. 'Dee said it was time.'

I looked up, momentarily confused. 'Ah, Dee, yes. What did Dum say?'

'He agreed,' she said. She looked past me and out of the window. I watched her smile and then frown and then turn back to me. She was *responding*.

'They don't like the idea, Doctor, but I think it's time to try some new medication.'

'I'm still a medical student, but I'll talk it through with the consultant next door. Why do you want it changed?'

Thus far she had been on a drug called Depixol for several years – an antipsychotic drug that in her case was injected every four weeks. She had been started on this 'depot' medication when she was twenty-five after her third admission, when it was clear she was non-compliant with tablets and every time she stopped them, her illness got worse.

When she was unwell, she went to her mother's home, verbally abused her, and on one occasion took a kitchen knife and tried to attack her with it.

'I tried to stab her in the abdomen,' she told me. 'I'd had enough of her trying to kill me.'

I looked at her in some surprise. She didn't look the dangerous type, whatever that looked like.

'I thought she had sabotaged the boiler and was trying to poison me with carbon monoxide as I slept – I'd heard on the news that a couple of kids had died from a faulty boiler. It made no sense, but I thought it was her.'

'Did you talk to your mother about the change in medication?'

'It was her idea,' she confirmed.

I checked it with the consultant and Rachel asked to bring in her mother the next week, so we could talk through the options.

They turned up as planned and I met Mrs Littlewood. Rachel sat quietly for most of the meeting and Mrs Littlewood told me what a loss it had been when she had left university and how, when she was better, she could return to her studies and get a degree and start working.

There was a faraway look in Rachel's eyes as she listened to her mother talk about her brother's success. He was working in the City and making a lot of money. Rachel hadn't been able to work for years, she wasn't as sharp as she had been in her teens and she didn't have the same drive or ambition. Her work in the charity shop amounted to two hours twice a week.

I sent her mother back to the waiting room and turned to Rachel. 'Do you really want to try the new medication?'

She nodded. 'I don't have much of a life, do I? I feel so empty all the time. Like I'm hollowed out.'

I got the consultant in at this point, and he switched her to a different class of drug and took the opportunity to increase the relative dose.

'There isn't really much evidence that one drug works better than another,' he told me. 'The choice is often determined by the side effects.'

Rachel came back a few weeks later for a quick chat to let me know how the new medication was suiting her and she said she felt more alert, more alive. She was right. She simply looked 'better'.

'Anything else?' I asked her.

'Still a bit paranoid about being poisoned, but no worse than before. I can live with it, but it's quite hard work.'

'What do you mean?'

'Well, it's quite hard work having to make all your own decisions.'

I treated her to one of my professional silences which, coupled with a half-tilted head and a friendly smile, I thought would encourage her to open up. These days, I realise, it's the sort of look that makes mothers tighten the grip on their child's hand.

'Are you OK, Doctor?'

'Yes, thanks. I'm fine. What do you mean about it being hard work making your own decisions?'

'Dee and Dum hardly talk to me now. It's like I've done something wrong.'

I tried to reframe the situation for her. 'It sounds like the new medication is causing the hallucinations to recede.'

'But they're my friends.' She looked out of the window unhappily. 'I can't hear them. I miss them.' She looked tearful as she got up to leave.

'I'll get you to see the consultant next week,' I called after her. 'It's my last week. I'm off to ophthalmology next.'

I had assumed that the voices, the hallucinations, were a bad thing. But in many ways, whilst she had sufficient insight to recognise they were part of an illness, they were real to her. And over the years, like bickering partners, she had grown accustomed to them, had used them as a sounding board and was attached to them. I think she even loved them, for better, for worse, in sickness and in health.

She did see me one more time. It was three years later, and I was training in psychiatry at that point. I was doing an outpatient clinic at St Jude's and I bumped into her in the waiting room.

'Hello, Doctor,' she began. 'Do you remember me?'

This greeting instils fear in me. It always has. I would probably not recognise my own brother if I saw him out of context. But then this woman spoke to me again. 'You don't recognise me, do you?'

My second worst sentence.

'What symptoms did you have?'

She laughed. 'Dum and Dee.'

And she slotted back into my mind.

'Rachel! How are you? Did the new medication work? How's your mother?'

'I'm really good, thanks. I got married and now I ignore my husband with the same skill I learnt to ignore my voices.'

She giggled. This wasn't the same person. She was bright and articulate. She was funny.

I grinned at her and then she told me her relationship with her mother was good. 'You saved my life,' she said as we parted.

I was lost for words.

So that's hallucinations.

Thought disorder next and then we do our finals.

Thought disorder:
Soliptic ambrigation

Just occasionally, some teaching comes along that has a profound impact on my understanding of medicine.

The first time, I was being taught how to use a stethoscope. The second was playing draughts with Graham. The third, bizarrely, was on a chest ward at St Jude's.

You never know when these things are going to strike.

The patients were old, they were smokers and almost everyone was bronchitic. They came in with lung infections that critically compromised their respiratory capacity and after we put out our own cigarettes and pulled ourselves away from *Blockbusters* in the mess, we would examine them and then start them on intravenous antibiotics.

After working through the night, we would see all the patients admitted to review their progress. During one of these *post-take* ward rounds, one of the SHOs gave me a cardboard tray with two pre-filled syringes and told me to give them to 'that patient over there'.

He pointed to an aged, breathless man on the other side of the ward and followed me to watch what I did. I vaguely recalled him as about the fifth admission from the night before.

To a mere medical student, a senior house officer is a remote and other-worldly figure. They have passed their finals and have survived a whole year on the wards. They have the battle scars and know where to hide the skeletons. If the consultant is your colonel, then the SHO is your sergeant major. If they say you should do something, you do it.

I took the cardboard tray and headed for my target. I told him who I was and that I was there to give him an injection. You could hear the crackles in his chest from the end of the bed. He looked at my white coat and nodded. He wasn't in any position to do otherwise.

The SHO watched me give the intravenous injection into the cannula. I knew it was a test and I wanted to do it right – I so wanted to please him. I followed the approved technique methodically, just as I had been taught, and then I looked up for his approval.

'What did you just give him?' he asked.

I froze, open-mouthed. I hadn't asked and I hadn't looked. I'd simply given him the stuff I'd been given.

'Who did you just give it to?' He rammed the point home. I'd given it to 'that patient over there', the bloke I barely recognised who looked like every other bronchitic on the ward.

I looked down at the man in the bed. I saw a name band round his wrist. I hadn't looked at it. He had a name. I didn't know it.

I saw him exchange a glance with the SHO who winked back at him. And then I looked at the empty vials on the cardboard tray.

'Sorry,' I said, thoroughly ashamed.

They could have been cyanide for all I knew. I had trusted the man in the white coat, and the patient had trusted the stupid medical student. I knew the research. I'd even studied it, but I hadn't actually applied the lesson.

Shame on you, Ben – forced obedience to an authority figure in the right uniform. It was an inspired piece of teaching.

I went home, grabbed a textbook and opened it at an experiment conducted by Stanley Milgram at Yale. He tasked volunteers to subject a 'guinea pig' to ever more serious electric shocks whenever they failed a simple memory task. The graduations on the dial went from an extremely mild 15 volts to a very severe 450.

In fact, the current was non-existent and the recipient was only pretending to be in pain. The only person not 'in' on the set-up was the one delivering the shocks. And if they hesitated for any reason they were given a simple instruction, ranging from 'Please continue,' to, 'You have no choice but to continue.'

Everyone went to 300 volts and two-thirds went all the way to the top, despite the victim's 'screams'.

Because someone in authority had told them to.

You have no choice . . .

Some years later, I saw a patient with schizophrenia on the ward. He was about my age, had a similar middle-class background, a good education and a university degree. We could have been brothers. He had been admitted by another doctor who had been on call the night before, so I was interviewing him for the first time. I asked him when he first noticed there was a problem. Looking back, that was my first mistake – unless you have insight, most people coming into hospital don't think there is a problem, so it was the wrong question to start with.

'It was the vision of dysplopia that set the sequential severances alight. I had no vision of the dilapidation or the excess of inadequacy countered by the dismembered conjunctive fight for freedom. I don't think we can be exploited by our inconsistent approach for aiming the inevitable paradesic challenge.'

He carried on like this for about a minute before he stopped and looked at me. I was only able to scribble down the first couple of sentences verbatim.

'I have the whole thesis here.' He reached into his bag and pulled out a large bundle, topped by a five-year-old newspaper folded open on the second page. 'Local boy, Paul Carrington, gets place at Oxford,' said the headline.

'We're so proud of him,' the headteacher said. 'He's our first pupil to get to Oxbridge.'

Paul looked young and excited in the photograph, clean-shaven and full of hope and optimism, not like the bearded and malnourished figure before me.

'It was a conspiracy of the highest armoury. They contrived and strived to semble the soliptic charm.'

I scribbled further notes. It was complete nonsense of course, but it was said with such fluent conviction that it took a while to realise he was completely thought disordered. It's one of the key signs of psychosis. Some of the words were simply misused, but some were neologisms – made-up words are not uncommon in schizophrenia.

Paul had to repeat the last year of his degree because he lost most of the time to unspecified illness. He scraped through but then went into a psychotic decline. A friend eventually went to see him and found him alone, suspicious and fearful at home, the windows covered in tinfoil and twenty bottles of Evian in the unplugged fridge. The TV was facing the wall and newspaper cuttings of conspiracy theories were pinned up on every available space. His friend called the GP and the GP called the community psychiatry team.

They went to see him and then organised the admission from there. He didn't think there was a problem.

Why would he?

In his thought disordered state he found it hard to articulate the nature of the conspiracy against him, but it was clearly real to him. He wouldn't let the psychiatry team in to see him, so they had to go to the magistrates' court to get an order under section 135 of the Mental Health Act that allows entry into a private dwelling. He was then detained under section 2 and brought into hospital.

We spent a few days assessing him. Physically he was OK despite being underweight. His drug screens were negative, but the historical narrative told us that it was more likely to be schizophrenia. I went to him after the ward round and told him that we needed to start him on medication – an antipsychotic drug to try to lessen his paranoia and free up his thinking.

'You're trying to ablute the poisoned chattel,' he said angrily, which I understood to be a refusal.

We decided to give him a few days to consider it and I saw him each day to try to explain why he needed medication so badly. He wasn't having any of it. It was during one of these meetings that he asked to go home to get some clothes. It was a risk that he might not return, but he was on a section, so if he decided not to come back, we could always call the police.

I went with him to his home. A Health Care Assistant (HCA) would normally do this, but I wanted to see how he lived, and it turned out to be a lesson in what schizophrenia can look like.

There were five locks on his front door and two video cameras. I made a mental note of the hatchet in the hallway and he clocked me looking at it.

'Intruders,' he explained.

I should have left at that point, but I was young and curious and risk assessment was not something much talked about back then. I later discovered that he was facing charges for having threatened his neighbours with an axe.

Rubbish was invading the hallway – discarded clothes to begin with, then food wrappers and takeaway cartons, half-eaten and left to rot. Newspapers, magazines and bottles of water were strewn everywhere.

By the time we got into the lounge, the carpet had disappeared under the tide of refuse. I tucked my trousers into my socks and tried not to inhale too deeply. The dim glow from a naked bulb reflected off the foil which had been carefully applied to the windowpanes, in which I could see little holes at eye level where he must have looked out from his self-imposed prison.

The foil was designed to stop the secret services monitoring him. The machines they used could alter his thoughts and made him think there was a conspiracy to control and kill him. He had long since stopped watching TV because it linked to the beams and commentated on what he was doing. He needed the cameras to gather evidence of the conspiracy to give to the police. It turns out they had known about him for a year because he made weekly trips to the local station to complain about the plot against him.

I asked him about the half-eaten food.

'Poisoned. Different. Evidence,' he replied.

We had found that whilst he was so thought disordered, he could get his meaning over better by just using single words. It was a testament to his intellect that he was able to recognise that others didn't understand him and adapt his own narrative. I soon discovered that he was going to random takeaways all over town, never the same one twice, to reduce the risk of being poisoned. He ate about one meal every three days or so, which accounted for his weight loss. He wanted to eat but feared for his life every time he did. He ate half of what he bought, so that if he became unwell, he could use the remainder as evidence for the police.

Poisoned. Different. Evidence . . .

He showed me what he described as the rest of his thesis, three large ring-binders full of paranoid conspiracy theories about the secret services and Big Pharma – the ramblings of a brilliant, psychotic mind. 'I just need to ambrigate it more,' he told me.

We came back to the ward without problems and I made sure that the clothes he had picked up were given a good wash. My conversations with him continued and while he was perfectly nice to talk to, we never seemed to get anywhere. From his point of view, there was nothing wrong with him. His delusions were internally consistent and meshed with experiences and hallucinations from the TV.

I went back to my consultant the following week. 'He's still refusing meds.'

'What are you going to do?' she asked.

'I'll keep working on him.'

'How long do you need?'

'Another few days, a couple of weeks.' It sounded like a statement, but was really a question.

'And if he's still refusing then?'

I didn't know what to say.

'Another month, another year?' she went on. 'Ben, he has no insight. You like him, and you're identifying with him because he reminds you of you.'

I looked at her and smiled at her observation. 'You're right. I'll tell him he needs to take medication. Give me twenty-four hours.'

She nodded at me and smiled. She had approved the plan.

I went to see Paul on the ward with a new approach. I wore a suit and tie and was more forthright than usual. I had stopped being his friend. I'd decided to become the authority figure. After a short preamble, I moved on. 'Paul, I need you to start your medication.' I was clear and I was assertive. I was the man in the white coat. I had stopped wearing it, and here I was, recreating it.

He put his hands up, palms facing me. 'It's disquieted rhythm that contrives the pharmaceutical negation. I can't have those drugs. They'll kill me.'

'Paul, I'm writing you up for Clopixol tablets. If you don't take them, we'll have to give you an injection.'

'That's not legal. I'll legate the unsolicitation.'

'Paul, you have no choice. You need to start the medication.' It just came out.

He looked at me and crumbled. He went very quiet and nothing was said between us for about five minutes. That's a very long time when you are sitting in a small room with someone. It was like a staring contest that you had to win.

'Today?' he asked eventually.

I nodded my head. 'I'll get it now.'

I went to the nursing office and got his prescription card. I watched carefully as the nurse took the dose out of the bottle and put it in a small gallipot. I filled another with water and went back to Paul. He was sitting with his head in his hands. I gave him the medication and passed him the water.

He looked at me intently while he took it, got up silently and went back to his room.

I didn't see much of Paul for the next few days. He had taken to his room and didn't want to socialise. By taking the medication, albeit reluctantly, I think he had acknowledged there was a problem and that the last few years of his life had been a product of his illness.

His mood went down as he started to regain some insight, and he needed antidepressants when he got really low and considered suicide.

I remember eating lunch with him in the canteen a few weeks later. He was improving and we were making plans for him to return home.

'Ben, can I ask you something?'

'Sure,' I said, trying to identify the meat in the stew and looking for a bit that didn't need the gristle cutting off.

'I've seen a lot of people come into the ward. Most of them get medication after a couple of days. They get held down. Why didn't you do that to me?'

I decided to be honest with him. 'Inexperience. And then my consultant told me that you remind me of myself.'

86

Paul smiled, looked down at his plate and pushed it away. I wondered if it was a residual symptom from his illness, but he read my mind. 'I saw how fat I'm getting – it's the bloody medication.'

And then he said something that has stuck with me.

'Thank you for your inexperience.'

Paul left hospital about a month later. He carried on with the medication and when I last heard he was lecturing in philosophy at university.

Finals:

Soap in my eye

When you reach the last year at medical school, when you realise that it's mid-March and finals are in June, you can start to empathise with patients with anxiety disorders or depression. They are quite close relatives. It's unusual to see someone with anxiety who isn't a little depressed, and it's uncommon to see depression without a liberal helping of anxiety.

I was still only twenty-two. Despite my obsessions having calmed down in my late teens, anxiety and a tendency to depression were never far away. I've been like that all my life. I probably shouldn't even use the term depression – it's not as bad as the disorders I see in my patients. I'm talking about ruminative introspection, a sense of loss and foreboding, and a side order of lassitude. At worst, I can't face the world, and it keeps me in bed for a couple of days each year. If I try to read, or work, my brain tells me to stop. My concentration is hopeless. I have no energy. I take things negatively. It's all I can do to watch daytime TV, and generally, that depresses me even more. So I sleep. That is my salvation and my cure.

I call them my black dog days. Even Winston Churchill had them, so I like to think I'm in good company.

I once spoke to a colleague about it – a friend actually, Milton. I see him when I am happy and when I am sad, so in that sense, he is the perfect friend. I told him about some of the recent stresses at work. I told him I'd had some problems sleeping and felt run-down. He listened to me, quietly and carefully, and then he shrugged. It wasn't an uninterested shrug. It was the sort of shrug that conveys hope, interest and 'maybe it's not as bad as all that'. If it was a private consultation, it would have been worth the fee alone.

'What do you do when you wake up?'

'I try to go to sleep.'

'What do you do if you can't?'

'I've put a wooden bench from my parents' home at the front of my house. I sit there and watch the sun come up.'

He smiled. 'Sounds nice.'

I cried a bit. 'It is.'

When my mood is high, I don't get pressure of speech, I'm not grandiose and I've never lost contact with reality, but there are times when I feel good, almost to the point of feeling supercharged, my synapses spark like lightning, I become uncharacteristically sociable and more extrovert, my libido increases, and my thinking speeds up. Actually, that's the key thing really, it's the speed my synapses talk to each other in my brain. My processing speed, which is quite reasonable anyway, goes up tenfold.

I can 'see' things, make connections and I get ideas. Some of them, many of them, are stupid, but sometimes it gives me projects or ideas that I can work on later, when my mood goes back to normal. And it does, soon enough – too soon, sometimes.

Everyone is talking about mental health these days, which is no bad thing, but conversations with friends in a coffee shop about mild depression are a long way from what I do. I tend not to treat people with anxiety, mild depression, OCD and not-quite bipolar disorders, things with which I feel some kinship. And I can't help but wonder whether I have chosen a field of psychiatry where I can maintain my sense of separation from the patient – a world of forensic psychiatry where I can look to external rules, rules set by society, marked by the courts and punished by the prisons, about what is normal and what is acceptable behaviour.

When we are dealing with an offender population, some of them are just plain bad – *send them to prison and throw away the key* – but occasionally, at the opposite end of the spectrum, you see a person who is so unwell, so completely and utterly psychotic that even the most cynical onlooker would be hard-pressed to ascribe blame to their actions.

I once did a report arguing that a person who had killed a stranger in a department store was so unwell that they were legally insane. The court agreed. When you kill someone because the aliens are swarming from the cash register to your brain and then you realise the person serving you is the leader of the aliens, intent on destroying earth, and once the deed is done, you go and sit down in electricals and cut your own throat, punishment seems quite low down on the 'things to do' list.

Similarly, when someone kills their much-loved father shortly after switching to a new insulin preparation which took away their ability to recognise an impending hypo-glycaemic attack, and then absentmindedly gives themselves another shot of insulin and goes to sit in the lounge with an unrecordably low blood sugar level, to be revived later with amnesia and minor brain damage, and when their consciousness at the material time was so evidently absent, the issue of culpability, or the lack of it, seems pretty clear.

But as they say, the easy cases are easy; it's the other 99 per cent that are difficult.

And so far, I have focused on psychosis. It's generally more straightforward to understand people doing bad things if they are deluded or hearing voices than if they are depressed. In part, it's because we don't immediately associate depression with threat.

A woman was attacked on the common just yards from her home. Police are looking for a mildly depressed man.

It just doesn't make sense.

But it does happen. People can do bad things when they are depressed. I once admitted an eighty-year-old man, recently diagnosed with Parkinson's disease, after he smothered his healthy wife of sixty years in what he said was part of a suicide pact. His children believed otherwise. He had then taken ten paracetamol thinking it was enough to kill him. It didn't. One week into the admission, he walked to the end of the ward, opened a window and jumped out of it. He died.

Depression isn't simply low mood, not in psychiatric terms anyway. Low mood is just one symptom of depression, which can be mild, moderate or severe. And at the severe end of the spectrum, you can get delusions and hallucinations. This used to be called 'psychotic depression', which differentiated it from so-called 'neurotic depression', which 'normal' people are allowed to have simply because of the vicissitudes of life.

Three months before finals, from my perspective, there were a lot of vicissitudes.

By this time, I was living with Jo, my future wife, in a flat in South London. We were both working very hard, and she was probably right that I was more anxious than I should be.

What's the incubation period of chickenpox?
How do you treat pain in labour?
What is the treatment for haematemesis?
How do you diagnose congenital myotonic dystrophy?
Who ate all the bread?

My circadian rhythms dictate I get up before 6 a.m., I work till 11 a.m., have a bite to eat, have a siesta, do some reading in the afternoon, and then, by 5 p.m., that's it for me. By 8 p.m. I am looking forward to bed, and by 9 p.m., it takes a special occasion or a medical emergency to keep me from it.

Jo, by contrast, started to come to life at midday. She would amble round the apartment being vaguely distracting until 4 p.m. and would start working in earnest at about 7 p.m. Quite when she finished, I never found out, but sometimes she would come to bed as I was getting up.

Just as well. It was a single bed.

'Why do you get up so early? It's like you're depressed or something.'

The accusation at this point was unfair, and yes, I choose my words carefully. It was an accusation. I once, some years later, suggested she might be a little depressed, and I have never seen her so angry, as if it were a mortal sin.

Jo was right, though, to question the possibility of depression based on my waking early in the morning. Sleep disturbance is one of those things that relates to mood. Whilst you can't be categorical about it, people with severe depression often wake up early in the morning.

I don't want to overstate the case, but I wonder now whether Jo and I just didn't see each other for the first fifteen years of our relationship. They say that a dog year is equivalent to seven human years. So given our work patterns, I wonder if junior doctors need seven times as long to have the same 'relationship' as normal people. Either that or it was the inhumane hours we worked as junior doctors that kept our relationship going and fostered a sense of co-dependence.

So, apart from sleep disturbances in depression, people stop enjoying things. It's called anhedonia and it's horrible – hardly surprising that people start to think about a one-way trip to Switzerland. People stop doing the things they normally enjoy: they stop eating, they're *tired all the time* – that's what 'TATT' means in your medical notes – they feel worthless, guilty and can't concentrate. If you feel all that, it's hardly surprising that your thoughts could turn to suicide.

Literally, whether to be or not to be. That is depression. And even that's not an exhaustive list. I'd make a diagnosis of depression based on just some of these symptoms, never mind *low mood*, the bit of depression that people seize on as its defining feature. It's that pervasive sense of sadness, hopelessness and empty desolation – like a wet weekend in Geneva.

As the days and weeks passed in our South London flat, our whole lives revolved around the impending examinations. Knowing as much psychiatry as any medical student reasonably could, I was naturally hoping for a psychiatry case in my medical finals. We worked it out: there was a 25 per cent chance of getting a psychiatry long case, which is very low, unless you are doing the lottery. There was the same probability of getting a paediatric case, and if we had a 25 per cent chance, say, of dying in the next year, most of us would file that under the heading of 'very bad' – I didn't really understand paediatrics.

Finally, there was a 50 per cent chance of getting a medical case, which was fine, because I could play with my stethoscope.

I went off to King's for my finals, just opposite the Maudsley, and wondered if I would ever work there. I stopped to look at it and suddenly felt a sharp pain in my eye. I started to wipe it and felt something like soap on my forehead. And not just on my forehead.

I found the nearest loo and made a beeline for the mirror. It might have been anxiety, it might have been a momentary lapse in concentration – I have never done it before or since – but I hadn't washed the shampoo out of my hair.

I can sweat on a frosty morning, and the day was already promising that humid London heat that makes everyone plan a barbecue and lie down under the plane trees. My anxiety and the stifling conditions on the train had combined to turn me from a slicked-back Gordon Gekko to a frothy Grand National runner-up.

I was all of a lather.

And quite a lot of it had leaked over my shirt collar and jacket. I took off both, rinsed them, put my head under the tap and took my second shower of the day.

As I was dressing, newly devoid of lather, a man came in to use the urinal.

'Rough night?' he said, as I was pulling on my sodden shirt. He was wearing a name badge, and whilst he will remain anonymous, I do remember seeing that he was a consultant paediatrician.

'No, I'm fine thanks. I've got my finals today.'

He looked at me, as I now realise, in much the same way as I have sometimes looked at my patients when they say something really strange.

I've got a little man living in my vagina.

It's not a microwave, it's a cosmic transporter.

'Good luck,' he said cheerily, and I couldn't help but notice he didn't stop to wash his hands.

I made my way to the exam centre and gave my name to the SHO who was organising the day.

'Are you OK?' she said.

'Yes.'

'It's just that you look a little . . . wet. OK, well, your case has just come, so if you go to room six, you've got forty-five minutes.'

I opened the door to room six and saw a woman of about thirty with a child sitting on her lap. Neither looked very happy.

'Good morning,' I said, introducing myself.

'Hi,' she said. 'I'm Jane.' Flat, monotone, no psychomotor retardation, no smile, no tremor, good eye contact.

'Who is the patient?' I asked, hopefully.

She shrugged and then gestured down to the child. 'Johnny here.'

Fuck. Paediatrics. Short straw. Life over. Retakes in November.

'What's up with him?' I asked. I thought I'd keep the questions open at this point.

94

'I'm not meant to tell you.'

Double fuck.

It's true. When patients are brought in for exams, particularly unhelpful SHOs tell the patients not to say what the diagnosis is. Some patients take them at their word, and give the aspiring doctor no clues whatsoever . . .

'So, what symptoms do you have?'

'I can't say.'

. . . and it seemed that I was in that situation.

I persevered and spoke to Johnny. He was five and he couldn't tell me much apart from he couldn't stand up properly. I let him play with the koala bear on my stethoscope, borrowed from Jo that morning.

'I fall over a lot,' he said. 'I can't get up the stairs.'

He got bored by this point, which I noticed a lot in paediatrics, and he went off to play with the toys in the corner of the room.

Jane just watched him go off and there was a tear in her eye.

'How are you?' I ventured.

She put her head in her hands and sobbed for what seemed like an age. I'd given up any chance of passing this exam by now, so I just let her cry.

Eventually she stopped and looked up and seemed to take me in for the first time.

'Why are you all wet?'

I told her and she smiled a little at first and then it seemed she couldn't stop. It wasn't affective instability, she just needed to break out of her morbid preoccupation about her son. She needed a tonic, a holiday, a funny film, preferably with an antidepressant, and what she got was a wet, anxious, medical student doing finals.

'Is it really bad for you at the moment?' I asked.

'Yes,' she said, settling down. 'I cry all the time. I'm tired, I don't think I can go on. I do, but it's for him.'

'Sleeping?'

She shook her head. 'Can't get to sleep. Drink myself to sleep. Wake up feeling awful at four in the morning.'

'Five-minute warning,' came the cry from the SHO outside, banging on the bell. I'd almost forgotten about Johnny; I hadn't even examined him.

'Can I tell the examiners how bad you feel? You need some help.'

She nodded. 'I'd like some help. I want them to know how difficult it all is.'

I looked down at my empty sheet of paper and she put her hand on mine. 'Let me tell you about Johnny,' she said. 'I'm a single mother. I'm thirty-two – he's my first and only pregnancy. He's got Duchenne muscular dystrophy. It's an X-linked recessive inheritance, but they think there's a lot of new mutations, so there's often no family history. I've tried to find the father, but he's left the country. Johnny told you about the weakness and that's typical – presentation at three or so, diagnosis with CK levels and biopsy. If you look at his legs, there's marked pseudo-hypertrophy. Prognosis is terrible.' She lowered her voice to a whisper. 'He's being measured for leg splints this afternoon. That's why I agreed to do this. They reckon he'll be in a wheelchair by the age of ten. Then it's progressive weakness, spinal problems. And cardiovascular complications, then . . .'

And then she trailed off and called to Johnny. He looked up at her and pushed himself up from a crawling position.

'Look at how he does it. It's because he has no strength in his hips.'

The SHO came in. 'Time's up.'

I took Jane's hand. 'Thank you.' And she winked at me.

'I didn't tell him anything,' she shouted to the SHO, who seemed to smile in an evil way and told me to go straight into the exam room.

There was a man of about fifty and a younger woman sitting on his right.

Fuck and double fuck.

It was the man from the loo, and it was immediately apparent he had recognised me, too.

'You didn't bring a towel with you,' he said sardonically.

'I'm not Ford Prefect,' I said. I was a big fan of *Hitchhiker's Guide*, and carrying a towel is quite an important thing, but I'd lost him.

'Tell us about the patient.'

He had a peremptory air. It was as if the woman next to him was only there to make up the numbers. She only spoke once in the next thirty minutes.

I put my hastily scribbled notes in front of me. One page for Jane and one for Johnny. I wonder now what came over me, but it seemed worth it just at that moment. I pressed the gamble button and picked up Jane's notes. 'I saw a thirty-two-year-old woman with a one-year history of low mood, sleep disturbance, anhedonia and feelings of helplessness—'

'Stop, stop, stop.' The paediatrician waved and then looked down at the notes in front of him. He turned to the woman on his right, but she was just staring at me.

'Why are you wet?' she asked.

'Hyperhidrosis,' I lied.

She leaned forward.

'It's excessive sweating.'

He looked angrily at her and took back the reins. She might have been a paediatrician too, but I never found out.

'You were sent to see Johnny, a child of five.'

'Yes, he was with his mother. But I interviewed a woman of thirty-two with depression.'

They called in the SHO, the one with the evil smile, and asked her if she had told candidate number 1656 that it was a paediatric case.

97

She looked at me and back to the consultant.

'No,' she admitted. The paediatrician was getting redder and angrier by the moment, which, being a nascent psychiatrist, I spotted.

'Let me tell you about the mother,' I suggested. 'And then I'll tell you about Johnny.'

Presumably because there was nothing in the playbook to preclude this, he nodded curtly back at me.

The woman on his right seemed to smile to herself.

'As I was saying, Jane is a thirty-two-year-old . . .'

I carried on to argue, successfully I thought, that she had a depressive disorder, caused by a lack of social support looking after Johnny.

'Are you Johnny's consultant?' I asked, finally.

'No.' He was stony-faced.

'Please would you contact his consultant and get his mother assessed. She needs antidepressants and she needs social support.'

He didn't so much reply as growl a little, which I took to be a 'yes.'

The woman on his right put her hand over her mouth and turned away from him.

Then it was his turn. I might have won the first game, but now he was playing at home. 'Now, you said that you'd tell us about Johnny,' he sneered. 'Please be so good as to present his case to us.'

The spectator on his right looked worried.

'Johnny,' I started hesitantly, 'is a five-year-old boy with a muscular weakness starting at three. His condition appears to be progressive.' I went on to list his mobility problems. 'I'd want to do a CK and possibly a muscle biopsy, but it seems likely he has a muscular dystrophy. He's got Gowers' sign already. It was the way he pushed himself up using his hands.' Something I actually knew. 'I've considered infantile myotonic dystrophy as the main differential, but considering the lack of facial or peripheral weakness, it's more likely to be Duchenne's.'

I stopped to let them take it in, and I saw them checking what I'd said with the notes in front of them. The woman nodded happily, and the paediatrician glowered at me. 'What about the prognosis?'

'Sadly,' I said, with the best 'giving-bad-news' face I could muster, which I had basically just copied from Jane, 'his muscular strength will diminish, and I suspect that he'll be severely disabled by ten or so. After that, well, almost certainly a wheelchair, and progressive weakness and all the respiratory and cardiovascular complications of that.'

'OK,' said the paediatrician, squaring up for a fight. 'Tell me about the genetics of Duchenne's.'

I practised my contemplative look as if to convey that I was recalling the information from several years ago. 'X-linked recessive I seem to remember. High new mutation rate though. Sadly, the father is not around and not contactable.'

'Thank you,' said the paediatrician, out of ammunition but still looking for something on me. 'Tell me, why were you washing in the toilet this morning?'

I told him. 'It's stupid really. I was so worried about today, I forgot to wash the shampoo out of my hair.'

It took about ten seconds, but I saw his body posture relax. 'What speciality are you going to do?' he asked.

'Psychiatry,' I said proudly.

'Thank fuck for that,' he said.

House jobs:

A doctor in possession of a white coat

It is a truth, universally acknowledged, that a doctor in possession of a white coat will get it covered in sputum, urine, faeces, vomit or blood by the end of the shift.

My proof of this was fifty-six hours into a long weekend and I was called to do some bloods on one of the wards at St Jude's. I didn't normally work there, so I didn't know the patient.

He had been admitted after vomiting some blood and was waiting to go to theatre. I read the notes before I went to see him. There wasn't much in the way of detail – of family background, whether he had children, what his job was. Just that he was jaundiced, drinking too much and had a history of depression. I loaded up my cardboard tray with everything I needed and went to his bedside. He was wearing bright yellow pyjamas, and it was impossible to tell where they ended and he began. One of the tests was to see if his liver was producing enough stuff to allow his blood to clot properly. A thin trail of fresh blood was coming from his nose.

After years of heavy drinking, when the liver is a hard bit of gristle that has long since forgotten its function in life, it is prone to upset the neighbouring body parts. Lots of alcoholics do this, upset friends and family, all the time.

Who needs a pancreas, anyway? All you do is make insulin. I sort out cholesterol, make hormones, make bile, detoxify everything, store energy, monitor clotting – all right, not so much of that lately, I grant you. Don't even mention the gall bladder. What's so bloody clever about storing bile?

This particular liver's beef was with the veins at the lower end of its owner's oesophagus.

All you do is watch food go by; call that a job?

Sadly, the years of abuse had caused the veins at its lower end to become varices, which are like piles, and we all know that piles can bleed. Varices bleed even more, and it's quite difficult to stick a little rubber band around them.

His liver wasn't always so bitter and twisted. It was once a normal, happy liver, full of hope and promise, but along the way and after a couple of drinks, it got a bit low, and eventually it lost respect for itself. Then it got angry and alienated those around it.

I was reminded of a woman I saw with chronic schizo-phrenia. Chronic, to a doctor, means the opposite of acute or sudden. It doesn't imply bad, but when you lose your initiative, drive and personality, it's a long way from good. I will admit its place in this story is tenuous but as with the oesophagus, it involves watching food go by.

She worked for a biscuit company and her job was quality control. I saw her in outpatients perhaps thirty years after her first onset of schizophrenia and her life had been in decline ever since.

I asked her what her job involved. She told me that she watched the digestives go past on the production line, and if any were broken, she would throw them in the bin.

'That's it?' I asked.

She nodded.

'Isn't that very boring?' I don't know why I said it, and I don't like myself for having done so.

'No.' She suddenly became more animated. 'Sometimes we swap over, and I watch the chocolate bourbons go by.'

Come to think of it, this story does fit here rather nicely.

It's all about loss of dignity.

I Googled the biscuit factory. It had closed before I met her.

After all these years, the fondest and proudest memory she had was watching the biscuits go by.

You want it darker? How about this. I don't think she would even get a job these days. When I ask patients what they want, they don't talk about their illness getting better or coming off medication. Without exception, they tell me they want a decent job – something to do, somewhere to live and someone to love.

There it is, the whole of human need, unfulfilled.

Mine is the shame.

Back on the ward, Yellow Man was perfectly nice with me, and as I wasn't being called elsewhere, we spoke for a while, but mostly I just sat and listened. He had no one in his life. His marriage had ended years before, and he had lost contact with his children. He was homeless and had lost his job long since.

Looking back, I think he knew he was dying, and he used his last few minutes with me talking about the few things he was proud of, trying to put things right and saying he was sorry.

Then he looked up at me and tried to say something, but all that came out was a litre of blood.

I know what you are thinking. A little blood goes a long way. And you'd be right. But when oesophageal varices bleed, they really bleed, and unless you can get a Sengstaken-Blakemore tube down it – which has a balloon at the bottom end to pressurise the varices – they just keep on bleeding.

And it was never going to clot.

I saw that a nurse was calling the crash team. He slumped forward and I held him. There was a lot of noise around us and curtains were being pulled shut, but everyone in the ward had seen it. All the patients looked on and watched intently, their faces impassive, imploring me to do something.

Please, Doctor. Save him.
Save me.

I was still holding him. I felt like I was looking at him from a distance. I was in a picture and I saw myself holding him, and he was vomiting blood over my back.

I put him flat on the bed and held him briefly whilst he was dying, embracing him, comforting him and holding his soul. It was the most I could do for him. For a short moment, it was just the two of us, there was no one else there, then the crash team came running towards us in slow motion, to tear us apart and start their unhelpful ministrations.

And the blood kept coming. My training took over. I stood and started to squeeze the bag through. He still had a pulse, just, and was trying to breathe when not vomiting.

The crash team were upon us and I walked backwards until I felt the curtain behind me and watched them for the next thirty minutes.

After they left, I wrote up the notes, and wrote RIP at the end of them. I went back and sat at the end of his bed. All of the other patients had their curtains closed so it felt like the ward was empty.

A nurse brought me some tea. 'Are you OK?' she asked. I nodded.

As she passed me the mug, she slipped on the bloody floor, reached out for the bloody sheets and they gave way. She slid to the floor to kneel in his bloody mess. I helped her up and we sat together. She watched me drink my tea and I looked at her and then we got up and walked out. I never knew her name. We were both broken and lame and bloody.

I recall washing his blood off later. I put my shoes under the tap to rinse them and watched the water form little rivulets on the polished leather.

I find myself crying while I reflect on it.

Years have now passed, and it's been a professional life-time since Yellow Man died in my arms. I still think about him. Not in an anxious way and the thoughts don't upset me now, but he still travels with me.

Yellow Man killed himself. It wasn't suicide but it might as well have been. He didn't stab himself, or burn himself to death, or jump from a bridge, but he might as well have. He did it slowly, with alcohol.

He didn't leave a note, but then few of us do.

Training to be a psychiatrist

'Why did you become a psychiatrist, anyway?' asks Elaine, bringing in some prescription forms for me to sign.

'Don't know really. Seemed like a good idea at the time. Why did you become a nurse?'

'It started off as something to do. I fell out with my parents. I was quite rebellious, you know.'

'No kidding.'

'Steady. But then it just clicked with me. I like dealing with people's problems. It's why we all do it, isn't it?'

'How are the kids?' I ask. One of them has an eating disorder and had stopped going to school.

'She's a lot better. She's catching up with her lessons. The school are really helping her.' She picks up a set of notes from my desk and flicks through it.

'Hey, they're private.'

'Who's Roy?' she says, ignoring me.

I take the notes off her and put them on my desk again. 'Roy was the first person I saw as a psychiatrist. On my first day, in fact.'

'Did you cure him, Dr Cave?' she asks, all wide-eyed and not at all like her.

'Bugger off. Lunch later?'

'Great. One o'clock. You can tell me all about Roy.'

'Not the canteen,' I shout after her. 'We'll go out for lunch.' But she doesn't reply.

I read Roy's notes before putting them in the 'keep box'.

It had been the first day of my first psychiatry job at St Jude's. He had come in complaining about shaking too much and the nurses had called me to assess him.

It was 11.15 a.m. By this point, I had been employed in the field of psychiatry for precisely two hours and fifteen minutes. I had done some bloods, seen a couple of people on the ward and found the doctors' mess.

St Jude's, it has to be said, isn't in the best part of town. It's a deprived area and for a time had the highest rate of domestic burglary in the country. Unemployment is high, incomes are low and drugs are rife.

Roy had schizophrenia. About one in a hundred people do. He was on antipsychotic drugs and said he was shaking all the time. I asked him about his illness, and he told me he had become paranoid when he was about twenty and believed that spirits talked about him and controlled his actions. When he was well, he co-existed with the symptoms. When he was unwell, he shouted at people in the street. He blamed his medication for his aggression, and he used ever-increasing amounts of skunk – a type of cannabis.

Over time, the amount of tetrahydrocannabinol (THC) in commercially available cannabis has gone up from 2 per cent to as much as 28 per cent, and with greater potency comes an even greater potential for psychosis and dependency. Without wishing to sound judgemental, I take the view that cannabis is a bad thing, especially if you already have schizophrenia. Roy had schizophrenia, and was smoking skunk, which has plenty of THC.

'The voices,' he said, 'they control me; they make me do things.'

Feeling that your actions are controlled is a well-recognised symptom of psychosis. It is a type of *passivity* phenomenon and it can be terribly intrusive. Sufferers feel that they have to comply with some outside force, exactly as if they were a marionette. They are robbed of their own free will to determine their actions. They are passive in terms of deciding what they do, or even what they think. I can't imagine anything worse than feeling you're being controlled like that.

When I saw Roy and he told me about his illness, you couldn't help but feel sorry for him. Fortunately, he was quite well, and it was obvious that he was taking his medication, partly because he wasn't shouting at me, and partly because he had really bad stiffness and his hands were shaking terribly.

His medication, a depot antipsychotic, was injected every few weeks. Once administered, it is gradually released into the bloodstream. Unfortunately, one of the side effects is a tremor that looks like Parkinson's disease. Fortunately, there is a group of drugs that can treat these side effects quite effectively. I'm pleased to say I'd read that bit of my text-book years ago, the same one now propping up my chair, and my first act as a junior psychiatrist was to give Roy a script for a month's supply of Procyclidine. He seemed quite happy with my treatment approach, thanked me and then left. It felt good being a psychiatrist and healing the sick, even if in this particular case the cause was iatrogenic – we had caused the problem in the first place.

I discovered subsequently, the same night in fact, that Procyclidine causes a mild psychoactive 'kick' that some people like and are willing to pay for.

After I finished my first day, I went with a colleague to the pub at the end of the road for what I thought was a well-earned pint. We sat and talked about the patients we'd seen, and I mentioned the script I had given Roy. My colleague shifted uncomfortably and looked a little uneasy but didn't say anything.

I then noticed that Roy had come into the bar. I waved but he didn't see me, and he made his way to the first table by the door. My observational skills told me that my treatment approach had worked well. There was no evidence of tremor, none whatsoever.

I had healed the sick.

One of the people he was talking to gave him a fiver and he moved on to the next table. His gait was normal, and he didn't look the slightest bit stiff. In fact, he was moving freely and was clearly demonstrating good manual dexterity as he dished out little plastic bags of what looked like cannabis, and other little plastic bags which appeared to contain a few tablets.

After working his way round the room, he came to our table. I looked up at him, and he finally smiled in recognition. 'Hey, Doc, nice one,' he said, extending his fist for me to hit.

I obliged, raised my glass to him, declined his offer of cannabis, took a mental note of what Procyclidine looks like, and went home to read up on the side effects of various medications, mostly to determine which of them were drugs of abuse.

It wasn't the best of first days.

It seems almost like a victimless crime, but I came to realise over the years that much of the violence I'd seen was due to alcohol or drugs – frequently both. Either people offend violently because of the drugs, or steal things when they're withdrawing.

But sometimes, the really smart ones like Roy, they get their doctors to give them the drugs for nothing.

The bitter red pill

Just before my membership examinations, I went to a revision lecture about 'insight' – that's the term used to describe how the patient understands their illness.

Generally, if you see someone with a phobia or a compulsive disorder, they know there's a problem and want help to sort it out. They have insight and they'll make an informed decision about the treatment you suggest.

But if you see a man who knows himself to be the Lord High-Priest of England and associated territories, who claims to be a billionaire, the Viscount of Milton Keynes (I never got to the bottom of that one), and is dressed only in a feather boa on London Bridge station, I would say with some degree of certainty that they do not have insight into their condition.

Psychotic disorders traditionally have poor levels of insight, and until the patient's condition improves, the voices are real and the delusions preoccupying. When the patient starts talking about the voices being part of the illness and when they are able to question their delusions, that's insight, and that's when the psychologists can start their work.

'In conclusion,' said the lecturer to a bored audience only really interested in passing their exams, 'it's the ability to label pathological experiences as being part of the illness. More accurately,' he added, trying to win us back, 'it's whether the patient agrees with you and whether they do as they're told.'

There was a polite titter from the students and then there was a lecture about postpartum psychosis. It turned out to be one of the questions in the exam paper and is, without doubt, the reason I am a qualified psychiatrist.

I'm not sure I fully understand insight even now, but whatever it is, two cases during my training years made me consider it deeply.

I was still quite inexperienced when I saw Alan. He taught me that regaining insight can be a painful process. He was on one of the general wards at St Jude's at the time. The consultant had asked me to discuss his medication with him to see if he would try something new.

'So', I concluded, after talking to Alan about changing his medication, 'what do you think?'

He looked perplexed. 'Tell me, how will the new stuff cure me if there is nothing wrong with me? I'll take it, but it's not going to get Sally back is it. They've still got her at MI6.'

I wasn't sure what to say. Sally, his daughter, had died with her boyfriend, Naveen, in an RTA six months earlier.

'Naveen knows what's happened,' he went on. 'That's why he's been taken too. They listen to me all the time now, to make sure I don't expose their secrets. You're in danger just by being near me.' Then he asked me to leave for my own safety.

Alan had been in and out of hospital for several years. After a degree in maths, he worked in electronics and then set up a number of highly profitable business ventures. I sometimes wondered if he had worked for the intelligence services himself. As time went by, and as his illness worsened, his business dealings became more and more erratic, and he ended up with nothing. He had schizophrenia and had become a revolving-door case – he got better with medication, then stopped it after discharge, relapsed and was readmitted to repeat the cycle over and over again.

When he was unwell, he spent his days reading about the British security and intelligence services and writing letters to government, specifically the foreign secretary whom he blamed for his daughter's 'disappearance'. When he was very unwell, he went up to Downing Street to protest his case.

This time, the medication wasn't having its normal effect. He wasn't getting better. He seemed more and more entrenched in his delusions. That's why the consultant was keen to try a new treatment approach. We didn't know if it would work, but frankly, anything was worth a shot.

I went to see him the week after he changed to the new medicine.

'Well, I don't have any side effects, which is nice, but I've not really seen a difference,' he told me.

I asked the nurses how he was. 'He's quieter than normal. He's not written so many letters the last couple of days.'

The next week, he seemed a bit down. 'I'm worried about Sally,' he told me. 'I'm worried something bad has happened to her.'

'What do you think might have happened?'

He shrugged. 'I don't know.'

His response surprised me. Normally he would point the finger at the security services, but his concern now was more measured, more nuanced.

I called to see him on the ward three days later.

'He's inconsolable,' the nurses told me. 'He keeps talking about Sally.'

He was shaking with emotion. He was rocking back and forth. 'I know what happened,' he said.

'What happened, Alan?'

'She's not coming back. She's dead.'

'How did she die, Alan?'

'In a car crash. She was with Naveen.'

'I am very sorry,' I said. I was sorry for him, but looking back, I don't think I appreciated the gravity of asking him to confront his loss. Back then, I don't think that I could empathise with his grief and how his recovery was tearing him apart.

He slumped forward and put himself on the floor. He pulled his knees up to his chest and sobbed uncontrollably.

He settled after a few minutes and looked up at me. 'Ben, I don't want the new medicine any more. I can't cope with it.'

It was a few years later when I saw the film *The Matrix*. It depicts a future where humans have literally become the batteries for the machines, and are kept suspended like a foetus in the womb and fed a computer-generated reality called the Matrix. Life has become what the Matrix gives you – everything is illusory, but you don't know it isn't real. A few resistance fighters survive in the real world outside the Matrix and their leader, Morpheus (Laurence Fishburne) visits Neo (Keanu Reeves) to recruit him to the struggle. In doing so, he offers him a choice between taking a red pill, which will bring him crashing back to reality in all its horrors, or a blue pill which will allow him to stay in his make-believe world. 'Taking the red pill' has become a loaded metaphor in modern society, but I'm using it in the literal medical sense of taking a pill and opening your eyes to reality, no matter how bad it really is.

I thought back to Alan. He had incorporated his daughter's death into his delusions. That way, he didn't have to grieve for her. She had been 'kidnapped' and was being held by 'the government' – it was easier that way. His recovery, and he did recover, took three cycles with the 'red pill'.

Each time he was able to grieve his loss just a little bit more, and eventually he accepted the medication regularly. It was a desperate and slow recovery played out over many months.

But he did get better.

★

'Celia's an interesting case,' said Vicky, my consultant, 'and she's stopped taking her medication. I'm worried about her.'

'She smothered her own child, didn't she?' I'd been reading the medical records of the patients on the ward and thinking about my own new-born daughter. 'Convicted of infanticide, wasn't she?'

Vicky nodded and looked at me closely. She had picked up on something. Maybe I was hesitant or sounded judgemental. 'Yes. But Ben, the question you should be asking yourself is, would she have killed her own daughter if she hadn't been mentally ill at the time?'

It was the first time I realised how perceptive she was. I think I've always been prone to moralism, but growing up in Stockport in the shadow of the 'Moors Murderers', Ian Brady and Myra Hindley, my prejudice to those who killed children was confirmed at a very early age. I always knew I'd find it difficult to assess people who harmed children, let alone treat them dispassionately and fairly.

Looking back now, I have to thank Vicky for making me take the case. If Alan taught me how difficult it can be to recover insight, it was Celia who confirmed for me that people sometimes need the respite of the blue pill – for a while at least. Sometimes people just aren't ready for change and the best thing a psychiatrist can do is to let them tread water. All we do is help them stay afloat until they're ready to swim to the shore. That's the difference between psychiatry and the rest of medicine.

Sometimes, I fear I've been too quick to prescribe the red pill and that's been my failing. I think it's because my medical training has sometimes got the better of me, with its insatiable demands for treatment and progress and measurable outcomes.

Celia was going to change all that. She was going to beat the prejudice out of me. Celia was going to turn me from a doctor into a psychiatrist. She wasn't just going to take the doctor's white coat off me, she was going to burn it.

Before I went to see her, I went back to the notes. It was clear that Vicky had been tireless in keeping Celia out of prison and in hospital for treatment. When she was first admitted, some eighteen months earlier, she was floridly psychotic with hallucinations and delusions of being possessed. She was irritable and had a low but changeable mood. Her condition had improved with medication but then, whilst out on leave with a member of staff, she had quite unexpectedly jumped in front of a fast-moving bus.

Now, six months on, Celia had just stopped taking her medication.

The first thing I noticed was how she held herself in her chair. She always sat upright. She never slouched. She seemed rigid, and I couldn't blame the drugs.

'It's to help my back,' she told me. 'It aches all the time stuck in this bloody thing.'

'What happened?' I asked, pointing at the wheelchair.

'I fell into the road. It was last year. A bus went over me.'

I nodded, letting it sink in. She looked down at her legs. The left one stopped just below the knee, the stump sticking out of her leggings. She seemed to be displaying it – a visible reminder to herself.

'I was in hospital for about three months, but they couldn't save my foot. They amputated it. I wish they had let me die.'

'I see that you've got an appointment for a prosthesis next week.'

She looked at me and shrugged. 'Whatever. I didn't go to my last one.'

'Celia, why have you stopped taking your medication?'

'Don't know,' she said. 'Don't like it. It's too much.'

'Side effects?' I asked.

'You could say that. I don't like what it does to me up here.' She pointed to her head. Her blonde hair was greasy. Her face was round and blank. She was hard to read.

'You can ask me about what I did,' she said. 'You need to know, like all the others.'

'Thanks,' I said, automatically.

How could you kill her?

'Tell me what happened.' I wanted to understand how anyone could do such a terrible thing. I knew she was ill at the time — I'd read the notes — but even so, surely, she could have exercised some willpower. I needed to know she wasn't a monster.

'What happened?' she repeated back to herself. 'I smothered Rosie.' She had a faraway look in her eyes. 'She was so little, so helpless, but in my mind it was like I knew she had been possessed by evil. Dr Vicky, she originally called it postpartum psychosis, but now she calls it schizophrenia.'

'How was she possessed?'

'She took the negative energies from those around her. It grew in her. It all sounds so mad now, but I thought she was the anti-Christ. I'm not even religious.'

'What did you do after you smothered her?'

'I don't really remember. It's all blurred.' She looked distractedly out of the interview room and into the large atrium in the middle of the ward. The patients tended to sit around the edges. Celia liked to glide in her wheelchair over the smooth wooden floor in the middle. It was like a dance floor, occasionally used for table tennis or keep fit classes.

'And now I'm better,' she added. 'Your drugs have made me so much better, that I want to kill myself.' I knew she hadn't finished, so I waited. 'I've got insight. That's a good thing, right?' She smiled to herself, pleased with the irony.

'Is that why you jumped in front of the bus?'

She looked at me sharply. 'Yes, you've read my notes. I think it would have been a rational suicide, don't you, Doctor?'

I didn't know what to say.

'I loved her you know,' she said, as if she were reading my mind. 'There was no choice in what I did. But now, I do have a choice about the medication.'

I said nothing and waited.

'Please, God, let me stay off medication. God give me salvation. I sacrificed Rosie. I have to sacrifice myself for things to be right.'

Each sentence was a staccato burst of gunfire, and it might as well have brought me to my knees.

'It's what I deserve. You know that. I have to be punished. I want to be with her again. Let me do the job properly this time.'

I have already used the analogy of the patient treading water before they swim to shore. Celia was asking me to let her drown. I thought back to Alan and his overwhelming despair as he regained insight. Celia was the same, but in her case, the guilt of having killed Rosie was just too much for her.

Imagine for a moment taking the red pill, and then waking from your comforting madness to realise you'd killed your child.

Would you take it?

Normally, we associate insight with an improvement in a patient's condition. That's when we can take a less paternalistic approach and give the patient back the reins to take control of their life again. It's when trust develops and when people recover.

But Celia wasn't ready. She might have been able to cope with the bereavement, but she couldn't cope with the guilt and the shame. She would have to acknowledge her part in it, even though it wasn't her fault − I saw that now. Her insight was too awful to bear. The better she got from her psychosis, the more suicidal she became. Her own broken body after going under the bus was testament to that.

I realised that we were going through the next cycle of her recovery − from psychosis to the re-emergence of suicidality. It was at the same point previously she had run off from her escorting nurse and jumped into the road.

It was my job to stop the same thing happening again.

There was a choice before her. Carry on with the red pill and the unbearable insight of what had happened, or take the blue pill, which was no pill at all, and retreat back into her comforting delusion where killing Rosie seemed to make sense.

I am not sure what I would do in the same situation.

I decided to prevaricate for a while – deliberately taking no decision and leaving her off her medication. That's sometimes the most difficult thing to do as a doctor.

We talked, we chatted, and we got to know each other over the coming weeks. I tried not to talk about Rosie and her death, but inevitably it kept coming up. I could see that Celia was struggling with exactly the same prejudice that affected me.

'How could I have killed her?' she sometimes asked me. 'I'm a monster. I don't deserve help.'

'You really should start on the medication again, Celia. You'll become unwell again and lose your insight if you don't. We could insist on it.'

She smiled. 'Do what you must, but when I was ill, before you gave me the medication, I felt like I'd done the right thing. Now, I'm just a murderer. I need to be punished.'

'Celia, I need to admit something. When I first saw you, I wondered how you could have killed Rosie. I think I was angry at you. But what you did, it was your illness. It was some biochemical abnormality in your brain. It wasn't your fault.'

'So, do you understand why I need to stay off the medication?'

'Yes, I do. But I've given it thought, and I've talked it through with Vicky, and I can't allow you to become ill again. That's not a life.'

'So, Ben, your treatment can be my punishment?'

I nodded.

'I'll start the medication again,' she said. She looked defeated and grey.

She took the tablets, and with some encouragement she carried on with them this time. There was no return of her illness and soon enough, she was able to embark on longer-term therapy with the psychologist.

For the first time in ages, she seemed to be making progress. She had the prosthetic leg fitted but didn't wear it all the time. She was even going out on escorted leave again. But despite this, she seemed ever more distant with me. Sometimes she didn't want to see me, or said she was too tired. When we did meet, she was closed down, inaccessible. I talked to the psychologist about it.

'She's quite angry with you,' I was told. 'You're a symbol of her recovery and all the pain that goes with it.'

The symbolism hit me the next day. I never asked Celia afterwards why she did it. We probably both reached our own conclusions. It wasn't even that serious in the great scheme of things. I think she just needed to manifest her anger. She needed catharsis.

The day it happened, I was standing with my back to her, chatting with some patients. They later told me what she did. Celia had been on the other side of the atrium. She sat watching me for a moment and then she leaned forward and pushed the footplates of her wheelchair down. She put her good leg behind them and then manoeuvred the chair to point towards me.

Then she pushed herself forwards. She gained speed on the wooden surface and pushed her arms down on the wheels again and again. Faster and faster she went, me still oblivious to what was about to happen.

Then she sat up, back into her rigid upright stance and used the built-up speed to carry herself to me. She touched the wheels expertly to keep her path straight. That's when one of the patients I was talking to looked past me, her eyes wide open with alarm. She didn't say anything, but she didn't need to. I turned around and followed her gaze.

Celia was almost upon me.

We locked eyes. She was sad. She was enraged. She was depressed. I had never seen anyone so full of anger. There was nowhere for it to go apart from this battering-ram charge, this headlong attack on the instigator of her misery. Then I felt one of the other patients try to push me out of the way. I half turned, but it was too late.

The weaponised footplate of the wheelchair did its job perfectly. She had harnessed her emotions to become a ballistic weapon.

Down I went like a sack of potatoes. It was my ankle that bore the brunt of the impact, my right Achilles tendon.

I told you it was symbolic.

Then the strangest thing happened. I knew I wasn't seriously injured. My ankle hurt but I knew, even if it wouldn't take my weight, I could still scramble away if needed. But I just sat there. I don't think we had stopped looking at each other. There was an unfathomable and unshakable bond between us that had just been consummated. She had to do what she did, and I had to sit there and take it.

There was no outward emotion in what she did next. Still looking at me, she started to reverse, her back upright and rigid, her hands flicking at the top of the wheels. Then, she brought herself to a standstill. I knew what was coming. I put my hand out to the nurse who had come to intervene. 'It's OK,' I said. 'Let her.'

It's my fault.

She thrust herself forward again. I saw her eyes watering as she came towards me. She hated me. She loved me.

I put my good foot out to absorb the impact, and I still felt myself being pushed back to the edge of the wooden floor, back to the edge of the carpet with the other patients, out of her domain.

Then she pushed herself away for a second time. I sat up now. I was crying, not with pain but with emotion. Her catharsis allowed me mine.

And she wasn't spent yet.

As a young boy in Stockport, my big brother decided that we were going to learn how to box. We had moved on from golf by this point. We persuaded Dad to buy us a punchbag and we hung it up in the garage. After we had abraded our knuckles sufficiently and realised that we needed sparring gloves, we used the bag quite a lot. It was one of the more successful presents of the many indulgences we were afforded. Sometimes the bag was just a bag, some-times it was a Russian paratrooper or an alien invader, and sometimes it was my brother or even my father. I could get quite angry as a child. But I do remember how much better I felt after I had spent twenty minutes whacking the shit out of the leather-filled sack.

I looked at Celia now, back in the middle of her domain on the dance floor. She didn't have much energy left but she pushed at the wheels one more time. I was her punchbag.

Slowly, so slowly she glided herself into me. I waited for her to come. I didn't move. I just let it happen. I was fascinated. I was enthralled. It was intimate. It was angry.

We were lost in each other's silent tears, our eyes locked together as she hit me for the third and final time.

She touched me so lightly I barely moved. We were like two boxers hugging each other, their strength gone at the end of the bout.

And there we sat. Me on the floor, her in the chair, now slumping forward, all her rigidity gone. I wondered if she had ever been given a punchbag by her father and whether it would have made a difference.

'I'm sorry,' she said, quietly.

'I'm sorry too. I'm sorry for your pain.'

After a while that could have been seconds or minutes, I got up and tested my leg. We nodded at each other, and I limped off to the nursing office to gather my thoughts.

I sat down and took off my shoe and saw my ankle was red and swollen. But it wasn't that bad. I started to write up the notes and the nurse went to get me some ibuprofen.

'400mg,' said the nurse, offering me the red pill. She looked at me. 'What are you smiling at?'

I shook my head. 'Nothing,' I said. 'Nothing at all.'

There is a wonderful and unused word: *respair*. Susie Dent tweeted about it at the peak of the pandemic. It means the return of hope after a period of despair. Sadly, the word has long since fallen into disuse, which is a shame, because we need more of it.

Celia found her respair and left hospital almost six years to the day after Rosie died.

That's the same time it takes to become a doctor.

If I lost my dignity that day, so be it. Celia taught me that psychiatrists treat people not diseases. She did more than anyone else in shaping the psychiatrist I would become. But she took something from me too. And I'd like to thank her for it.

She took my prejudice.

Buzzzz

Electroconvulsive therapy has been around since the 1930s, in the days before any safe or effective medication for depression. It rapidly gained popularity, and, like many new inventions, people started to use it for conditions where its efficacy was questionable, more than questionable, where it was no use at all. These days there are very specific indications and very clear legal controls governing its use. I've reached for it ten times in my career and, of those cases, seven did really well. One almost died from a pulmonary embolus and it made little difference for two. For very serious conditions with high mortality rates, that's a pretty good result.

If I have treatment-resistant depression, I want ECT. If I have catatonia, or mania so severe that I could die from dehydration, I want ECT.

That's my advance directive sorted.

It's not always been that simple. It was an emotive issue in my childhood home because my uncle had ECT in the 1960s and my mother reckoned it led to him killing himself.

When electricity goes through the brain, it causes a seizure like the tonic-clonic fits you might see in epilepsy. The discharge from the brain goes to the muscles and they contract, not in a coordinated way, but all at once. So, in your arm for instance, your muscles would be trying to flex and extend your elbow at the same time, and it's like that through the whole body. After this 'tonic' phase comes the clonus, the repetitive jerking movements that others see as the 'fit'. The patient is unconscious and won't know what is going on, but it looks very unpleasant and the uncoordinated muscle contraction and the jerks of the seizure can break bones. Which is why ECT is now always 'modified'. Patients are anaesthetised so they are unconscious and given drugs that paralyse the muscles for a short period.

The paralysing drugs we now use, euphemistically known as 'muscle relaxants', come from modern versions of curare which the indigenous people of South America used to coat the darts in their blowpipes. It paralyses little animals when out hunting and it paralyses big animals like us too. But now it is used by people with stethoscopes, so it's OK.

And that is the message I tried to give my mother, but she didn't believe me and in fairness she had a point. She had seen her brother George given the unmodified ECT and she knew it was not nice, and the people with stethoscopes sometimes knew sod all about anything.

But that was a long time ago, and this is a digression and I have sufficient insight to know it is simply to delay my blushes.

Whilst I was training on an acute psychiatry ward at St Jude's, we had a rota to give ECT. I noticed that my turn was coming up. I hadn't done it before.

Nerissa Johnson was a severely depressed woman of about forty. She had first become unwell when she was in her twenties and took to her bed for three weeks. She stopped her nursing studies and overdosed on amitriptyline, an anti-depressant drug that was widely used before Prozac was invented. Amitriptyline is a good drug, on the whole, but can be positively dangerous in excess. It is prone to stop your heart, which is a very bad thing, because people who are depressed tend to take overdoses.

She recovered and returned to her studies, only to lose contact with reality just before her examinations and hit a patient under her care. She was never charged or prosecuted but it did effectively end her nursing career.

After that she fell victim to a crippling depression which confined her in hospital for about a quarter of the year, too depressed to move or feed herself. For a quarter of the year she shuffled around at home in a dressing gown, and for half a year she wrote children's books whilst probably wondering when her dark days were coming back. She didn't like the medication we had to offer her, and perhaps as a consequence of this, her consultant had offered her ECT some years earlier. She accepted with some degree of trepidation and found it worked really well.

The downside was that she lost her memory the day she had ECT and also got really bad headaches, both of which are quite common side effects. She would normally have two treatments a week, for about a month. Then she went home, giving her eleven months a year to do the things she liked. All in all, she had received seven courses of ECT, each comprising around eight individual treatments, so was no stranger to its side effects.

Whilst I was working on the ward, I found myself quite fond of Gemma, one of the student nurses. She was beautiful and intelligent, and the only thing that would make you question her judgement was that she seemed to fancy me. She hadn't seen the treatment being administered before, so I suggested she should come and watch. Nothing like a bit of ECT to cement a medical romance. She brought a couple of colleagues, who were also ECT virgins.

I had read all the books there were to read on this subject. I knew the hardware; I knew its output, and I could find the correct spot to put the electrode paddles on both temples of a recumbent head. I had practised on Gemma.

Once the button on the paddle was depressed, the machine I was using had a three-second fixed delivery. Writing this now, I realise how old-fashioned this sounds. Technology has really moved on since then. Mrs Johnson was lying on the bed. Gemma and her pals were standing at her side. The anaesthetist did his stuff, then took his place at her feet. 'She's ready for you, Dr Cave.'

I assumed my position by her head and reached for the paddles I had set up earlier. I flicked the on switch and started to place the electrodes on Mrs Johnson's head.

'You might want to use the electrolyte solution,' the anaesthetist murmured.

Fuck, I thought. I was about to burn her skin. Three pairs of student nurses' eyes locked on to me and saw me for the fraud that I was.

'Yes,' I mumbled, pushing the end of the paddles deep into the pink solution, liberally coating the electrode, and, at the risk of giving away the punchline, also coating its handle, my fist, my shirt cuff and probably, in truth, most of my forearms. I might as well have had a bath in the bloody stuff.

My father never liked the idea of me being a psychiatrist. He was a teacher who went into my mother's family business after they married. He was a practical man who taught me how to wire a plug and change a light bulb. I had studied physics, maths, chemistry, biology and even general studies at school. I knew that flying a kite in a storm was a bad idea and I am pleased that I have instilled basic knowledge of electrical properties in my children. The little one, whilst walking with me in the Alps, pointed her metal walking stick at an angry-looking cloud as it discharged one billion joules of energy. It missed her, but she won't use walking sticks at all now.

Put simply, electricity is known for its habit of following the path of least resistance. It is something that Dad taught me, I learnt at school and my daughter will attest to. But this bank of wisdom eluded me as I hurriedly applied the electrodes to her temples and pressed the button on the paddle with my right thumb.

I found myself gripping the paddles much more tightly than I expected. My arms were flung outwards and my body stretched towards the ceiling. And there I stood, like Jesus on the cross, with three pairs of student nurse eyes and the anaesthetist gazing at me in astonishment.

The worst bit was knowing that I was going to be crucified for three whole seconds. The second worst bit was seeing the anaesthetist's expression change from surprise to hilarity. The third worst bit was watching Gemma's friends turn to her with a look of sympathy, not for me, but for her.

It was a very, very, very long three seconds.

When I was eventually released, I slumped on to the chair behind me and tried to stabilise my breathing. My head hurt and my arms tingled curiously. To his eternal credit, the anaesthetist kept his cool as well as his smile, and went to the head end to give Mrs Johnson some oxygen.

Then he turned back to me. 'She's still under. Would you like to do that again?'

Anaesthetists are really good doctors and there is no truth that they lack any discernible social skills. Definitely.

When lecturers say: 'Who is the most important person in an operating theatre?' they hope that the answer will be 'the surgeon', which allows them to adopt a solemn face and say that actually, it's the patient. This is, of course, nonsense. Just ask anyone who is concerned at the prospect of waking up paralysed during an operation.

I declined this anaesthetist's gracious offer to repeat my mistake, made my excuses and left.

I was back on the ward later the same day, mostly recovered, apart from a ferocious headache and curious memory lapses, when Mrs Johnson appeared. I'd been planning to come and let her know what had happened. The duty of candour hadn't yet been invented, but it's what we seemed to do naturally. It seemed only right to tell patients what went wrong and why.

But I didn't have a chance even to open my mouth. She bounded up to me. 'Dr Cave, would you do my ECT next Thursday?' Compared to me she seemed positively manic. 'I've had over fifty treatments, and you're the first person not to give me a headache.'

I spoke quietly because it felt like the reverberations of my voice were performing a temporal lobectomy with a cheese grater. 'Mrs Johnson, we need to have a chat . . .'

You've probably got the idea by now that I don't see too many people on couches. And the number of times I was invited to see Gemma on a couch after giving myself ECT went into rapid decline. It's very difficult conducting a relationship when her friends put their arms out and make buzzing noises every time you see them.

After a suitable interval of several years, I told my dad what had happened. 'Stupid plonker.' He laughed quietly to himself and took another sip of wine.

I told the same story to my mother before she got dementia. She was just depressed at that point. She asked if Mrs Johnson got better. I equivocated, and she pressed me for an answer.

'Yes, Mum, she got better,' I lied. Well, not *lied*, exactly. She did get better, but I knew the end of the story by this point. Mum was a perceptive type and knew she hadn't got the whole truth, but she pressed no further. She paused and looked quite serious. 'ECT isn't a laughing matter, Ben.'

Mum died two weeks ago. I started to write this book the night before we buried her.

It's probably just a coincidence.

I never asked my mother if she read her brother's suicide note, or even if he wrote one. I should have. It was such a massive trauma in her life – my family's life.

The health lottery

When we write suicide notes, they come in all shapes and sizes. Some are hastily scribbled, others are carefully documented. Many give reasons – they might blame someone, or indeed themselves – but it's unusual to have a written narrative that completely describes a person's mental state.

This final note does. It's real, the names are real, the people are real. She was a patient and I knew her well.

Feel flat all the time – mornings worst
trying to force myself to be cheerful but feels FORCED
like behind a glass screen losing touch with other people –
no connection, speech forced,
smiles forced, words hollow everything's an effort no drive
or motivation
tired all the time thoughts churning all the time
forgetful, more accident-prone pulling on clothes, bath,
cooking daily chores all an effort like climbing mountain
everyday phone up various people to get tasks done so
something moving hoping for a change
Getting more and more mixed up
No enjoyment in previous interests – psychiatry losing its
fascination
Programs like Inspector Morse A touch of Frost etc which I
used to enjoy before don't do anything for me any more
Used to enjoy listening to CDs but music does nothing for me

Feel useless
  as a mother
  as a wife
  as a woman
See no hope for the future
Trying desperately to see hope for the future but becoming
more + more difficult
sleep unrefreshing
food forced down because my baby needs nourishment
Focusing on my precious baby Freya – she means
everything to me, I desperately want to be a good mother
to her but I'm starting to feel I'm failing her in a big way,
that everyone can see I'm a useless mother that I'm no
good.
Finding it difficult to hand [sic] *on to positive things*
anyone says, can't hang on to it for long – hits me in
early hours of morning – thoughts churn round + round.
Starting to think that Dave hates me, wants me out the
way, wants me to go crazy so he can get another wife
who's better for him.
Finding it difficult to hang on to reality – am I bad +
wicked?
I don't deserve good things, who am I kidding?
Is this all a bad dream or really happening?
Is there really hope for the future?
I've tried to put a smile on, to hand [sic] *on to positive*
but getting more + more difficult to know what's real.
Losing reason? Losing sanity?
Freya needs me, I can't let her down. Need to get myself
back to normal for her. She + Dave mean world to me –
I need to sort myself out for them. Fear I'm cracking up.
No point in counselling cognitive therapy whatever, I
couldn't take it in anyway or make use of – thoughts too
mixed up, don't hang on to any one thread for long,
no clarity anywhere, not got will or energy

I've been down this road before, don't want to breakdown or end up on psychiatric ward having ECT. Want to avoid that at all cost – I've got my baby to think about. Got to keep going for her she's everything to me, more than life itself. She needs me + I'm going to be there for her, whatever it takes.

The surviving families are normally left perplexed and bewildered. Rational suicide does happens, but usually the reason someone takes their own life in an unexpected way is mental illness.

The note you have just read belonged to Daksha. It displays the sense of utter hopelessness that pervades severe depression. You can tell that she is detaching from reality and that she recognised her inability to benefit from counselling as she slid into psychosis.

I got to know Daksha when I was training in psychiatry. She was a graduate and had excelled in her chosen field despite the hurdle of serious mental illness, a bipolar disorder, first diagnosed after a large overdose whilst she was still at university. Subsequently she'd been in hospital five times and had ECT on three occasions.

She came from a humble background and was always modest about her achievements. When she was manic, she got bubbly, spent money and was generous to everyone. When she was low, she suffered from poor concentration and had difficulty sleeping. She would try to minimise her depressed feelings from her doctor and developed suicidal and paranoid ideas.

We met every week for a while, and I got to know her well. We liked each other and she didn't wear her illness on her sleeve. Our meetings eventually stopped, and I lost touch with her. It's like that with busy jobs, but I occasionally heard how she was doing from colleagues, and I was happy for her. Then I heard she had come off medication in order to start a family. Freya was born on 4 July.

Three months later, on 9 October, she stabbed Freya, stabbed herself, covered them both with an accelerant and set themselves on fire. Freya died of smoke inhalation and Daksha survived for another three weeks, before dying from her injuries. Perhaps mercifully, she never regained consciousness.

She had asked her husband before he went to work that day if there were 'bad forces' at play against them. Dave discovered their bodies when he got home. He knew about Daksha's illness and mood changes, but was unaware of her paranoia, part of the psychosis that accompanied her relapses.

You can hear the paranoia in the note – she was worried that he hated her and that he was looking for another wife. She knew she was losing touch with reality and she was scared by it. She also knew that she wouldn't be able to use counselling or therapy – she was too far gone.

The coroner said that Daksha killed herself while the balance of her mind was disturbed, and Freya's death was classed as an extended suicide.

There was an inquiry into what happened and why. It made far-reaching recommendations, notably about the post-code lottery of care, her cultural and religious background, stigma and how mental health professionals are treated when they become unwell. It also said the team looking after her should have involved her family more. If Dave had known more about her relapse indicators, including the paranoia, then he might have recognised the warning signs for what they were.

Maybe. I don't know.

But it is true that patients tend to follow the same pathway into their illness. Someone who gets obsessional before their depression the first time is quite likely to follow the same path the next time they get depressed.

I find Daksha's case troubling because I knew her, and managing such relationships when you can't hide your emotions behind the veneer of professionalism is complex, to say the least.

You may have formed the impression she was my patient, but she was in fact a fellow psychiatrist. We worked in the same places and sometimes found ourselves on call together. She was a work colleague and a friend. She was about to start her first consultant post when she and her daughter died.

The purpose of sharing this is simple.

Woman kills her own child. I need to explain the back story to headlines like this. The answer is mental illness.

When I remember Daksha, it is quite impossible to reconcile the person I knew with what she did. To say that her actions were born out of mental illness is self-evident, but let me trumpet it loud, if only for Dave and other families in the same situation.

It's the mental illness, it's not the person.

At Daksha and Freya's funeral I watched as Dave prostrated himself before their coffins. He was literally mad with grief. It was as powerful a display of human grief as I have ever seen. It was raw and unrestrained, and it felt almost a violation to witness it. I found myself averting my gaze and, as I did so, I looked around at my colleagues – all our colleagues. Everyone was there. We were sharing the loss of Daksha and Freya with her loved ones and our hearts went out to them.

Some were crying openly. Some tried not to. Perhaps I was projecting my hidden fears, but I recognised something behind the distant gaze, behind the tears and the sense of loss. A look I'd seen before, binding us together. The awful realisation that one of us had been taken, and it had been a lottery all along.

I went across to the psychiatrist who had previously been treating Daksha. I knew him and loved him well. I gave him a hug. He barely acknowledged it – his arms hung limply by his side.

I was holding Yellow Man again, as his life departed.

We were hugging and I was looking at the faces of the other patients on the ward.

Save him, they seemed to say.

Save me.

And heal thyself.

Mr Couteau

I open the bottom drawer of my office cabinet and look at all the case files where there has been violence to members of staff. Even in hospital, some of them were due to alcohol or drugs, and even then, only a few of them were prosecuted. Some of them weren't even interviewed by the police.

Well, they're in the right place already, aren't they, Doc?

I run my hand over the spines of the folders – each one about a member of staff. The first name in the file is mine, and the last belongs to Elaine.

My 'baptism' took place quite early in my career. It happened in the middle of a clinic waiting room. I'd simply called his name – that's all.

You can probably imagine what the room looked like back then.

These days, they all seem to have a TV on the wall telling you to get a flu jab, that the trust has zero tolerance of violence to staff, or it's telling you to lose weight and exercise more, then offering courses on self-confidence. Some have a café, where you can buy crisps and doughnuts.

But this was before all that – this was 'old school'. You've probably sat in one just like it: the stale smell in the air, like a child's satchel crossed with air freshener; the centrifugal seating arrangement, with all the chairs pressed against the wall so that everyone is made to look at each other rather uncomfortably; and the old coffee table with out-of-date issues of *Country Life* and *Good Housekeeping*.

My personal record was finding an issue from 1975. Thinking about it now, I wonder if in fact it was a brilliant piece of unintentional 'reminiscence therapy' for patients with dementing illness. There was a very prescient piece about Harold Wilson renegotiating the terms of Britain's EEC membership. He was going to resign a year later.

I went into this waiting room and I called for Mr Couteau. I had a letter of referral from the GP which was spectacularly unhelpful. These things are now generically termed, *'please see and do the necessary'*, because they show a careless disregard for the nature of the problem, the social history, the treatment so far and what is wanted from the consultation. Here is what I knew about the patient:

> *Dear Mr Cave,*
> *Please see Mr Couteauo,*
> *He complains of social problems and would like to see a psyhologist.*
> *You're advice is much apreciated.*
> *Yours sincerely*
> *Etc*
> *Dictated but not singed to avoid delay*

For fuck's sake. Even the patient's name was spelt incorrectly. 'Mr Couteau,' I called. Everyone around the edge of the room glanced up, but there were no takers. I eyeballed each of them in a slightly accusatory way and said the name again. I raised my voice for no particular reason, having decided to give it one more go. 'Mr Couteau,' I snapped.

Finally, as I was about to move on, a thin-faced man of about thirty decided to stand up. He looked in my direction but didn't seem to be looking at me.

I said his name again in what I thought was an enquiring and supportive sort of way. 'Mr Couteau?' which medically translates as, 'Mr Couteau, I have a full waiting room and two new admissions back on the ward. Please get your arse in gear and come and talk to me.' I even smiled at him, which was a clear sign of irritation.

Unfortunately, Mr Couteau did not get his arse in gear. Instead, he reached into his satchel. I can still remember the sideways glance he gave me. It was hurried and expressionless. It didn't say, 'I've been waiting for over an hour,' or, 'I don't really need to be here, but my wife made me come.'

In fact, he seemed to look right through me. There was no connection.

Something was wrong.

He scrutinised the contents of his satchel, purposefully and slightly clumsily. The only thing I knew for sure was that he wasn't looking for his appointment card.

Something was very wrong, very wrong indeed. He hadn't acknowledged his name except to stand up. He hadn't made eye contact, not meaningfully, and he seemed flustered.

I've never had a premonition before, but absolutely every part of my brain was screaming 'ALARM'. My adrenal glands started to do what adrenal glands are built for, and I could feel my pulse double and my breathing deepen almost to the point of hyperventilation. Time went a bit Dali, and I was able to look around the room and see four people, all waiting to see me, two men and two women. I still remember where I was in the room and where all the patients were seated.

My premonition clarified and I came to the absolute and irrevocable conclusion that Mr Couteau was going to take a gun out of his bag and shoot me. And if he shot me, I decided he was probably going to shoot everyone else.

I can't really explain it, but I knew that's what he was going to do.

By now, he was clearly looking to orientate his hand to the gun at the bottom of the satchel. To this day, I don't know why I formed this view. He was a normal, if under-nourished, sort of chap.

My brain was regressing. All the blood was heading for my muscles and I had a very narrow focus on things. He now had my complete attention. Nothing else existed.

He reminded me of how I imagined Ratty from *The Wind in the Willows* to look, and I liked Ratty, so there was no clue there. His lack of eye contact might have raised a hackle or two, but not my overwhelming visceral reaction.

Eventually his hand stopped moving and there was a faint smile on his thin little face. At this point, I realised, in a regressed Pooh-like way, that something had to be done. My overriding thought was that if he shot the patients, then it wasn't going to be a good starting point for their treatment.

That would be a bad thing.

There were four of them and me, against Mr Couteau, against Ratty. If I ran away, he would shoot the other patients. None of them seemed to have noticed what was going on, and they didn't look like they would be able to defend themselves anyway.

So there was nothing else for it.

His hand was slowly edging out of the bag now, grasping something. I looked past him and saw the receptionist through a glass screen in the adjacent room. I knew from bitter experience that she had a hearing problem of the kind that renders the sufferer unable to hear a ringing phone, even at close range, whilst preserving the ability to engage in normal conversation with her friends in the office. It is, in my experience, a reasonably common condition that needs more attention and research.

His hand was now nearly out of the bag and his Ratty smile was a bit wider and his teeth a little pointier. I knew I had to make a decision.

Which I did.

First, I shouted 'ALARM'.

When I say I shouted 'alarm', you should know that if I had the ability to pitch my voice, I would be a good operatic baritone. As I can't pitch my voice, the best I can say is that I can be very loud indeed. The woman on my left immediately fell off her chair and the receptionist broke off her conversation to look at me.

I decided to close him down. I knew I'd need to wrestle the gun off him, and I'd mentally prepared to break his arm if necessary – frankly, whatever it took. I flipped through my repertoire of martial arts skills designed to disable a man with a gun.

And came up short.

I had been on the control and restraint course – we all have to do it – and nothing there was going to help me. I had been on the breakaway course, but unfortunately Ratty was not holding my shoulders, nor had he grabbed me from behind, nor was he holding my hair, all eventualities for which I was thoroughly prepared, and in thirty years of clinical practice, have never been able to use.

I propelled myself past the coffee table towards my target. *Close him down. Close him down.*

My eye was inexplicably caught by the front cover of *Country Living*, and more specifically a picture of a nice farmhouse table that would look good in my kitchen.

'Yes, I got the idea at work, love. There was even time to read a magazine . . . Yes . . . Quiet day, not much happened.'

Finally, I wrenched my eyes away from the rather smart Smeg appliances on display in an open copy of *Homes & Gardens* and looked up at Ratty.

His hand emerged from the bag and his face took on a triumphant expression.

By this point, most of the room had been rendered deaf by my stun-grenade shout. I had incapacitated an already vulnerable woman who had hit the floor behind me. I'd decided which kitchen table to go for and discounted the

Smeg fridge on the grounds of cost. Now I got a good look at Ratty's hand.

It was not wrapped around a gun, but it was wrapped around a fairly significant knife – about five inches long, and like one of those you see for sale, for no good reason, in Bar Tabacs all over France.

20 Gauloises, des timbres-poste, oh, et un couteau de chasse, svp.

It's a knife. It's a fucking knife. It's only a fucking knife. Thank God.

And it's true, there are no atheists on a battlefield, or a busy psychiatry outpatient clinic either. I really do apologise for my use of profane language. This is what my internal dialogue sounds like. It's not pretty, but it's really difficult to describe my overwhelming sense of relief when I realised it was 'just' a knife.

I was closing down a person with a knife. I don't know how, but I knew that you close down on a gun and run away from a knife. It makes sense when you think about it.

But by now, all my momentum, which is the product of my mass (large) and my velocity (high), and which could probably be better described as a 'rhinoceros-like charge', was aimed, suddenly and completely, in the wrong direction.

There was about a metre between me and Ratty, and I was closing very fast. The receptionist was now looking at her phone and seemed to be wrestling with her cognitive ability to determine whether having a woman on the floor with acoustic shock and a shouting doctor charging at a patient with a knife constituted an emergency.

There really is no protocol for this sort of thing, but if she had been paying careful attention to my expression, she would have spotted a moment of relief when I saw that it was 'only a knife', but then seen it change back to 'terrified' as he thrust it towards me.

Fortunately, if I put one middle fingertip on the floor and stretch the other as high as it will go, the pencil mark will be six feet and four inches up the wall. Which is an inch taller than I am. I am now eternally grateful for that, because I have no doubt that it was the combination of my outstretched arm, held like the barrel of a gun from a tank turret, coupled with my mass and velocity, that launched my opponent off his feet and prompted him to soar majestically on to the wall behind him.

He bounced off it, reverberating as he did so, then stumbled back towards me, so I found myself able to grab his wrist, turn it in the wrong direction and watch the blade drop harmlessly to the floor.

At this point, the movie hero may fail to remove the weapon from the bad guy, thus allowing him one last chance to get even, but I have always found this a tiresome plot device, so I kicked the knife towards one of the watching patients. Perhaps unsurprisingly, I had their rapt attention. All except one. She was obviously more involved in her internal dialogue than even this episode could intrude upon.

I witnessed the same reaction on 11 September 2001 when the planes flew into the World Trade Center. I was on the medium secure unit at St Jude's at the time and staff and patients were shoulder to shoulder watching the TV. About four of the patients were so unwell they couldn't focus or concentrate on those momentous events, and it was the same phenomenon here.

Ratty was now disarmed and I was holding his hand. There was a slightly awkward moment when we both realised that the game was over and wondered what to do next. By now, the full effect of my earlier adrenaline surge was kicking in and it seemed a shame to waste it. So as he then struggled to get away, I picked him up and put him back down on the floor sufficiently firmly to make sure that he bounced a bit more, and to remind him, lest he was in any doubt, that getting up again before the police showed up would be a very, very, bad idea.

At this point, I realised that my older brother, who went off to university when I was still in short trousers, had probably saved my life. Swiftly bored by academia, he had decided to learn how to kill people and joined the Parachute Regiment. During his training, he'd frequently used me to practise unarmed combat skills. It usually began with me coming at him with a stick, or one time, a golf club, and invariably ended with me lying face down on the floor, my arm pointing upwards at an unnatural angle and my wrist losing the will to live.

'Try to get out of it . . .'

I heard his voice now. Followed by a sound like the first drop of rain on a tin roof.

Then more drops. A chorus of them, in fact.

Three of the four patients were clapping.

The one lost in her own experiences did not, and I made sure I spent some time talking to her later. She was very unwell, and in due course I walked her to the ward.

The other patients were very charitable. The receptionist had galvanised herself sufficiently to take them to another room and even made them some tea. The police arrived, I gave a statement, and saw Ratty again in court some months later. Only this time, his teeth weren't as pointy as I remembered and he didn't remind me of Ratty anymore. He was just an ordinary fellow called Mr Couteau. He pleaded guilty to possession of an offensive weapon. After that, he went into hospital – he was autistic, had a psychosis and had been using cannabis. At least he ended up getting the help he needed.

And that was it, really. I finished my ward work, wrote up the non-applauding patient for some sedatives and anti-psychotic drugs and went home.

I found myself strangely emotional that night and saw that my hands were shaking.

I got to know the receptionist better over the next few months. She made me tea a few times. It turns out she had schizophrenia and found social interaction quite challenging.

It's all too easy to judge people without the full picture.

Expert witness collywobbles

'Are you ready?' I call to Elaine.

'Yep.' I get my coat and we leave the unit. 'Pizza or Turkish? There's a new place.'

We don't say much until the hummus, olives and pitta arrive.

'Will your shoulder need surgery?' I ask.

'I hope not.' She sounds uncertain. 'Have you ever been assaulted?'

'Yes, but not like you. I didn't know the patient which I think made it easier.'

'What happened?' she asks.

'Nothing really. Just a man with a knife. But the first time I saw a nurse being assaulted, it was about a week into my first job.'

'What happened?'

'I was seeing a man in A & E. He was in on a section 136. The police had found him wandering, shouting at people near the shops. They thought he was psychotic, so they brought him in. It was routine really. I was interviewing him with Cathy, don't think you know her, she was the deputy ward manager. Anyway, I looked up, and Cathy was running across the room towards me. The patient had got up and was coming for me.'

I take some of the taramasalata that has just arrived. 'It's very good. So, she puts herself in front of me just as he is taking a kick at me. It was like Owen Farrell taking a conversion. Anyway, she took the kick right in her groin.'

'Was she OK?' asks Elaine.

'I think so. She doubled up with the blow. We didn't really talk about it back then. It was just part of the job.'

Elaine looks thoughtful. 'Still is, I think. What happened to him?'

'He ran off. Security were useless. We reported it to the police, but we didn't hear anything more. So, I finish the day and I go to the local off-licence and I buy Cathy a little miniature of brandy. I put it in an internal mail envelope, remember those, and put it under her wipers on the windscreen.'

'That's nice.'

'No, that's just it. I came into work the next day and the car was still there – it hadn't moved, and the brandy was still there under the wiper.'

'Why?'

'Well, I saw Cathy when she arrived and asked her why she'd left her car at work. She told me she'd gone to her car the night before and seen the envelope. But it turns out that she was having a bad time with a boyfriend – he was violent to her. She thought it was from him, and she couldn't face opening it. She walked home. Then I felt really bad, so I took her to the car and made her open the envelope with me. I told her it was to make her feel better. She just stood there and cried. I think she was just holding it together until she could let it out.'

Elaine is welling up. 'I just need the bathroom,' she says.

She comes back a short time later with red eyes.

'Are you talking to anyone about what happened?'

'I've got a counsellor if I want,' she says.

Then the waiter brings the shish kebabs. I pick mine up and push the meat on to the plate. 'Do you want some?' I ask, waving the skewer at the meat and then dropping it between us. Elaine looks down at it, silently, and then gets up. 'I'm just going for a cigarette.'

She looks a bit more settled when she comes back. 'I thought he was going to kill me.' She moves the food around on her plate, but she doesn't eat anything. 'He was on top of me with the metal bar. He tried to hit me over the head, but the end of it hit the ground. Then he changed his grip and used it like a dagger.' She sounds cut off from what she is describing. 'I think he was trying to stab me in the chest. I moved at the last moment and he got my shoulder. That's when the C & R [control and restraint] team arrived.'

'They did a good job.'

'I'm pleased you got him into Bramworth.'

She's trying to close the conversation down. It's not the first time she told me what happened – each time a little more, but she's still blaming herself for having snapped at him.

That's the bit she can't cope with. 'What you did, Elaine, it wasn't your . . .'

She cuts me short. 'We need to be getting back. I need to plan the rota.'

The shutters have come down. I pay and see she's outside again having another cigarette. The waiter wants to know if there was something wrong with the food. 'No, it was good, thanks,' I try to reassure him.

Back in Lakeview, she seems to relax as we go through the familiar security checks. It's comforting and ritualistic. We're about to go our separate ways, me to my office and her to the ward when I turn to her. 'I'm kind of worried about you.'

'I'm OK,' she says. 'Earlier on, Ben, you said that you'd been assaulted by a man with a knife.'

'Yes.'

'Were you OK after that?'

'Yes, fine,' I lie.

She seems reassured and turns and goes. Back at my office I see the notes on my desk, still waiting for me. I sit down, feel wobbly and kick the textbook back in underneath me. I'm a little anxious, a little unsettled. I haven't been entirely honest with Elaine.

I felt quite stressed in the immediate aftermath of Mr Couteau. It slowly subsided but then I had something resembling a 'flashback' when I was at the Old Bailey giving evidence in a different case. It might have been that my mind was sensitised to knife attacks because the case involved a man who had stabbed his friend in the chest. He survived, but only just. All I had to do was turn up and answer a few questions about his diagnosis, his risk and say that he needed a hospital order and a restriction order. It was routine, more of a formality that the court needed to go through. It wasn't even contested – his defence team wanted him in hospital as much as the prosecution wanted him safely off the streets.

Eventually, after a lot of waiting around in court, I was finally called to the stand. On an impulse, I decided to take my thirty-page report with me.

I shouldn't have.

If they want to question you about it, it'll be there, waiting for you. Besides, it looks suspiciously like a crib sheet to a jury, so it never plays well. But with my lack of experience at the time, my report was my security blanket, my transitional object and I needed it as much as I had needed my koala bear when I was four.

In retrospect I would have been better off taking Koala with me. The bag I had was a leather satchel. It was a nice leather satchel, and it contained my report. I reached in, and suddenly it felt as if my hand was no longer my own. It was different somehow, and suddenly I thought that it might be looking for something altogether more dangerous. I pulled out my hand in a quite deliberate way as if to confirm to my eyes that it was just some paper it was holding and, as I did so, I dropped the report. I watched as it fluttered down the steeply banked stairs leaving pages in its wake.

As I walked down, I picked up page 20. 'Mr Allen attacked his friend with a bread knife believing him to be threatening his life.'

Next was page 24. 'Since the assault Mr Allen himself has experienced nightmares, intrusive thoughts and occasionally relived his experiences.'

Page 29. 'Mr Allen was suffering from a paranoid schizophrenic illness and had ongoing symptoms consistent with PTSD.'

The judge peered down. 'You won't be needing those,' he said, judgementally.

I left the remaining papers to be picked up by the usher and made my way to the witness box. I felt cold and sweaty, and I suspect if I could have seen myself, I'd have been cardiac grey.

As I was sworn in, I started to hyperventilate, each section of the affirmation spat out in a condensed expiratory note.

'Idosolemnlysincerelyandtrulydeclareand,'

(rapid inspiration)

'affirmthattheevidenceIshallgiveshallbe,'

(rapid inspiration and wipe brow)

'thetruththewholetruthandnothingbutthetruth.'

Then I was ready for questioning.

'Is your name Dr Ben Cave?'

As questions go at the Old Bailey, it was probably one of the easier ones, but by this point all I wanted to do was lie down in a nice dark room for half an hour. I could feel my peripheral vision going.

'Doctor,' said the judge, peering down at me like a pre-Raphaelite painting, 'are you quite well?'

'Yes, my Lord.'

Oh Gawd, what do you call them? Is it Sir, your Honour, my Lord?

I turned back to the barrister. 'I am Dr Ben Cave.'

Nothing happened. It was a knife. It was only a fucking knife.

'Are you a qualified doctor and psychiatrist approved under section 12 of the Mental Health Act?' said the barrister, looking carefully at me.

'Yes,' I managed.

'And have you seen the accused to provide a report to the court?'

'Yes.'

'Is it your view that he needs hospital treatment?'

'Yes.'

'Does he need a restriction order?'

'Yes.'

I had got through it so far. My name and four yesses. The judge peered down again. 'Would you like a glass of water, Doctor?'

I was shaking. I was hyperventilating. I was hyperalert. I was scanning the court for any threat.

I should have bought the Smeg fridge.

'Yes,' I said, in a rather strangled voice to the judge, and he looked to the usher, who nodded and poured me some water.

Nobody else seemed to want to ask me anything so I was excused.

'Well,' said the judge eventually, fixing his gaze on Mr Allen in the dock, 'the doctor's evidence was clear and cogent, and I am persuaded that you need to receive treatment and not punishment. You will be taken back to Lakeview House, and I make a hospital order with restrictions without limit of time.'

It was an inauspicious start to my career as an expert witness. Still, it did the job. My patient ended up on the right section and as I left the court, I took my tie off and sat down on one of the benches. I turned my phone on and saw a message from my brother.

'Are you OK? Fancy a drink?'

'Fuck, yes.' I replied.

His offices were just on the Strand. I went to an off-licence on the way, bought a bottle of wine and took the lift up to the fifth floor. He was there waiting for me with a glass of wine as the door opened. 'God, Ben, you look terrible.'

I accepted the glass from him, drank it and then reached out for another. 'Looks like you need it,' he said, topping me up.

'Hi, Phil,' I said in a delayed greeting. 'How's tricks?'

'Good. What are you doing this way?'

'Not much,' I answered, slightly enigmatically. He'd need to work harder than that to get me to open up.

'Right,' he said.

We ran out of wine and decided to go for a curry.

'I was giving evidence in an attempted murder case,' I said, whilst he was ordering some poppadums. I didn't think that giving evidence in an attempted murder case was getting sufficient attention, so I tried a different tack. 'It was quite fun looking back on it. I mean not at the time. I dropped all my notes. But I enjoyed it.'

'You enjoyed it,' he echoed. He seemed detached and he was looking at the empty Cobra bottle next to him and waving to the waiter.

I've already referenced that we were much-loved but little-hugged children and we both have different thresholds for emotional expression. I have always thought that Big Brother needed a higher blood alcohol level than me to reach the same level of emotional insight. I had reached my zenith, but he was still a Cobra and a large red from it.

'I'm envious,' he said. 'You have it all sorted.'

I looked up sharply. I've always admired Phil and often privately wondered what he thought about me. To hear such a comment from him was not only unusual, it was sobering, so much so I wondered if a hamster had been eating his mind.

'I'm going to get a divorce,' said Phil.

I sat quietly, not surprised but still stunned.

'Sorry,' I said, quietly. I didn't need to share the problems Jo and I were having, so I quietly wiped some of the mango chutney off my tie.

'Are you OK, gentlemen?' enquired the waiter, no doubt troubled by the two silent men sucking the atmosphere from the room, looking down at their food like the statue artists in Covent Garden.

'Yes, we're fine, thanks,' I said. 'We're fine. We're OK.'

It was two days later during a meal when Jo asked me where I'd been on Tuesday night.

'I went out with Phil,' I said.

'You snored all night. You were really pissed when you came back.'

'I know,' I said. 'It was a difficult day.'

'My day was difficult too,' said Jo.

'How was it difficult?' I asked uncertainly.

'I had a child with meningococcal sepsis. She'd been sent home twice by her GP who didn't recognise the rash.'

It didn't sound particularly problematic in the great scheme of things. 'So?' I asked.

'She was septic. She lost her hands yesterday. We had to amputate. I think she's going to lose her feet. We did everything we could, but it was too late.'

I put my fork down on the plate. 'I'm sorry.' I don't think I had anything else to say, and I knew it wasn't enough. It felt like the conversation I'd just had with Elaine. I knew there was a problem, but I couldn't put it right. It was like trying to tell my mother things would be OK to reassure her. But it wasn't OK. Jo's patient, a little child, had just lost her hands. Sorry just wasn't enough.

Whatever I have experienced, I can only sit and admire Jo's ability to cope with something that I could not. In fact,

I am in awe of the whole range of paediatricians, surgeons and oncologists – the list is long – coping with endless crises and heartbreak.

Mr Allen, the man who took a bread knife to his friend, was treated for schizophrenia and then he was treated for PTSD. He did really well.

I sense Elaine is unlikely to take up the option of counselling. Jo never did. Neither have I. We're all very good at treating people. We cope with stress – that's what we do. And we keep coping right up to the point that we can't cope any more.

The problem is, we don't notice when we reach that point.

Just as the psychotic patient loses contact with reality, so does the carer. We lie to ourselves about how we feel, we put the stressful day behind us and try to forget all about it, and when that doesn't work, we blame our partner for our mood. I know I did.

Denial, repression and displacement. It's how we cope and we're really good at it.

I need to get on with my packing. I swivel on my chair and notice the textbook under me isn't quite the right size. I push myself round to the bookcase behind me and reach for the first book that comes to hand. It's another *Dice Man* exercise. The book that comes out is a thin tome by Freud. I look at it speculatively and then put it on top of the other book. I try the chair again and it seems to work nicely.

Wobble-free.

I smile to myself. I look at the bottom drawer of the filing cabinet and I know I'm prevaricating. Time for some late quartets. I need some Beethoven. It's meaty. It's visceral.

Prison is waiting for me.

Prison

'Ben, dear boy,' said Anthony. 'I've come to see if you'll carry on working here?'

'Good afternoon, Dr Franklin,' I say, mirroring his language. 'Sadly, I think I must be going.'

'No regrets?'

I look at the prison cases now on my desk. 'Regrets about leaving, no. I've enjoyed myself here, but it's time for a change.'

'You won't like it you know.'

'What?' I ask.

'You won't like senior management. When the CQC came here last year, they asked me what the management was like and I told them it was brilliant.'

'Why did you say it was brilliant?' I ask. I know the drill – you have to ask for the punchline.

'Because they leave me alone. That's the best type of medical manager. Let the clinicians get on with it.'

'I'll still be doing clinical work.'

'Good. Listen, I heard you went for lunch with Elaine. How's she doing?'

'She's finding it tough going. She's blaming herself. She's only coping by keeping busy.'

'Mmm, that's what I thought. Did you hear about my court appearance? I got an insanity verdict.'

I pull a deliberately suppressed smile. 'Did you, Anthony? I'm not surprised – you're very good.'

He laughs and calls back as he's leaving. 'Don't forget, you're only here because of me.'

It's true. He set me on my career path. I'd done some research whilst a registrar, and he had heard me teach on the subject. 'Get a job in prison and then do your forensic training,' he told me.

And that's exactly what I did. Of all the jobs I've done, I learnt more at Campsmoor prison than anywhere else. I was a research fellow. I had already passed my membership examinations for the Royal College of Psychiatrists, so I was able to assess prisoners, prescribe and do court reports.

I even got an office of my own, though the bars on the windows made it feel like a prison cell, albeit with a desk and a computer. The architects had either run out of ideas, or perhaps correctly anticipated we'd be locking up more and more of our population in the future.

It looked out into a shady atrium with more cell windows peering at each other. The cells to my right belonged to my psychotic patients, the cells on the left, the ordinary prisoners, and the cells opposite me, the vulnerable prisoners.

By and large, 'vulnerable' at Campsmoor meant 'sex offender'. If armed robbers were first amongst equals, then the vulnerable occupied a lower place on the food chain than boiled potatoes.

'Ordinary' meant violent and dangerous, and the difference between them and my psychotic prisoners, I concluded, was whether I'd interviewed them yet.

The amount of severe mental illness in prisons never ceases to amaze me.

It's odd, looking back. I think I have a very visual memory, but all I can recall about that office-cell is the sound of constant shouting across the internal courtyard.

'You fucking nonces, I'll kill you,' yelled the ordinary prisoners from the windows on the left. Unfortunately, the psychotic incumbents on my right, who were already hearing voices, tended to get confused about whether these voices were real or imagined.

'Shut up,' they'd shout, which confused the ordinary prisoners, because they weren't shouting at the psychotic prisoners in the first place, and didn't like being shouted at by anybody.

'I'm not fucking shouting at you,' they shouted.

And the angrier the ordinary prisoners got, the more they shouted, and the more the psychotic prisoners thought they were being shouted at, the more disturbed they became, and the more they shouted back.

The sex offenders largely steered clear of this cycle of abuse. Perhaps they were made that way. As children, they didn't bellow when they were being abused; maybe they didn't even realise they were being abused. Most of them didn't even think they were guilty. They all knew deep down that the person they had abused or raped was secretly asking for it, or if not of an age to consent, then they were a lot more mature than the average ten-year-old.

Their capacity for denial always staggers me.

Children these days, Doctor; they're so grown up, don't you think?

The shouting bothered me for the first month. By the second, I had acclimatised to it. It was 'white noise' in the background. By the third month, I missed it when I went home – like birdsong, you only notice when it stops.

I remember one evening, soon after I started, looking out into the atrium through my bars. I caught the eye of a man standing like a reflection of me in a window directly opposite. We looked at each other and I quickly became uncomfortable and turned away.

It's remarkable how resilient we are, that we get used to the environment we are in. By the end of the first year in prison, I was quite happy in my little room with a desk and a computer. Maybe the architects were smarter than I thought, making us all live in the same little cells.

There were two things that made it all bearable. First, I had a set of keys, and I could go home whenever I liked. Sometimes, quite often in fact, I tapped my key pouch, just to make sure they were still there. The second thing was the addition of some vertical blinds. That way, I could look to the left at the ordinary prisoners, and on other days, I could look to the right at the psychotic prisoners, but I never again wanted to be seen by the person opposite me. I wasn't to know it at the time, but that meeting would come soon enough.

Before I got to know the system, my consultant, Vicky, would decide which cases I was going to see. We had worked together before at St Jude's, and she was something of a mentor to me.

'Here, Ben, take a look at this chap.'

I opened the prison file and looked at the reception record. He had come in the night before and the nurse had sent him to the health care centre because she was worried about his mental state.

The medical information collected at the point of entry into prison was fairly cursory. It recorded the offence as the prisoner reported it, so it was often wildly inaccurate. Sometimes I don't think they actually knew why they were there. Then it went through their medical and psychiatric history, their use of drugs and alcohol, and because the form had been designed for all prisons, details about gynaecological history and pregnancy.

I'll be honest, as I opened the folder, I was hoping for a serial killer.

His pulse was sixty-five.

OK. If not a serial killer, then perhaps a terrorist. There was a category A prison here after all.

His blood pressure was 130/86, which was probably lower than mine at that moment. I would settle for a murderer.

It turned out he wasn't having periods and he wasn't pregnant.

Then I got to the all-important bit. The charge.

Speeding.

Speeding?

'Vicky,' I piped up.

'Yes, Ben,' she said.

'He's in for speeding.'

'Yes, Ben.'

'Well, it's not exactly cutting-edge forensic psychiatry, is it?'

'No, Ben,' she said, 'but consider this. I've never seen anyone remanded for speeding before. It's new ground.'

To this day, I don't know if Vicky was serious, or just brilliant at personnel management, but either way, I took the folder and started to feel quite proud that I was the first forensic psychiatrist to examine someone for speeding, certainly in the UK.

And then she gave me another one.

'Burglary,' I said, completely ignoring his cardiovascular and gynaecological history. To be honest, I was not impressed.

I took my two cases and trundled off.

First, I saw the person charged with speeding in the health care centre. The HCC catered for a mixed bag of prisoners with both physical and mental health problems.

There were clinic rooms, just like any modern general practice, even a dentist, but there were also some locked wards where six prisoners shared a large room, and then several cells round the corner where more sensitive and high-profile patients could be treated.

In the middle there was a small interview room with a couple of old chairs and a Formica table. There was some graffiti carved into it, but I soon realised that if I positioned my papers right, you could only see the *Muth* and the *ucker* on either side.

It was the spelling that bothered me most.

There was a big red button on the wall with *ALARM* written on it, in big letters. This made a big noise, I was told, and if you pressed it, six big men dressed in protective Kevlar body armour, helmets and bite-proof gloves, descended upon you, the first to drag you out, and the others to subdue the prisoner.

There was also a smaller button, a green one, placed under the table, but no one ever told me about this. I had been happily interviewing a patient who was doing quite well. We had a good relationship and he was accepting the medication – he was really making progress.

Unfortunately, during one of our meetings, my knee accidentally came into contact with the small green button. We carried on our discussion, oblivious to the fact that six big men and an alarming amount of Kevlar were advancing towards us.

I looked up as the door was thrown open, and before I could say, 'Excuse me, but this is a medical interview,' I had been grabbed by two of the Kevlar-coated officers and bundled out of the room.

'Are you all right, Doc?' they demanded.

I saw my interviewee faring less well, a mild look of surprise on his face as he was bundled to the floor.

'What was he doing? Why did you press the alarm?' came the questions from behind one of the face shields.

It took about a minute for me to explain that the whole thing had been a terrible mistake and that the patient had actually been very well behaved. The officers, somewhat grudgingly, let the prisoner stand up and he brushed himself off and straightened his tracksuit.

My 'rescuers' seemed put out that I was not offering them effusive thanks and decided to lecture me in the proper use of silent alarms.

'So, if you press the green button under the table,' explained my principal tormentor, the sarcasm dripping from each word, 'the silent alarm goes off, and we come and rescue you.'

★

Chop put his head round the door. 'Are you ready for him, Doc?'

'Yes, thanks.'

'And you do know about the alarm systems,' he asked.

I looked at him grinning under his big moustache. 'Yes,' I said, 'I know about the alarm.'

He brought in Mr Matthew Chester, the speeding villain. A world first – a forensic psychiatrist seeing someone going 40 in a 30mph zone.

'Call me Matt, everyone does. Matt's the name, what's the game, sugar and spice and all things nice. Nice to see you. Nice to see you I said, to see you nice. Price of petrol. Filled up in Chelmsford, had to ford the car, they found my star, the one that guides me, slides me. Te he. Mach-ete. Can't believe they stopped me, pigs, had a mission to do, vision to do, evil to slew.'

I put my pen down and looked up at Chop. Matt was still talking nineteen to the dozen, standing behind the chair, and I beckoned him to sit down. He ignored me. Manic people do that. He had pressure of speech and was rhyming and punning on words.

'Mr Chester,' I tried to interrupt, but it was impossible. By this point his conversation had moved on to religion and he was talking about repenting his sins and the smiting of demons. I talked over him. 'Mr Chester,' I explained, 'I need to start you on some medication.'

'Station, nation, creation.' Then he stopped abruptly. 'He's still there,' he cried, sounding suddenly mournful. 'The Devil's still there and I care . . .'

Chop put his hand on his shoulder. 'Matt,' he said, 'we need to go back to the cell now. We'll come by in a bit and give you some of the medicine the doctor prescribes.'

He seemed to listen to him, a bit anyway, and nodded slightly.

157

I went to my cell and put his name in the computer. It told me that he had been stopped for speeding, but the officers had recorded him driving erratically and going through a red light and nearly knocking down a pedestrian.

He was breathalysed and this was negative, but then things became a little unusual. He wouldn't stop talking. He started to preach and at this point the officers decided to search his car. Reading between the lines, they thought he was on drugs. When he opened the boot for the officers, they found a large sword.

Rather endearingly, the officer's notes at this point refer to the suspect 'looking a bit shifty'.

It's difficult to define what 'shifty' looks like and I've never used the term in a court report. You'd get worked over by the barristers.

Dr Cave, in your experience as a forensic psychiatrist, what exactly is your training in so-called shifty facial appearances?

Naturally, the officer asked him what the sword was for. Most people at this point would say that it was ornamental, or they were on their way to Sandhurst for their passing out parade, but Mr Chester just said that he was on his way to kill the Devil.

The officer wrote in his notes: 'I was surprised at his response and I asked him where the Devil was living.'

I love police notes – they're full of understated heroism, like, 'I became worried for my safety after he took the sub-machine gun out and pointed it at me.'

You can almost hear the sergeant reading the original report back at the station, telling the still-shaken PC, 'Just change the bit about crapping yourself, Stanley, and say you got worried. The court don't need to know about your bowel movements.'

I'll do any report if there are lots of police notes and I carried on reading. 'The suspect had the address down on a piece of paper. He said he was going to knock on the door and behead the person who answered it. Then he went on to preach a little and invited me to repent my sins.'

I saw Mr Chester on my daily rounds, and once he took his medication, he settled down quite quickly. He started to sleep better and he wasn't as intrusive to people around him so that he was able to come out of the cells and stay in one of the six-bedded wards.

By the end of the week I interviewed him again. He was still a bit high, fidgety and kept getting up and down, but he could hold a decent conversation.

'How are you, Mr Chester?' I asked.

'Never felt better. Hundred and ten per cent,' he grinned.

'So how did you end up in prison? What happened?'

He winked at me. 'I'm not in prison. I'm working for the government. I'm part of the prison inspectorate. Undercover branch.'

'I see. Do you do any other work?'

'Well, I'm a teacher. An English teacher.'

'And have you ever seen a psychiatrist before?'

'They were useless. They were giving me lithium and it slowed me down. I had so much to do and that's when it all came to me. Psychiatrists are doing the Devil's work and they were trying to stop me on my mission. They came round to section me, I mean, can you believe that?'

'When did you last have lithium?'

'About four months ago. I feel so alive now.'

'You're taking a medicine called olanzapine. Would you take the lithium again if I prescribed it for you?'

'No, I only take the olanzapine because you'd inject me if I didn't.'

I didn't tell him that the Mental Health Act doesn't apply in prisons. He was in a prison health care centre, not a hospital, so I just said, 'Yeah,' in as non-committal sort of way as I could, and then threw in a 'definitely' for good measure.

'Where do you live?'

'Chelmsford.'

'How come you had a sword in the boot of your car?'

'I've been through this. Are you a psychiatrist?'

'The police notes say that you were going to kill the Devil.'

'You're part of it, aren't you?'

I did my expressionless poker face that seemed to work quite well in prison. 'What can you tell me about the Devil?'

'Well it's obvious, isn't it,' he said excitedly. 'There's a plot to stop my divine mission. I am the chosen one. I shall kill the Devil.'

'The notes I've read say that you have the Devil's address.'

He nodded proudly. 'It came to me in a dream. It's 66 Deverill Close.'

'Is that two L's?'

'You see, don't you, it's got the word Devil hidden in it.'

'Yes,' I nodded. I guess it was a short road too.

'So, when you got there, what were you going to do?'

He looked at me like I was a bit slow. 'Rid the world of evil.'

'Yes, but how?'

'I was going to kill the Devil.'

'What if you were wrong? What if the person was an accountant, or an estate agent?' I said, immediately regretting my choices.

'You're part of it, aren't you? I'm terminating this conversation.'

And he did. He got up and walked out into the corridor and waited for one of the officers to let him back into his six-bedded ward.

'Put him in a fucking cell by himself,' shouted one of the other prisoners.

I saw Chop outside the interview room and beckoned him in. 'He's really not that much better. I think we should get him back into a single cell. I'm worried he'll decide one of the other prisoners is the Devil in the middle of the night.'

'OK,' agreed Chop. 'Are you going to transfer him?'

'Think so. He's got no record, but he's quite deluded at the moment. Low security I reckon. Do we have any next of kin details?'

'Sure.'

Chop brought a printout and gave it to me. 'It's his wife in Chelmsford — Sharon Chester.'

I called her straight away. 'Thank you for calling,' she said. 'I've been worried sick.'

I asked her to flesh out his history.

'Well, I didn't know he'd stopped the lithium. He wasn't sleeping well and that normally seems to be how it starts, then he goes high and gets all these mad ideas. What is it now — on a secret mission?'

'Something like that,' I confirmed, aware he had said I was not to share any details with her. But that didn't stop her sharing details with me, I reasoned.

'Anyway,' she went on, 'he came back from school one day and told me he'd resigned. I mean, we need the money, and Andy, he's our son, he's only three.'

'How long do his highs last?'

'It's bad — normally he's off work for about three months. He's really brilliant you know. But he always thinks people are putting him down. Has he told you about the voices?'

'No. What does he hear?'

'Well, depends on his mood. But his psychiatrist at the hospital thinks he needs a depot because of his compliance. He really doesn't take the medication properly. The consultant said he thinks it's more of a schizoaffective disorder.'

'Could be. Listen, I'm going to try to get him moved out of prison. It's not the right place for him. Can I suggest you get in touch with the school and tell them he was unwell when he resigned — see if they will keep his job open for him.'

Over the next few days, he refused the olanzapine, and just as he had improved with the medication, he started to deteriorate again without it, but he had no insight into the changes in his mental state.

I got in touch with his psychiatrist in Chelmsford and they immediately agreed he needed to come in and found a low secure bed by the end of the next week. By this point he was literally raving. He was telling anyone within shouting distance, which was most of the house block, that he needed to kill the Devil once again.

Normally, once a prisoner is transferred out to a hospital, that would be the end of my involvement with them. In this case, I found myself driving through Chelmsford a fortnight later after seeing a bare-knuckle fighter who had started to get into more fights than usual. The boxer was also disinhibited, probably not because he was manic, but because his frontal lobe had been bashed around too much. He had exceeded its design specifications.

On an impulse, I phoned the unit, and the consultant was very happy for me to call in – I think he was secretly hoping to recruit me into a vacant post.

'So, we gave him intramuscular olanzapine when he came in,' he told me, 'and then we've given him a depot. He's still refusing lithium. Let me know if you think he's better than he was in prison.'

He opened the door to a well-appointed interview room where Matt was waiting for me.

'Hello, Matt.' I sat down opposite him, and he slowly looked up to make eye contact. 'You are wicked. You are evil.' He stood up and put his hands on the table between us and then spat in my face.

Matt walked out and the consultant hurried back in. 'I'm so sorry, I saw what happened.'

'It's fine,' I said, pulling out a handkerchief to wipe my face. 'Have you spoken to his wife? She was worried about his job.'

'Yes. The school were very happy to accept his resignation. It's not the first time he's had problems. Reading between the lines, it sounds like he's been sexually disinhibited before.'

'Will you do a section 37?'[1]

'Yeah, if he gets convicted. I suspect the CPS might drop the matter. We'll put him on a section 3 if they do. Same thing really.'

Matthew was a law-abiding family man with a wife and child. He was a teacher, a good one, and had a good life and a good career. And now, through no fault of his own, he had a severe mental illness, he had lost his job, they didn't want him back in teaching because of his disinhibition when he became unwell, he'd almost killed someone driving, he was going to lose his licence, he was being medicated compulsorily and he was getting worse not better. He was possibly going to get a criminal conviction and he was out of touch with reality.

I left the unit with the consultant asking me about my career plans and I was driving home and listening to a comedian on the radio. He described himself as a 'little bit bipolar'. The way he said it, it sounded more like my sort of ups and downs. Then he made a joke about people with mania. I felt indignant and turned the radio off to brood in silence. The comedian said he had bipolar so he could make a joke about it. Maybe he did have bipolar – I don't know, but it was self-evident he had a key to his little cell, just like I did.

I found myself tapping at my waist where I would normally carry my prison keys. They weren't there of course – you are issued them when you go into prison, and you give them back when you leave. It's ironic. When you are mentally

---

1 Section 37 is a treatment order imposed by the court after a conviction. It's effectively the same as a section 3, which lasts for up to six months and is used outside of forensic practice.

ill and you need your keys the most, they're not there. Mr Chester didn't have any keys. Either his illness or his employers or maybe society as a whole made sure of that.

He was a mentally disordered offender. He was dangerous, and I wondered to myself if I was part of the problem or part of the cure.

He was going to be in his little cell for a very long time. I was just visiting.

Fraggle Rock

It's normally very difficult to prove a negative outcome. For instance, if a surgeon operates on cancer and the patient is cured, it is an obvious and positive outcome. And the patient says thank you and buys some chocolates for the nurses.

If a psychiatrist treats someone for severe depression and they don't kill themselves as a result, it is a good outcome but it's impossible to say that the treatment stopped the suicide. The outcome is positive but hidden. And more often than not, the patient thanks the team.

If a forensic psychiatrist treats someone who is a danger to others and does a good job, nobody gets killed. But nobody notices someone not being killed. Nobody says thank you. In fact, people complain about how much the service costs and the patient complains about their detention being unjustified. And if they buy you chocolates, well, it's probably best to give them to someone you don't like and probably won't meet again.

So, it's quite a big thing to get to see the hidden positive outcome, and see how the system works, sometimes.

Mr Chester was a good example of this. It was lucky that the traffic officers stopped him. Imagine the devastating effect if he had reached 66 Deverill Close and made good his threat. But there was no fanfare of celebration at the absence of a catastrophic event.

The next case I saw was much the same. Nobody died and that's the great thing really and it's why I want to tell you about it.

I was waiting for Mr Potts in the same little interview room I had used earlier.

Chop brought him in, a thirty-year-old man in a wheel-chair – both legs in plaster and sticking straight out in front of him.

He smiled at me and said hello in an unmistakably Brummie accent. He was a good-looking chap and wouldn't have looked out of place on the set of *Peaky Blinders*. He had convictions for fraud, burglary, drugs and violence, and some of the charge sheet suggested more than a passing interest in offensive weapons, specifically a Samurai sword, found at his side when he was arrested. Intriguingly, his own address and the address he was alleged to have broken into were next door to each other in a terraced row.

I will confess to a degree of prejudice when it comes to Mr Keiran Potts. There was a time in the 1990s when everyone seemed to have a Samurai sword. They were widely advertised in newspapers so that inadequate men could display them over the gas fire and tell their friends they were into martial arts. I suspect that most of them might have exhibited a corresponding lack of expertise in the marital arts.

'Mr Potts. Nice to meet you,' I said.

'I don't need to see a psychiatrist. There's nothing wrong with me. You're not going to fraggle me off.'

Being *fraggled off* is the term used to describe being trans-ferred from prison to a psychiatric hospital. Prisoners called the health care centre on F wing at HMP Brixton, Fraggle Rock.

'I'm pleased there is nothing wrong with you. Is it OK to call you Keiran?' I responded pleasantly. 'Perhaps you could let me know why you ended up in prison.'

'Burglary.'

'From your next-door neighbour?'

He half nodded and half shrugged.

'Let's start with your legs. How did you hurt your legs?'

'Fell down, didn't I.'

'Do you need painkillers?'

He suddenly seemed more interested in our conversation. 'It's really bad at night,' he said. 'Codeine might help it a bit.'

'I'll make sure you're written up for something. Were you using any drugs before you came here?'

'A bit of Charlie.'

'A bit?'

He looked sheepish. 'A lot. About £200 a day, sometimes more.'

That was more than I was earning. 'How long for?'

'Three months or so.'

'So why the Samurai sword when you were picked up?'

'Do I have to say?'

'No.'

'It was to get him to admit what he was doing.'

'What was he doing?'

'Having an affair with my wife.'

Poker-face routine.

'She was drugging me. I'd wake up and she wasn't there. She was next door fucking him.'

'Did you ask her about it?'

'I was in the loft, getting evidence. With a camera.'

'Camera?'

'Well, she always denied it. Said I was mad. So I hid in the loft.'

'With the Samurai sword?'

'Yes.'

'And a camera?'

'Yes.'

'To prove that your wife was having an affair.'

'Yes.'

Quite aside from making your nose drop off, cocaine messes with your brain. That's why it's called 'psychoactive'. The euphoria and sense of wellbeing and energy it induces goes hand in hand with making you think that your missus is shagging your neighbour, or the entire Aston Villa squad, come to that. That could make anyone jealous, but this man's jealousy had become an article of faith. It's never quite enough to be sure of something yourself, however. Others have to believe it too.

'Why did you break in next door?' I asked him.

'I didn't really. I crawled from my loft space into his, and then I made a little hole so I could see into his bedroom. That way, when they were at it, I could photograph them through the hole. That's the proof.'

'And the Samurai sword?'

'If he denied it, I'd make him tell me the truth.' He seemed quite matter-of-fact about it.

'How long were you going to wait there?'

'A day or two. I had a KitKat.'

'What were you going to do if they admitted it?'

'I'll decide that at the time,' he said.

His use of the future tense worried me, and I decided to lighten the mood. 'How would you piss?'

He looked a little embarrassed but didn't answer me. Months of dopamine depletion had taken their toll on his reasoning ability.

'So, what happened?' I asked.

'The ceiling gave way. I fell down on to the floor.'

I pointed to his legs, and he nodded. 'They said it was a Pott's fracture, but I think they were taking the piss.'

'No,' I said, 'it really is a Pott's fracture. That's what ankle fractures are sometimes called.'

He looked at me suspiciously.

'Why burglary?' I asked. 'What did you nick?'

He appeared to relax. 'I took his watch from by the bed. And then I got downstairs, and the pain was so bad I called an ambulance.'

'Right.'

We all have slightly odd or idiosyncratic beliefs. Delusions, on the other hand, are convictions, and no amount of contradictory evidence will make you change your mind. If it did, it wouldn't be a delusion, it would just be a strongly held belief, and we're all allowed to have those.

The range of beliefs about which you can be deluded is infinitely varied. If one is capable of having a belief, it is possible to be deluded about it. It can be about love or religion, poverty or grandeur, jealousy or reference, perse-cution or anything else, come to that.

If Prince Charles is sending you secret messages of love when you are watching *EastEnders*, then you have an eroto-manic delusion. If you think you are Prince Charles when, in fact, you work in the café at Asda, then it's a delusion of grandeur. If the BBC news presenter mentions something about you whilst covering the latest crisis, it's a delusion of reference, unless you happen to be the prime minister.

The thing that binds all delusions together is that they don't change when you try to reason them away. They are fixed and people tend to act on them. The person who thinks Prince Charles loves them goes to Buckingham Palace and demands an audience. Everyone goes to Buckingham Palace. The person who thinks they are Prince Charles changes their name to Charles and tries to collect rent from the Duchy of Cornwall. The person with reference from the BBC writes angry letters to the broadcaster.

Dear BBC, I would like to complain about Amol Rajan's continued references to the size of my feet . . .

You will have gathered that delusions of persecution are the commonest type of delusion that psychiatrists deal with. The most dangerous is a delusion of jealousy. Professor Paul

Mullen, a forensic psychiatrist, describes jealousy superbly. He asks you to imagine you are walking along a beautiful beach on a warm evening. In the distance you can see a couple sitting at the best restaurant and being served champagne. As you get closer you see they are relaxed, happy and intimate with each other, and you think back to your two-star hotel room with a view of the railway siding.

The emotion you experience is envy.

But as you get closer to these two lovers, you have a sense of familiarity with the woman. You hasten your stride and eventually, despite her not normally wearing such a revealing dress, it becomes unmistakably clear that the woman is your wife. And then she leans forward and gently kisses the man on the lips.

The emotion you feel at this point is jealousy.

It transcends envy and binds together love and loss and anger. Of all the emotions, it is jealousy that makes us kill people close to us.

The next consideration is why the person holds the delusion, and this, more than anything, gets to the heart of things.

For instance, if I think my wife is having an affair, it might be true or it might not be true. If I believe she is having an affair because I've found sex texts to another man on her phone, and someone else's underpants under her pillow, hastily shoved there when I return early from work, it might well be a true belief.

So, it's not delusional.

But if I come home early from work looking for evidence of her infidelity based on the *Telegraph* crossword clue that seems to have special relevance (6 down, frosty tart), and the stranger sitting opposite me on the bus uses telepathy to tell me that my wife is a brazen hussy, it is delusional, even if she is actually spending quality time at Villa Park every Tuesday afternoon.

Just in case you are wondering – 6 down is *whore,* and she's not. I've checked. Villa have a training session Tuesday afternoons.

It's not the belief that makes it delusional, it's why you believe it.

I resumed the interview with Keiran the next day. I'd spoken to his wife by this point.

'Something else I was wondering, Keiran. Why do you think your wife was drugging you?'

Keiran looked at me closely. 'She's very clever, you know. She never leaves a mark, but she injects me when I'm asleep.'

'Right,' I said.

I think he felt he was losing his audience. 'You see,' he said, 'I think she discovered that I was having an affair, and now she's trying to get her own back.'

'Right,' I said again.

His wife, Olivia, had sounded perfectly nice on the phone. She didn't sound like a promiscuous poisoner but, in truth, I've never met one. I'll go further – she sounded really lovely and whilst she clearly cared for Keiran, she couldn't stand his endless threats and accusations. 'It's the drugs he takes, Doctor. He was always jealous, but since the cocaine, he's just insane.'

'Once,' she told me, 'he held my neck to the wall, to try to get me to tell him *the truth.* I blacked out.'

I was reminded of a Sunday newspaper colour supplement with thumbnail pictures of a hundred or so women on the front cover, all of whom had been killed by their partners. It's increasingly clear that women might be as likely as men to be abusive in relationships, but men are generally stronger and can cause more damage. And it is often when the woman finally 'acknowledges' that she has been unfaithful, simply to appease her accuser, that the knife goes in. It's never a good idea to come out with a white flag just to shut them up: in fact, it's a really dangerous thing to do.

'Never admit it,' I advised her.

Then she asked me what would happen to him. I told her I would ask the local psychiatry services to come to see him. He had delusional jealousy and needed to be in a hospital with a locked door and a high fence. It wasn't yet clear what the cause of his psychosis was. It could be the drugs. It could link to his underlying personality, or it could be the start of schizophrenia or a delusional disorder.

I was always taught that delusional jealousy was a big predictor of violence – that and 'command hallucinations', where the voices tell you to do things. Sometimes it's 'Brush your hair,' and sometimes it's 'Kill him.'

The teaching was right. I've seen a lot of violence committed by jealous men. Jealous men are no good and I should have told her to leave him – that is what I would tell her now.

'Ben, how did it go with the two cases I gave you?'

'Fine thanks, Vicky.'

'What did you do with the man speeding?'

'He wanted to kill the Devil. I sent him to hospital. Bipolar or schizoaffective. It was a near miss.'

'Oh. What about the other chap; burglary wasn't it?'

'Delusional jealousy. He was going to kill his wife. And possibly the neighbour too.'

'Oh. Were they having an affair?'

'I don't know. Doesn't really make a difference. I sent him out too. Might be too much cocaine, but he needs an inpatient work-up. It was another near miss.'

I like 'near miss' events. It's why I do the job. So it's fortunate for everyone I never became a pilot. Near miss events for them are a bad thing.

Captain Cave, when you were landing in Las Vegas, are you saying that the main boulevard looked like the runway approach?

Psychiatry is different. For us, a near miss event might be as good an outcome as we can hope for. I can never say that these two men would have gone on to kill, but both looked like they were going that way.

There was no failure of care. Nobody let them down. There was no bad decision-making. The system, from the traffic officers to the custody officers to the prison reception process to the forensic in-reach service, it all worked. And it all worked seamlessly to create a hidden negative outcome. No fanfare. No headlines.

Murder didn't happen.

But sadly, no one knows. And I don't have a tin of Quality Street sitting on my desk.

'Right,' said Vicky. 'Are you enjoying it here?'

'Yes. Yes, I am. It's more about how society responds to crime than psychiatry. What's next?'

'Have you seen any sex offenders yet?'

'No.' I said. 'Sounds interesting.'

Sex offenders:
Matchstick man

There is a link between me getting covered in urine, the film *The Great Escape* and a demented paedophile charged with rape.

I think it needs some explanation.

As a young doctor, I'd joined my consultant on a home visit to an elderly confused woman. He was standing up and asking her all sorts of questions about her memory. I've never really liked standing up, so I sat down and sank back into her richly upholstered Victorian chair.

The consultant had just diagnosed her with dementia and a urinary tract infection, a UTI, which explained both her confusion and her incontinence.

She must have really loved that chair.

When I came out, the consultant laughed at me. 'Beginner's error,' he shouted through the window of his new BMW, driving off and leaving me standing on the pavement. 'The hospital's a mile in that direction.'

Next, you need to be aware of a scene from *The Great Escape*. This tells the story of Allied prisoners of war trying to escape from a German camp during World War II. The pivotal moment sees actors Gordon Jackson and Richard Attenborough trying to board a bus, and having their papers inspected by a suspicious Gestapo agent. Their papers are in order but as they get on the bus, the agent says, 'Good luck,' in English, to which Gordon Jackson, says, 'Thank you.'

Unfortunately for him, he said it in English.

So, when I pull out the case of the demented paedophile from my grey filing cabinet, I know immediately what I am going to do with it. It's going in the 'keep box'.

After my conversation with Vicky, I'd been contacted first thing that Monday morning by a firm of solicitors to see a sixty-year-old man already at Campsmoor. They had tried to take instructions from him but felt that he was very confused. The problem was, they told me, he had a court hearing on Wednesday to enter his plea of guilty or not guilty.

'He doesn't even seem aware he's been charged with six counts of indecent assault and rape,' they told me. 'He seems frail and we would like you to comment on his ability to stand trial and his fitness to plead.'

Being 'fit to plead' is central to the way the courts operate. Actually, it's a bit more than saying you are guilty or not guilty when the judge says, 'How do you plead?' and without an answer, the courts are a bit stuck – they don't know what to do next.

Up until 1772, if you said nothing when you were asked to plead, you were taken down to the cells, tied down to the floor, and then a board was put on your chest and abdomen. Then heavy stones were piled on to the board, effectively crushing you. And that's how you stayed. There were just two possible outcomes. Either you died, or you said you were guilty or not guilty.

And if you did make your plea, I imagine that you were untied, given a nice cup of tea and then taken back into the courtroom for your trial to continue.

I only mention this because the psychiatrist has now taken the place of the weights crushing the person to death. It is now our role to advise whether a person is fit to plead. And it's important, because whatever else happens, if you are unfit to plead, you won't end up going to prison.

I looked up the 'demented' paedophile on the computer system and saw that he was in the house block with the other sex offenders, which made me wonder what was going on. If someone was as cognitively impaired as the solicitors implied, I'd have expected the prison officers to have referred him to me for an assessment.

I called through to the landing.

'Yes, we know Warren . . . No, he doesn't come out of his cell much, but he's OK . . . No, he says he can't remember things . . . Doc, I don't mean to be talking out of turn, but he's faking it. There's nothing wrong with him.'

I saw him the next day, Tuesday, on the house blocks. I was taken to his cell and I introduced myself to him. 'I'm Dr Cave, I'm a psychiatrist,' I repeated three times before he seemed to get the idea.

'Why am I here?' he asked, weakly.

'Where are we?' I asked.

'Is it a hotel?' he said. 'How long have I been here?'

It was starting to sound like that game where everything you say has to be a question.

'How long do you think you've been here?' I asked, getting into the swing of things.

One of the female prison officers came to the door. 'You OK, Doc?'

'Is that my wife?' asked Mr Warren.

'Do I look like your wife?' It was a question, but it was more of a statement really.

Warren turned to me. 'May I go to the toilet please? I keep having accidents.'

I nodded and watched him walk out of the cell and turn left. There was no hesitation. He went along the central corridor and turned right to the toilets.

'He seemed to find them all right,' I muttered to myself.

I went back and sat down on Warren's chair. I was testing my hypothesis.

It was dry.

When Warren came back, he nodded at me as I got up to give him his chair, but he didn't ask me who I was.

I went through a full dementia assessment, and the scores showed that he had a moderate to severe dementing illness. The problem was that it made no sense. He scored very low in areas where you wouldn't expect it. When my mother got dementia, she would have no problem repeating a person's name and address whilst it was fresh in her mind, but five minutes later when you asked her what the address was, she'd look slightly worried and ask what you meant.

Warren didn't understand the subtlety of memory impairment in dementia, and worse than that, he was taking me for a fool.

'Well, I've finished Mr Warren.'

'Finished what?' he said.

'I've finished the memory tests.'

'Did I pass?'

'No, you failed everything. You've got dementia. It's quite bad. I'll write to your solicitors.'

I got up to go and had just reached the cell door. I stopped, half turned, and channelled my inner Columbo and the Gestapo agent from *The Great Escape*. 'I'll come to court this Friday to give evidence, Mr Warren.'

'It's tomorrow, Doctor,' he corrected me. I think he realised his mistake whilst he was talking. 'The hearing is Wednes—'

I turned back to him and we looked at each other for quite a while. 'I hope justice is done on Wednesday, Mr Warren. Good luck.'

On an associated matter, I'd also like to thank the severely 'demented' man who had recently moved into a probation hostel near Guildford. Your instructions for me getting back to the A3 were spot on, and with my satnav broken, it was most helpful.

★

Sadly, there have been other times I have been covered in urine.

I was on a ski holiday with Mike, some other friends and our respective partners. It was a sunny spring day, and with the temperatures rising, the snow by mid-afternoon was slushy and wet. So, we started early and once it felt more like waterskiing, we stopped for the day and found a restaurant with a good view.

After the third or fourth isotonic rehydration drink that some people call beer, my kidneys had rediscovered their purpose in life and I needed to have a pee. Realising that the toilets were out of order, I trudged off to the block at the top of the ski-lift station.

As I was going round the back of the restaurant, I saw a big snow mound banked up against the wall, glistening in the afternoon sun. I took off my sunglasses and saw that there were little holes in the snow bank, each with tell-tale yellow trails. I had discovered my own private pissoir, and thank goodness, I needed it.

I climbed halfway up the slope, past some of the other holes and started the laborious process of unzipping everything. My enormous relief was matched only by my infantile pleasure in trying to make my own little piss hole, which, given how productive my kidneys had been, was progressing nicely. I looked around at my competition, kept my aim straight and noticed that there were holes everywhere. To my left, to my right, in fact right under me, and in some places, more holes than snow.

I was standing on a giant honeycomb.

I didn't move. I calculated that I needed another thirty seconds and would then slide down the hill behind me, to avoid any unnecessary impact stress on the thin crust of snow on which I was standing.

178

Some skiers caught in an avalanche talk about hearing the snow break away. I was five seconds from finishing when I heard the 'crack', and saw it open all around me, linking hole to hole. And then I dropped a full six feet into what now revealed itself as more catacomb than honeycomb.

Fuck.

I tried to get out, but I was stuck. I tried to get purchase with my feet, but it felt like they were set in concrete. I flailed my arms a bit, but all I succeeded in doing was creating my own urine-coloured Slush Puppie.

Then a very jolly group came past, en route from the ski lift to the restaurant. I felt like ducking into my oubliette of shame, then manned up and poked my head as high as it would go.

'Help. *Au secours.*'

That was it, really. They came over, turned out to be French, had a bit of a laugh at my expense and pulled me out.

And you think we smell of garlic.

Being covered in urine is one of those context specific things. It can be a funny memory, or it can be the stuff of nightmare, and if there were ever a case to make me realise that offenders are often victims first, it is this next case, and I put it firmly in the 'keep box'.

Gary was forty years old when I met him at Campsmoor, and he was serving a life sentence for sexually assaulting two ten-year-old girls. Sarah and Sophie were twins. When his house was searched, thousands of images of children were found on his computer. Since 2014 they would be described as category A images, which involves penetrative sexual activity or sexual activity with an animal or sadism. He liked all those things.

He lived near the girls' parents and often helped them out when they needed some shopping or a drive back from the supermarket. He seemed 'an honest sort' and he was always in and out of their house. My impression was that he was seen as a simple soul, and if the girls' parents were honest, I think they would probably admit they were exploiting his good nature.

At Christmas, the parents of the girls were let down by their babysitter and they phoned Gary. Everything was fine, and before long he was babysitting on a regular basis. It was six months later that one of the girls drew a picture at school that set the alarm bells ringing. It was anatomically correct and graphic in a way that a child of ten should not be able to draw. He had raped them both, repeatedly.

That was five years ago and I had been asked to see him because he had tried to kill himself whilst serving his sentence.

'I know who you are,' he said, but I still introduced myself.

'I understand that you tried to kill yourself, Gary. I'm here to work out how to help you.' I could see the residual bruising around his neck – there was still a marked indentation where the nylon cord had dug deep.

He was sitting opposite me in a private visiting room just off the main area with thirty or so tables and chairs where wives and partners saw their loved ones. He had refused to come to the health care centre to see me. The room was clean, spartan and two CCTV cameras were monitoring us.

'They wouldn't bring me here during visiting hours,' said Gary, looking at the large room behind me. 'The kids come here to see their fathers.'

I glanced round and saw plastic toys and even a small tractor with pedals. I had one just like it when I was a child.

'Would you like to talk with me, Gary?'

He shrugged. 'Got nothing else to do, have I.'

'Where would you like to begin?'

He didn't say anything for a while, but then seemed to make a decision to engage with me. 'It wasn't the girls. It wasn't about them. They were good kids. Are they OK?'

'I don't know,' I said honestly.

'Can I write to them to say how sorry I am?'

'No, you shouldn't have any contact with them.'

'You know I loved them as if they were my own.'

I thought about my two girls. 'Tell me about you, Gary.'

'Not much to say.'

I waited.

'It was a normal childhood really. It's not something I talk about.'

'You've refused all the prison courses. You've refused psychology. You've refused psychiatric assessment until now.'

'Yes.'

'Why?'

Again, he shrugged. 'No point really. I did what I did. That's the end of it.'

'Are you ever interested in why you did it?'

'I know why I did it.'

'Why?'

'Love.'

'How so?'

'I loved them. They were pure. They were good.'

'Were you loved?'

'My dad, my stepdad, he said he loved me very much. He loved me so much, he said he'd show me how much he loved me.'

Gary was looking down at the table now. I wasn't there in his head.

'He used to make me suck him. And if he didn't come, he'd beat me. I was OK with the beatings, but I didn't like sucking him. That was the start of it really. He made me watch when he fucked Mum. I had to go and get him cigarettes afterwards. I was never horrible to the girls.' He paused and made fleeting eye contact. 'I was at home and I didn't know he was in the bathroom. So I went in and he was sitting on the toilet. He was really angry that I'd disturbed him. I'd never seen him so angry; he threw me into the bath and he took his belt and he . . .'

He was rocking back and forth to comfort himself, and like the images of the Romanian orphans under Ceauşescu, it seared itself into my mind.

I didn't want him to be telling me this. He was an object of revulsion. He was the person to be avoided on the high street. He was the bogey man, the evil rapist to be reviled, but all along he was just a broken, miserable child in a man's body.

'. . . he took his belt and he beat me until I stopped crying.'

'How old were you?'

'I was ten. Then he took his dick out and I thought I would have to suck it so that's what I went to do, and he pissed in my face. He pissed all over me.'

I could hear some doors slamming shut in the distance and some muffled shouts.

'I felt ashamed. It was like I stopped existing,' Gary said. 'I stank of piss. I've never been so ashamed.'

There was a long silence.

'So, Doc, what next? Send me off to hospital. Give me antidepressants. I've been on them half my life. Tell me to go on an offender management course.'

'Do you want to address your offending behaviour?'

He hesitated. 'That's what I was trying to do.' He pointed to his neck.

I left the interview feeling confused and ill at ease. I confess I've never found dealing with paedophiles easy, but Gary really got to me. He was never destined to be a paedophile, and were it not for his most terrible abuse, I don't think he would have been.

Some years later, I was at a Child and Adolescent Psychiatry conference meeting in Birmingham. I was trying to recruit a consultant for a new service. I took a couple of prospective candidates out for a meal and one of them told me about a girl of fifteen he had treated, one of a pair of twins. They had been raped when they were ten.

'Sarah and Sophie,' I blurted out. I was surprised I remembered their names.

'Yes, do you know them?'

'No, I assessed the man who raped them. What happened to them?'

'Not good. Sophie did OK, I didn't treat her myself. But Sarah, my patient, died by suicide when she was eighteen – she'd just gone into adult services and couldn't cope.'

'Christ.'

'She wanted to talk to the assailant – she wanted to know why he did it.'

'Really?'

'Yeah. It was a shame she couldn't.'

'Why couldn't she?'

'Don't you know? He killed himself in prison. Would you like another beer?'

When I was training in psychiatry, I worked quite closely with Jackie Craissati. She was then an up-and-coming forensic psychologist and she was championing the treatment of paedophiles. I watched her on a daytime TV talk show, and she was saying how this group of offenders need support and treatment to reduce their reoffending rates.

They booed her.

Now that's madness.

My third unfortunate experience with urine was in Thailand. I was with Jo, who was still my girlfriend at the time. We were on a stopover, returning from a period of study in Melbourne, where I had broken my leg. Still on crutches, and whilst in the queue for customs, I realised that we were behind two other medics from St Jude's. After laughing at my leg, they persuaded us to meet for a 'night out'. A night of 'local culture and dance', they promised.

Now, crutches don't work well on wet tiles – it's basic physics. In fact, a little water between the tile and the rubber cup at the bottom, makes them skid around like Jeremy Clarkson on a greased Teflon racetrack.

Women will already be familiar with my next observation in behavioural psychology. Unless a man is happily making snow holes or chasing a fag end around in the urinal, they do not have very good aim, which explains why the floor in most men's toilets is perpetually wet.

Having consumed more beer than was good for me and grown tired of the 'local culture and dance', which seemed to consist of young women playing ping-pong and darts, I hobbled off with my crutches to the toilets behind the 'theatre'.

I made my way cautiously over the wet, tiled floor and then balanced myself by the urinal, tripod-like, with one leg and two crutches wedged under my arms.

Next, somewhat unexpectedly and certainly uninvited, a young man walked up behind me and reached round my waist. Either, I thought, he was trying to help a beleaguered traveller, or he was trying to steal my crutches, or he was trying to offer me relief of an entirely different sort.

Whatever the truth, the sheer surprise of seeing a pair of hands reach around my waist meant that I put all my weight on my crutches. The left one immediately decided to do its best Clarkson impersonation, put itself in launch mode and shot away from under me. I stamped down on my broken leg to try to regain my balance, and the intense pain made me cry out in anguish. I collapsed backwards and my fall was cushioned by the young man who, and I'm being charitable here, had come to 'help' me.

Thinking that I'd probably killed him, I rolled off as quickly as possible, basting myself thoroughly in the toilet juices on the floor. Fortunately, he seemed unharmed and he sprang to his feet, helped me up and passed me my crutches.

I normally tip staff in restaurants for good service, and I tip taxi drivers if they don't ask if I'm analysing them. I'm not overly generous, but as things are cheap in Thailand and I felt sorry for him, I reached deep into my wallet. I had just extracted a thick wad of notes that would buy him a couple of decent meals and was passing the money to him when my friend, having heard my cry of pain, ran in and saw me passing the bundle of cash to a wet-looking chap with the beginnings of a moustache.

'I fell over and he helped me up,' I explained.

'Your flies are still open,' he said, taking it all in.

If there is a moral to my three experiences of being covered in urine, it is never to sit down on a home visit, that the French are a decent bunch after all, and that people really are innocent until proven guilty.

I fear that I have too often accepted their guilt based on the accusations made against them and taken their denials as confirmation of their guilt.

Let me explain.

We had a tropical fish tank in one of the rehabilitation wards at St Jude's. The ward manager thought that it was good for the patients. Sadly, one by one, we found the fish crushed under a large stone at the bottom of the tank.

The only thing I knew for sure – it wasn't suicide. We investigated it, we questioned staff and the patients and there was talk about calling in the police. I had my suspicions of course. I was at the time looking after a man with chronic schizophrenia who had raped a woman. Whenever I tried to talk to him, he told me to 'fuck off'.

Actually, it's the only thing he said to me for about three years. Twice a week, he would come into the ward round, and I'd ask him how he was, and he'd say, 'Fuck off.'

He applied for a tribunal and I wrote a fairly negative report discussing his poverty of thought, his social decline and his need for treatment. The nurses, encouraged in their reports to say something positive about their patients, wrote: 'He sees the consultant regularly, he is consistent in his views, articulates himself clearly and has a good sense of humour.'

He was obviously the fish killer.

About a year later, I was seeing another patient on a different ward whom I recognised. 'I know you,' I said. It was meant to be a friendly greeting, but he took it the wrong way.

'I am really sorry about the fish,' he blurted out, 'they just kept looking at me.'

There is another incident, and it still troubles me, where I made a false assumption.

The man I had been asked to see had been remanded in prison and was charged with raping a minor. The notes told me that he had just tried to kill himself. He had earlier declined an offer to place him with the other vulnerable prisoners and it proved to be a mistake, one that got him beaten up. His arms were stamped on, they kicked him in the head and then a group of men stood around and urinated over him.

He stumbled back to his cell and it was there that he tried to hang himself. No matter whether or not he was guilty, everyone had decided he was. His wife had left him, his children weren't talking to him and he'd lost his job.

Fortunately, the prison officers checked on him, found him half dead, cut him down and then called me to see him.

He stank of piss. He was shaking with fear. He was too traumatised to cry.

Send them to prison. Throw away the key.

I should have been able to empathise with him, a 'not guilty' man covered in piss, but all I saw was another sex offender who said he didn't do it.

I remember my interaction with him. I treated him professionally, but I was emotionally cold. I treated him well, but I was matter-of-fact. I advised him objectively, but at no cost to me.

In short, there was no investment in him. That's when I realised that the therapist, the psychiatrist in this instance, is as important as the medication we prescribe. It's not just a science, it is an art. We paint a picture of ourselves and then we paint a picture of hope and recovery, and then, if we're really good, we teach the patient how to paint it for themselves. At least, that's what we should be doing.

When the court later found him not guilty, I confess that my first thought was 'lucky bastard'. I thought that he had got away with it. Then, about a year later, new DNA evidence emerged, and it pointed to the real culprit.

Now, it wasn't just the court saying he was not guilty, there was a scientist in a white coat saying he was innocent. My preconceptions were wrong. His wife and children got it wrong too. So did the papers, and so did society. I imagine he'll be tainted by the association of guilt for the rest of his life.

It's probably true that most of the people I see are guilty of the offence for which they are charged. Being human, we tend to acclimatise to the situation in which we find ourselves, whether it's our own cell or the one the patient is put in. I'm not sure we ever know for sure in which cell people belong.

So I made a promise to myself that day, that I'd treat everyone the same, no matter how bad they were, no matter how insightless or inhumane they had been, I would invest in them.

I would treat them with respect and dignity. I'd make sure I mentally put a computer on their desk, give them a set of keys and a picture of recovery to put on the wall.

There is a pragmatism to it. It's the only way I can cope.

★

Let me finish by mentioning a man, Justin, who is still in prison and will be there for many years to come. The incident has stuck with me because it was a living re-enactment of one of my father's favourite jokes about a psychiatrist showing the patient some Rorschach ink blots – the symmetrical splodges that people are meant to describe, and then the psychiatrist interprets.

The man says the first ink blot looks like a naked woman, the next like a pair of breasts and the last, a woman looking provocatively at him. The psychiatrist observes that the man appears to be preoccupied with sex, to which the man retorts that it's the psychiatrist who's showing him all the dirty pictures.

It emphasises the subjectivity of most of psychiatry. But there is one thing that is quite objective, and it is based on the observation that it is possible to tell whether a man is sexually aroused. When a person convicted of raping a child tells you fifteen years later they are 'better' and no longer aroused by paedophilic imagery, and this is exactly what Justin was saying, there is a way to find out if he is telling you the truth.

We use a machine called a penile plethysmograph. Put simply, a spring-loaded clip is put on the male member and then the individual is shown carefully selected pictures that may cause sexual arousal. The arousal causes the clip to expand and that expansion is measured electronically and displayed to the person in the white coat in an adjacent room. It's hard to believe, but plethysmography is all done very tastefully.

I was seeing this man as an outside expert. I'd been given his history and couldn't escape the fact he was a victim first. He'd been abused just before his tenth birthday. When he was forty, he raped a child of seven.

The report was for his parole hearing, so it's no exaggeration to say that his freedom depended on my report and the parole board agreeing with it.

He told me all the right stuff. 'I can honestly say that I am better now. I have learnt so much in prison about myself and why I committed that awful crime for which I am sorry . . .'

You get the idea.

The question was whether he was telling the truth. I wrote to his lawyers and suggested plethysmography.

The lawyer seemed quite convinced that his client was a reformed character. 'He's not been in trouble for over fifteen years,' he told me. I hesitated to point out that he had been in prison for fifteen years and had not had much access to seven-year-old boys.

After he'd had his plethysmograph, I went to see him to go through the results.

I explained that the tests showed that he appeared to be aroused by just about everything. Even the person taking the test was surprised at the results. It was off the scale.

He looked a bit sheepish and then confessed that he still had strong paedophilic fantasies and masturbated compulsively.

'Doc, I've been like this since I was ten. I mean, have your fantasies changed since you were a kid?'

I didn't answer him, but if I were truthful, I'd probably have said, 'Not very much.' And then it struck me as rather facile to think that any fantasy would suddenly rewrite itself if other people said it was wrong, illegal, immoral or pathological.

I looked at his arousal pattern on the report and decided to confirm it for myself.

'I'm going to draw you a picture,' I said. I drew him a picture of a matchstick man. It had a round head, a line for the body and a line for each arm and leg.

That was it.

He looked at the scribbled picture, he held it up, gulped and leaned forward, conspiratorially. 'How old is he?' he asked.

As I said, he is growing old in prison. He'll get released one day – one day when he smells of urine and is too infirm or too senile to get out of his chair.

Self-harm:

The maroon chair

I'm used to people hurting themselves – it's part of the job. And it needs to be said that people hurt themselves for all manner of complex reasons.

The emotionally unstable way of dealing with stress works like this: *I feel hurt and out of control, so I hurt myself. You see how distressed I am, and you care for me. I am grateful for your care and I idolise you. You are wonderful and you will cure me. But what if you can't fix me? What if you're just like all the rest. You're going to reject me, so I'll reject you first and I'll make you reject me. You don't care about me. You hate me. I feel hurt and out of control, so I hurt myself . . .*

This pattern doesn't end. It just keeps looping round and around.

Depressive self-harm is quite different: *I hurt myself because I want to die. I'm indifferent to your help. I'm indifferent to you. I'll take your medication, but it probably won't help. I feel a bit better. I don't want to hurt myself now. I go home.*

In prison, it's often played out very differently. *I hurt myself. I don't care about myself. I don't care about you. I don't care if you help me or not. We are way past that now.*

The self-harm I have seen in hospital is like nothing I have seen in prison. It may reflect the fact that prisons are not hospitals, and prisoners are not being treated, but I think it goes deeper than that. There is a deep sense of hatred and loathing and disgust carried by some prisoners that I don't see in a non-prison population. The self-harm is not to manipulate those around them, it's not necessarily to kill themselves, though they might. It has become an end in itself, ultimately to redress the sense of shame that many prisoners carry but can't acknowledge.

Tyler was in the house blocks and was having counselling with Megan, one of the mental health nurses. He had a history of self-harming before he came into prison. It was the emotionally unstable type and he had gone from one hospital to the next. Eventually he gravitated to taking drugs and then he committed a string of burglaries to finance his growing habit of smoking heroin. He liked heroin. It dulled his senses and made the time pass quickly. Then he progressed to robbery, was caught, charged, convicted, imprisoned and tried to hang himself.

At this point he had graduated to the depressive type of self-harm, and for a while he was in the HCC. He started on antidepressants, and then was sent back to ordinary location on the house blocks.

Megan kept in touch with him each week, much as a community nurse might stay in touch with their patients, and then had become sufficiently concerned that she had admitted him back to health care. He had been seen by one of the prison doctors and his antidepressant dose had been increased. It was all quite routine, and sadly predictable.

One evening, just as I was leaving for the day, Megan asked me to see him.

'What's up, Megan?'

'He's not right. He seems really distant, and over the last couple of weeks, he's not been looking well. I think he's anaemic.' She handed me copies of his medical notes and I scanned them.

I saw he had previously had iron-deficiency anaemia which was probably caused by his repeated cutting. He was a regular at the local A & E who sutured him up and sent him home without even troubling the on-call psychiatrist any more.

'He's two years into a six for robbery,' I said. I had wondered if it might be 'gate fever' – it's quite common for a prisoner's mental state to deteriorate towards the end of their sentence. Deep down, they know that they won't be able to cope with freedom.

'I could see him tomorrow morning, first thing.'

'He's really pale.' Megan pulled a little face, which from an experienced nurse meant the advice you've just given is wrong.

I knew I was beaten. I took off my coat and hung it over the back of the chair in the nursing office.

'Take me to him,' I said, in a put-upon voice.

If you go looking online for white paint, there are plenty of varieties to choose from. There's Chantilly Lace, Cloud White and Strong White. If these aren't right for you, you could try Paper White, Vanilla Milkshake or even Moonshine. You get the idea – there are lots of sorts of white. But none of these colours did justice to Tyler, lying in bed in front of me.

If you want to see what white looks like, try meeting a person with a haemoglobin count of 40. To put this in perspective, a fit young man's haemoglobin should be between 130 and 180, so 40 is low, very low, so low that his two little coal-black eyes gleamed in his snowman face, and the sheets looked grey against his alabaster chin.

But there was a clue, and I stumbled upon it almost immediately as I approached his bedside. I'd like this to demonstrate great wisdom on my part, but in fact my foot simply kicked the mug that he had put under his bed, much as I put my cup of tea there each night for my wife to kick the next morning.

I reached down to pick it up, just like my wife does, and then I said, 'Fuck,' just like my wife does. But it wasn't dregs of tea sloshed across the carpet that troubled me, but the congealing blood that spilled out of it and on to the tiled floor. I stood up quickly and tried to wipe my finger surreptitiously on his bed sheet as I pulled it back to feel his pulse. I held up his hand and as my finger slid round his wrist in search of his radial artery, it was a bit more slippery than I was expecting. I gingerly turned over his hand.

Normally there's stuff in the way when you feel for a pulse, but not on this occasion. He had sliced through his tendon, the palmaris longus – the one you can feel under the buckle of your watch strap – and then all the way up his forearm. It looked alarmingly like the cadaveric dissection of the forearm that I had done years earlier as a medical student.

Oh look, there's the median nerve . . .

I lowered his arm and washed my hands at the basin by the bed. Blinding white? Not really. Arctic white? Still short of the mark. No, this was *fuck me, he's so fucking anaemic he needs to go to fucking hospital right fucking now white.*

'But I don't want to go to fucking hospital,' Tyler said when I let him know what was on my mind. Megan and I looked at each other and then we looked back at Tyler and spoke in unison. 'You're going to fucking hospital.'

He did go and had six units of blood and surgery to repair his forearm. I interviewed him when he got back to prison.

'I'd lost everything when I came here,' he told me. 'It's like begging on the streets. It's the point where any dignity is gone.'

'The cut I saw, was it different from the other cuts?'

'Yes,' Tyler said. 'Before, I didn't want to die, I just needed people to care. Then I came in here, and I was getting some drugs, and I got into debt on the wings. And I couldn't pay, so I had to do some favours and I really hated myself. I think I got really depressed. That's why I tried to hang myself.'

'Favours?'

'You know.'

'Ah. Why the cut up your arm? You'd actually cut through your tendon.'

'I didn't care any more.' He shrugged, unable to express himself.

I don't think I have ever seen anyone look more hopeless than Tyler did at that moment. 'Didn't it hurt?'

'I think I dissociated,' he said. 'It hurt later, but then I got used to it.'

Tyler should be a teacher. He clarified my understanding of self-harm – he was my transition from textbook to experience.

I see a lot of dissociation and Tyler's description of it was spot on. Have you ever 'come to' when you've been driving and suddenly realised you've been on autopilot for the last ten miles? You've been thinking about home, or what your wife or husband said, or some voice from the past has come back to you and you were lost in reverie – that's dissociation. You're still driving, but not conscious of the complex motor activities or the decisions you're making. Your brain's doing two things at once. It's a pretty impressive thing, your brain.

Some people can dissociate on demand. Some people live with it as a way of coping with their distress. They dissociate to be able to cope. Some take it to extremes and have whole personalities constructed in a dissociated form.

Most of us probably do it from time to time and it's quite a useful way of dealing with things, if only in the short term.

Tyler did quite well. I sent him to a prison that specialised in group therapy and his level of self-harming drastically reduced in both frequency and severity. He gave up early release to get himself treated.

It turned out that stories like Tyler's were not uncommon. The governor was always sending people out for urgent treatment of one sort or another. In fact, I'd stopped recording all the cases because it became routine.

★

'Routine' is not how I would have described Mr Lango. I look at his notes on my desk at Lakeview and peer out of my window. I get up from my grey desk and check the corridor, but there's no one around for me to talk to; there's no distraction to be had.

I go back in and try not to look at the maroon chair. It's making me feel unsettled, uneasy. I don't want to sit on it. I sit on the side of my desk and pick up Lango's notes again.

At the back of the HCC at Campsmoor there was a special room to contain the most troubled prisoners. It wasn't used much – I'd only seen one other person in there.

Lango, I was told, had been trying to kill another prisoner on the wings. The prison officers had intervened and in the process of controlling the situation and taking him to the segregation unit, one of them had sustained a broken arm. Lango was put in seg but he didn't settle. He remained violent and aggressive and was screaming through the night. Eventually, they'd had enough and thought that he might be having a 'breakdown' and moved him to the special cell.

He was in prison for violence and when the prisoner who had been attacked was interviewed, he said that Lango had earlier accused him of trying to poison him.

I checked his notes. He had been physically abused as a child by both his parents – how can you trust anyone in life after that? He was taken into care, but he'd never been able to form bonds with the foster parents who looked after him.

He drifted into a life of crime and violence and self-harm. He had repeatedly broken his hand by punching walls; he had frequently run at the same walls with his head. He had done it so often and so severely he had needed treatment in hospital on two occasions.

Gradually he must have realised that he enjoyed hurting other people more than himself. He hurt people, and the more they hurt, the more he enjoyed it. He grew into sadism, and eventually he took it as far as he could: he had tortured a person to death for sexual gratification. He was the first real sadist I had ever met, and I'm not talking about the *Fifty Shades* variety, I'm talking about fifty years in prison.

When I first saw him, he was lying on the floor. He had been brought over from seg and deposited there minutes earlier. Six highly trained officers were still cleaning his spittle from their riot gear.

He was violent and his violence seemed equally at home whether it was directed towards himself or others. He was paranoid, but at this point it didn't matter whether it was caused by illness or personality. When someone's behaviour is so abnormal, I am inclined to think that the traditional concepts that separate emotion and depression and psychosis start to break down.

I walked towards him and heard the door close behind me. I glanced upwards and saw two pairs of eyes watching me through the observation hatch.

The walls around him were made of soft rubber. The floor was too, and felt springy underfoot, like a country meadow. The whole room was pink, and unusually warm, since most of the prisoners in this padded cell were close to naked. Lango was no exception. He was wearing a pair of canvas rip-proof shorts and a body belt with cuffs at the front designed to stop him hurting himself, or anyone else, come to that.

I suspect that I was only in the room for thirty seconds or so, but it occupies far more time in my mind. I never really got to know him; our only interaction was a single exchange, me standing and him lying at my feet.

'Hello, Mr Lango; my name is Dr Ben Cave.' I thought it was one of my better introductions, but he didn't seem impressed.

'If you talk to me again,' he said, 'I am going to bite my tongue off.'

He didn't say anything else after that. Not a thing. That was it.

Fortunately, I knew that you can't bite off your tongue. There were no lectures at medical school about what part of your body you can bite off, it's just one of those bits of innate wisdom you carry around, probably based on how very difficult you think it would be to bite off your own tongue.

I should have learnt my lesson when talking to the man who amputated his own penis. If you are psychotic all the rules about what you can and can't do to yourself go out of the window. The same was true of Lango. I made the mistake of seeing him through the prism of my own reality, which was getting wobblier by the second.

I once saw a young man wrap himself around a hot steam pipe that he had managed to find on an old ward. When I interviewed him later, he found it difficult to recapture the mindset that encouraged him to sear the muscles of his forearms and inner thighs to the bone.

'It's hard to explain,' he told me. 'I knew it was painful, but it was like I was anaesthetised to the pain.'

I realise this is a bit of a horror show, but I want to drive home the point that by the time you get to psychosis and then go beyond it, you can't talk it away. It's not amenable to reason or logic or reassurance or any form of counselling. Sadly, in this particular case the delusion was mine. I had adopted the firm and unshakable belief that you can't bite off your own tongue and the evidence of my arrogance hit me a moment later.

Each second now became a minute. I watched him as he extended his tongue and then clamped down on it with his teeth. He was looking at me. I think he was biting my tongue off at that moment.

He guillotined the end of his own tongue with his own incisors, then he spat it at me.

It was like the arc of a golf ball over a pink rubber fairway, the blood, the divot nebulised by the club, falling away as the tongue soared to its zenith and then began to descend. My brother was screaming and I was rooted to the spot, swaying slightly in the heat, the spectators watching intently as the tongue hit my shin and then slid slowly down my trouser leg and on to my shoe. It bobbled for a moment on my polished toecap, like the ball dancing around the hole, and finally came to rest on the floor.

I moved my gaze from the chunk of gristle that had once been a tongue to Lango's mouth. He was already in the recovery position and bright red blood was flowing freely on to the pink floor beneath him.

Most caring doctors would no doubt think about the patient's plight at this point. Most would do something clever, something to take control of the situation and generally be heroic.

I am sorry to report that I failed on all fronts. I was frozen, dislocated from any reality and lost in memories of a man vomiting his life blood over my back.

In normal situations I would probably have called for gauze and tried to stem the flow of blood from his tongue, but having seen what had just happened, I was pretty sure that my fingers should not go anywhere near his mouth, and if they did, I'd want to know that he was unconscious first.

All I could do was look at the blood pooling by his mouth and calculate how long it would take before it reached my shoe.

I eventually managed to wrench my eyes away from the crimson tsunami and towards the observation hatch. 'He's going to need a blue light ambulance.'

I saw them nod and whilst they were making the appropriate arrangements, I left the pink and red room and phoned the nearest hospital capable of dealing with such an emergency. I found one with an on-call ENT surgeon. Finally, we were connected, and he proceeded to lecture me on the impossibility of what I was telling him. I listened carefully, and each time I felt like nodding, I focused on the contents of the plastic bag sitting in front of me.

Some of my more enlightened friends have told me that my mental detachment was a defence mechanism.

They're wrong.

The truth is that, for the briefest of moments, I felt he really was attacking my shoes, and that was all I could think about. The blood hadn't touched me yet, and I was determined it wasn't going to. My friends didn't know about the vivid images of Yellow Man I keep in my head.

The blood wasn't going to touch me.

Not again.

I went back to the pink room after Lango had been sent off, escorted by a large number of police and prison officers.

Some of the ones who had seen what happened were still there, debriefing.

'Will you nut him off, Doc?'

'I don't know. I didn't really get to talk to him.'

'He needs to go to Bramworth, that one. He's Upminster.'

'Upminster?' I frowned.

'Upminster. End of the District Line.'

'I don't get it.'

The prison officer laughed to himself and put his arm around my shoulders. 'A long fucking way past Barking.'

Funnily enough he was right. Lango went to Bramworth and he's still there now.

I saw a nurse arrive with a large roll of blue paper towels. I gloved up with her, went into the room and knelt down next to the puddle of congealing blood. I needed to do something. It needed to be cleaned up.

It needed to be expunged.

The voices in my head

When I hear about people who have done terrible things, I feel myself morally outraged.

When I talk to those same people, I am normally able to explain what they did because of illness, drugs or personality. By and large, I feel sorry for those with illness, troubled at how society deals with a massive drugs crisis, and angry at those with abnormal personalities.

I am not sure it is either logical or scientifically defensible, but my response is human, and I think that most of us are the same.

Most psychopaths I have seen, have themselves had very disturbed childhoods. So when I saw Robert, given that he was front page news at the time, I expected that I would find him to be a predatory psychopath with a history of having been abused. So I would feel some level of moral outrage but that would be tempered by his awful life experiences.

What I didn't expect was that our meeting would be terminated prematurely.

It was the only time I wanted to kill my patient.

Robert was the man in the cell opposite my office. The man who had been looking over at me from the other side of the atrium when I first started at Campsmoor.

He had been on remand for almost a year and had just been convicted of a series of violent and sexual offences against elderly men and women. He had refused to answer

questions during police interviews and declined to testify in
his own defence, so whilst the DNA evidence of his guilt
was incontrovertible, nobody really understood why he
had committed the offences. The judge decided to adjourn
sentencing and asked for psychiatric reports. My job was
to provide the court with some explanation of his actions,
and decide whether he was mentally unwell. He seemed to
listen as I described my role, and was willing to talk to me.
More than willing, it turned out.

'I can tell you about it now,' he said. 'I was found guilty
last week.'

I went through his background, his childhood, his attach-
ments with his parents and extended family, his education
and then his work history. There was some tension with his
mother after she divorced. She remarried when he was about
ten. His stepfather had beaten him and he had six broken
bones at the point he was taken into care. His schooling was
chaotic and he got into trouble from the age of fourteen.
He never learnt how to control himself. He didn't really
have any understanding of punishment.

Six broken bones from your caregiver can distort your
perceptions.

'I don't know why I did it, really,' he said. 'It's like I
have to. Call it a compulsion, if you like.'

He gave a thin smile and put his hand on his chin. He
looked almost wistful. 'It's when I go into their houses —
that's when it comes over me.'

'Am I right that early on, you would go to their homes
to rob them?'

'Yes, that's how it started, but the other stuff, it was so
exciting.'

'Sexually?'

'Yes . . .'

I realised that I was mirroring his body posture and I sat
upright on my chair and put my hands on the table between us.

'. . . and I get so excited . . .' he went on. A fleck of spittle appeared at the corner of his mouth and I followed its journey on to the table between us.

I wondered if he had sprayed spittle over his victims as he inveigled his way into their homes. I had read the impact statements of two of them.

'I don't go out now. I lie awake all night listening in case someone comes in.'

He carried on describing his offences, and there was a slow, clear change in his demeanour. He wasn't so much recounting them, as reliving them. The person I was talking to became lost in his depravities.

The next impact statement had read: *'I felt like killing myself after the third operation on my cheekbone . . . I'm frightened all the time now.'*

And he was telling me all about it. There was no inconvenient court case. He could sit and replay his fantasies as often as he liked. He told me what he had done, he told me everything, every action, every nuance. He left out no detail. He described going into his victims' homes and he told me what he said to them. And then he told me what they said, and how they looked and how they were so 'unsuspecting'.

'I liked that,' he said.

'What?' I asked, jolted back from the unfolding horror story.

'I liked that they were so unsuspecting.'

He described what they were wearing and their particular frailties. He kept talking but I started to hear him less and less. 'I should have done it years ago . . .'

Occasionally I made some notes and then I stopped, transfixed by his commentary. 'I hated my mum.' His mouth was moving all the time and then his arm started to move, slowly at first and then with greater frequency. 'That's when I'd hit them,' he said. 'And then I'd lean over them and undo my flies.' And then he did just that.

During my medical student attachment in psychiatry, we went out to one of the old asylums and I sat in on a ward meeting. The patients had been there for years in a highly abnormal social environment. They had lost their grasp of normal social behaviour, and so had the staff. Halfway through the meeting, the man on my left started to masturbate. I looked around for the person in charge to tell him to stop, but no one did. In fact, nobody said anything. The meeting carried on as if nothing unusual had happened. The therapist approached me later on.

'We try not to be prescriptive in telling people how to express themselves,' she told me earnestly.

But that was a professional lifetime ago, and I have become a fairly prescriptive type of person. I tell the staff on my ward that we have to prompt our patients continuously about socially acceptable behaviour.

'No, we don't hit people because they're talking about us . . .'

'Yes, washing more than once a month is a very good thing.'

Robert was now in full flow, and he didn't have a misguided therapist or a mental illness to excuse his behaviour.

'Please would you stop masturbating,' I said, but it fell on deaf ears.

'Ask me about the other offences,' he said. 'I can tell you about the old man. He was like my stepdad.'

Stop, please just stop.

There I sat, listening to him, and watching his arm go back and forth. I put my pen down, took off my glasses and looked down at my hands, and saw them clench into fists. 'You must stop,' I said, quietly and firmly, tears of emotion in my eyes. I could feel the alarm button to the right of my knee.

He didn't stop. He started to tell me about the old woman who seemed so frightened. 'She said it was nice to have a visitor.'

I looked to the side of the table and at the alarm button on the wall. I thought about my own mother living alone, calling me up because she had been fearful that burglars might come into her home. 'There's nothing to worry about, Mum. They're just people on the street. They're not going to steal from you,' I told her. 'Please try to relax.'

The person sitting opposite me was an average-looking man, neither old nor young, the sort of person you sit next to at work or on the bus. He was quite unremarkable. I could hear my own pulse, faster with each passing second. He wasn't real any more, he was a cardboard cut-out, a carefully animated stage prop. Unremarkable and insignificant.

I heard my father's voice in my head. *Ben, I know what I'd do if someone hurt you or your mother.*

There was no mental illness here. He was not psychotic. His violence, his awful sadistic violence was intimately associated with his sexual drive. He didn't have any self-restraint.

Then I heard my mother's voice in my head. *Dad is wrong, Ben. Vengeance is not justice.*

He was masturbating vigorously now. I had become his tool for sexual arousal, a proxy victim.

Ben, why do you want to help these people?

If you want a child to do well, you look after them and give them love. When they cry, you comfort them; when they do well, you praise them; when they are naughty, you discipline them. As they get older, you educate them, teach them how to behave in company and protect them from harm. You let them test their boundaries, make some mistakes and put them right again.

The person sitting opposite me had never had these advantages. He had told me about his childhood. He had old bone fractures to confirm that he had endured discipline, not learnt from it. His relationships were chaotic. He had no self-control.

I could hear my parents.

No one is born bad.

He's a psychopath. He needs to be punished.

By now, he had as little resemblance to a human as I have ever encountered. Every bit of my education told me that he was a victim, but I didn't see him as such. His mother and stepfather had dehumanised him, and here I was, doing it again. I identified with his victims – my mother was the same age as one of them. He was a monster and that was all there was to it.

I identified with my father's demand for retribution. *He made a decision about what he did. He should be hanged for it.*

It was his casual indifference to his victims that got the better of me. It was his inability to see them as real people, with lives and loved ones. Nobody had ever got to me like this before.

I could almost hear my mother. *He's a victim. He needs love. He needs forgiveness.* I was there to assess him. But I wanted to kill him. I didn't want debate. I was focused and detached. I have never had such clarity of mind. I could examine myself as if an outsider. I was physiologically aroused, my breathing was fast, my pulse was rapid, and my clenched fists made my arms shake with rage.

STOP.

'STOP,' I shouted.

He was still talking – his mouth was still opening and closing. His arm was still vibrating. The only thing I knew for sure was that he needed to stop talking. And stop moving.

His crimes and his sexualised retelling of them had reduced me to his level. He had stripped away the liberal values, the professionalism and the altruistic desire to help. We had absolutely nothing in common except our primitive urges. His were sexual. Mine were violent fantasies of retribution and of revenge.

I needed to stop listening to both my mother and my father. I needed to become myself. I had a choice to make.

I had loving parents and a good education. What discipline I had received was fair and focused. Philosophically, I had always argued that the price we pay for living in a just and reasonable society is that we give up the right to personal vengeance. My own voice was emerging.

Hold that thought, Ben. Hold it tight.

And then I made my decision. Looking back, it was probably the most important decision of my life. The decision that defined my beliefs.

I triggered the silent alarm with my knee. I picked up my pen and paper, put on my glasses, stood, and just to drown him out, also pressed the alarm button on the wall. I walked out of the interview room with the siren wailing, but all I heard was the pulse in my head, soon to be replaced by the pounding footfall of six officers in Kevlar.

I was starting to hyperventilate when they arrived, and I put my hand out to stop them charging in. I saw my hand shaking and I gulped at the air and told them what had happened.

'So you thought about killing him?' one of the older officers asked me later, his helmet now resting on the chair next to him.

'Yes,' I admitted. 'I suppose I was thinking about killing him.'

He looked thoughtful. 'Sometimes I want to kill them too,' he said. I think he was trying to be reassuring. 'It's not what we think, it's what we do that's important.'

I'm still not sure if he was talking to me or talking to himself. But I do know that in ninety minutes, Robert forced me to accept both my parents' positions and I realised that they weren't as contradictory as I'd once thought. I still feel sympathy and anger towards Robert, but my emotions live happily with each other now. Anger and love are intimate bedfellows.

Purple man

Purple is not a common colour for prisoners to wear. When they come into prison via reception, they are mostly wearing blue jeans or matching tracksuits. There is the occasional suit, but mostly that is to make a good impression with the judge or magistrates. The flow of prisoners in and out of Campsmoor is endless. Many of the prisoners are still on remand – they've not been convicted, so they're going out to court for hearings or trials and the lucky and the innocent don't come back. But the guilty do. After a while, it's easy to stop seeing them as individuals, each with their own story of how things went wrong. They just become a succession of dull eyes hiding an undercurrent of anger, resentment and perhaps most of all, fear.

I want some methadone.

I need some sleeping drugs.

I drink a bottle of vodka every day, I have fits if I don't.

I can't be in a shared cell. I get violent.

I hear voices.

He was asking for it.

They're trying to kill me.

The judge got it wrong.

One man, just twenty-one years old, came in front of me as part of this tired procession. He had just been sent down for ten years for a violent robbery with a firearm. He had previous offences, less serious and committed whilst a juvenile, so he was used to spending nights in the police cell and then going to court to be given a probation order or a community sentence. The worst he had done was two months at Feltham Young Offender Institution.

Sadly, he just didn't get it. There is a cartoon that my brother bought me when I started at Campsmoor – it's Joe Martin's 'Mr Boffo, unclear on the concept'. It depicts a man in a prison cell with a guard sitting outside, and the man says, 'OK, I'm ready to apologise.'

'When am I going home?' asked the twenty-one-year-old.

'What?'

'When am I going home?' he asked again. He sounded sincere.

'You got ten years,' I answered incredulously.

'Yes, but can my mum pick me up tomorrow? My barrister said I was sorry when I went to court.'

I looked at him through squinted eyes and sent him into the health care centre so the nurses could keep an eye on him. He was the sort of person who might become 'clear on the concept' at three in the morning and hang himself.

Some of the prisoners coming through reception made an impact, but in truth, mostly they merged into a single mass.

Then, all of a sudden, a man was sitting in front of me dressed entirely in purple. He had purple boots, purple trousers, a purple shirt and a purple bandana wrapped around his disappointingly black hair.

I tried to keep a straight face.

'Mr Reynolds?' I enquired. 'How are you?' I forced myself not to stare and looked down at his notes. His blood pressure was a little high, but nothing else from the health care screen jumped out at me. Convicted of attempted murder – no sentence yet and on judges' remand, or JR-ed. He seemed a little agitated, even distracted.

'Mr Reynolds, how are you?' I enquired again. He seemed to notice me, raised his purple arm, pointed at me and wrote something in the air between us.

'What's that?' I asked.

'The alpha,' said Mr Reynolds.

'The alpha?'

'The alpha,' he confirmed. Then he made the sign of the 'alpha' in the air again, and this time seemed to do another sign.

I pulled a 'go on' sort of face.

'Omega,' he said, succinctly. 'I am the Alpha and the Omega.'

Alpha and omega are the first and last letters of the classical Greek alphabet. The term is used in the Book of Revelation to mean that God and Jesus are eternal. It wasn't the sort of symbolism I was expecting on a rainy Thursday night at Campsmoor prison, so I got him into the health care centre.

'But I'm not ill,' said Purple Man, as the nurse came to take him off. Then he stood over me quite threateningly and used his finger to draw on the table. It was the alpha and the omega again.

'I am eternal,' he said, through the purple haze. 'I am God.'

I was always taught not to collude with a delusional belief, but when a man dressed in purple, one you know to be violent, stands over you in a prison reception clinic and announces that he is God, my best advice is not to contradict him.

'OK,' I said, neutrally, 'but I still need to send you to health care.'

He went without a fuss and I wrote an entry in my diary to see him the next day.

It may not have come through in the case histories I have reported on, but court reports are very detailed. My interviews start with me asking about their background history – where they were born, memories about their families and early experiences. It's not so much the specific answers they give, though this can be quite revealing, it's seeing how they fit into their world, and how they interact with others.

It's only then that I get into the story about the offence. That's when it gets detailed and specific. I once took a senior trainee with me to interview a man charged with rape and murder. His guilt was not in doubt, but his motives were only revealed during the interview.

So, when did you first have sexual fantasies?
What are they?
When did they become violent?
When did you decide to enact them?
Why did you choose the woman in the park?
Do you like all redheads?
Why did you use a condom?
Are all women dirty?
Tell me about your mother.
Does she have red hair?

My trainee had been quite chatty and in good spirits on the way to Campsmoor, but on the way back she seemed quiet and out of sorts.

'I didn't realise it was in such depth,' she said.

'What did you think it'd be like?' I asked, but she didn't answer my question.

'He kept looking at me.'

I looked over at her pale skin and her short red hair. We decided she shouldn't come back for the second meeting after the police found lockets of red hair in his loft.

Mr Reynolds, the Purple Man, was still dressed in purple the next day when I came to review him.

I had looked up his records and knew that there was police intelligence linking him to high-value drugs impor- tation, so I assumed that the attempted murder conviction would be gang-related.

I had barely introduced myself when I saw that he was distracted by my ring. I wear a signet ring engraved with a horse's head; it's a thing my brother and I did years ago and has no significance whatsoever. Strange really, because neither of us like horses that much, but Mr Reynolds was fascinated by it. 'May I see it?' he asked, leaning forward.

I put my hand across the table, wondering where this was going.

He nodded gravely. 'You're here to test me.'

'I'm here to interview you,' I retorted, trying to get back to some sort of normality.

'I'll tell you everything.'

'OK. Where do you want to start?' I asked.

'I think that I was twenty-six when I first realised who I was. My mother was not my mother. She was an imposter.' I glanced at his date of birth – he was in his early thirties, but his pockmarked skin made him look older.

'I'd see people looking at me, like they knew something about me.'

'Did you challenge them?'

'Sure I did. I don't like people looking at me. Knowing my business an' all. Some of them, they started saying things about me. They were testing me. My faith an' all.'

Mr Reynolds had then cut himself off from his family. That period was when he started to use ever-higher amounts of illicit drugs. Any discussion about his mother, or at least the person he now believed was her imposter, was met with implacable resistance, so I returned to his interest in my signet ring.

'It's a Masonic symbol,' he explained.

I could understand his concern if the engraving were of a square and compass, or the all-seeing eye, but a horse's head? It was more Mafia than Masonic.

'I can prove I'm God,' said Mr Reynolds.

'How can you do that?' I asked.

'I will smite my enemies. You don't believe me, do you?'

For several years Mr Reynolds, whilst no doubt involved in the drugs importation trade, had been quietly developing a variety of delusional beliefs.

First, his mother was not his mother. People followed him in the street and made negative references to him. He sometimes challenged these people, and the implication was that he sometimes got into fights with them. He told me that his absent father was a Mason and that people with signet rings, such as mine, were involved in either a conspiracy against him, or testing his faith, so that he could then, if 'righteous' enough, be admitted into the 'Kingdom of Masonic God'.

'Why do you think you're God?' I asked.

He took off his purple shirt and pointed at his acne scars on his chest. 'That's where the bullets went in. I couldn't have survived unless I was God.'

Mr Reynolds had started life as a God-fearing youngster, fatherless and schooled in the Church. He was teased and bullied because of his dreadful acne that left him scarred and friendless. He used drugs to help his self-confidence and as a result was disowned by his mother. The drugs he used became his trade and he defended his growing business with ever-increasing amounts of violence.

Gradually he started to believe things that weren't true. He had always been a violent man, but as time went by, as his psychosis became more entrenched, his violence became less business-focused and more to do with proving or disproving his delusions.

By the fourth time I interviewed him, things were not going well between us. I had started to broach the possibility of him having grandiose and persecutory delusions and suggested he start on medication.

That's when his views about me went from 'Masonic doctor testing my faith' to 'disbelieving doctor needs smiting'. His religiosity started to become more and more apparent and he would walk around the cell with his arms outstretched, reciting biblical verses he had learnt at school. He was refusing to wash, and the reason again seemed to be linked to some religious delusion.

'What is your name, Doctor?' he asked me during my final interview with him. I had by this stage found a bed for him at Bramworth and he was soon going to be transferred out from Campsmoor.

'Ben Cave,' I told him.

'Dr Ben Cave,' he repeated, slowly. 'You know what, Dr Ben Cave, I am not a forgiving God.'

I last saw him through the hatch to his cell. He had been urinating and defecating on his bed.

Mr Reynolds, the Purple Man, was the person who wrote my name on the wall of the cell, the one that I was called to look at by Chop. He was the person who set me on my professional course.

I did the right thing getting him out to Bramworth, but I was left very unsettled by the implied threat.

'Dr Ben Cave, Dr Ben Cave, Dr Ben Cave.'

His psychiatrist called me up some years later as he was about to be transferred from Bramworth to a medium secure psychiatry unit.

'We've got you down as a person who might be at risk,' said the doctor.

'What did he say about me?' I asked.

'Not much,' said the doctor. 'I'd say that any Mason is at about the same risk from him. He's on a depot and he doesn't need high security any more. I reckon he could even be discharged at his next tribunal.'

'I'm not a Mason.'

'Whatever,' he said.

I felt troubled by the news. It's much easier having someone in front of you saying threatening things, rather than someone 'out there' when you have no idea where they are or what they are doing or thinking.

I asked the doctor at Bramworth one last question. I asked him why Mr Reynolds dressed in purple.

He laughed. 'No fucking idea.'

I hung up the phone and looked up 'Home alarm systems'. It was about time to get one.

As a postscript I should add that Mr Reynolds did come out of Bramworth, was released from medium security and went on to commit another very serious offence in the course of his business dealings. This time he was sent back to prison for life, and I have never had to test the effectiveness of my home security system.

Consultancy:

Breakfast at Gloria's

I was at a party quite early in my consultant career with an accountant friend, Jas, who had a lovely warehouse conversion overlooking the Thames. I was looking out at the City opposite, quietly musing on my career choice when there was something of a commotion in the kitchen.

One of the younger accountants, Laura, was having an argument with a man called Rupert. Both of them were somewhat disinhibited from too much alcohol. I did not know either of them at this point and truthfully, I am not sure that I would ever have met them were it not for what was about to transpire. It was difficult not to listen to them and I was quickly brought up to speed: they had been going out for three months, Rupert was, according to Laura, a useless fucker, a liar and a cheat, and Laura was, according to Rupert, a stupid, neurotic bitch who always thought he was cheating on her.

I did wonder briefly if Rupert was confusing the terms neurotic and paranoid but, being an intuitive sort, I decided to keep my mouth shut. The dispute between them seemed to have something to do with Jenny in accounts, who Laura thought was a slut and even Rupert didn't seem to disagree with this appraisal.

It started to settle down and Rupert was doing his bit by professing his love for Laura, but then Jenny in accounts arrived at the party and decided that this was a good moment to announce that she and Rupert had been intimate with each other for the last month and that Rupert had promised he was going to leave Laura. Episode two was proving much more interesting than episode one.

By now, this was the focus of the party and thirty or forty people were listening in rapt attention, as if it were the last ever episode of *The Archers*.

Rupert denied he said he was going to leave Laura, and this sent Jenny in accounts into paroxysms of rage, which forced her to say very uncomplimentary things about the size of Rupert's testicles.

Laura seemed to agree with some of these comments, and Laura and Jenny from accounts had a brief moment of solidarity with each other until Laura remembered that the enemy of your enemy is not always your friend and decided to teach Rupert a lesson he wouldn't forget.

She took the wine glass she was holding and smashed it against the sideboard, which left a sharpened jagged stem, which she promptly drew across her left wrist.

It was a plot twist none of us were expecting.

Nothing happened for about a second and then there were gasps of surprise, quickly replaced by sounds of either irritation or sympathy, roughly in equal measure.

'Ben,' called Jas, meaning me to follow him, as he shepherded Laura to one of the bedrooms. I saw him look at his bloodstained raw oak flooring that had cost him £81.99 per square metre just a month earlier.

'Get the varnished ones next time,' I suggested, but he mustn't have heard me.

Rupert followed us into the bedroom and Laura tightened her grip on the glass stem but Jas told him to leave.

I nodded at him. 'Probably best,' and he looked at me quizzically. He was about to ask me who I was, probably to demonstrate that his testicles were not the size of peas, when Jas took his arm and whispered something to him and led him out of the room.

'I'm Ben, I'm a doctor,' I said to Laura. I sat down on the raw oak flooring which seemed to be everywhere. 'Jas asked me to have a chat with you.'

She nodded her understanding, but she looked pretty vacant. It put me in mind of telling a young woman who presented a week after a large paracetamol overdose that her liver was so damaged it was likely she'd need a transplant. If she wasn't depressed when she took the overdose, she was then.

I looked at Laura's arm and saw some old transverse scars, some red, some white, and it was to these that she now turned her attention. She sat down and used the glass clutched tightly in her right hand to cut herself six times along her forearm. Each was four centimetres long and equally spaced and parallel to the next. They were very neat, very neat indeed.

I thought about stopping her, but she knew what she was doing, and it wasn't going to kill her. 'It would be good if you could stop cutting yourself,' I said.

'I'm not in control,' she said, somewhat icily and in a fairly controlled sort of way.

The first cut, the deepest, was the embodiment of desperation, of lost love mixed with alcohol. The next six, they were to damage herself in a very specific way and regain control.

These were not the actions of a suicidal person, but the learnt behaviour of a person trying to overcome emotions that would otherwise overwhelm them. Men tend to hit people in this situation. Had it been two men arguing over a woman, there would have been the same blood damage on Jas' floorboards, but the blood would have come from a broken nose.

Laura and I spoke for a while and she was starting to be able to externalise her anger towards Rupert but she didn't want to let go of the glass stem. She told me that she might need to cut herself a little more. I believed her, so I was fairly relaxed about her holding the glass on her lap. It had become her comforter – a bloody and jagged symbol of her mental state.

'It's the emergency operator,' said Jas, throwing open the door and passing me the phone. 'They want to know what's going on.'

I explained the situation and looked up at Laura to ask if she wanted to go to hospital. She nodded back at me.

'Yes, she wants to come in.' I figured that she might need the first of the cuts sutured and the remainder cleaned and dressed with Steri-Strips.

'Is she armed, sir? The caller said that she was holding some broken glass.'

'Well, she's holding a broken glass stem, but she's using it to cut herself.'

I held out my hand to Laura, requesting that she pass me the glass, but she shook her head.

'I'll have to send the TSG round with the ambulance crew.'

'I don't think that's necessary . . .'

'She is armed, sir. I would suggest that you leave the room for your own safety and wait for assistance.'

That was it. The police were coming and I knew that they would have helmets and visors and sticks and Kevlar. The TSG is the Territorial Support Group of the Met Police, and, amongst other things, they deal with domestic disorder.

Jas sat next to Laura and took a fairly direct approach with her. 'Look, Laura, this is really out of order. The police are coming to my new home and I'm not going to have a fucking siege. Now give me the glass.'

I looked at him in surprise. It was a paternalistic no-nonsense approach. I had been trying to be emotionally neutral, but I realised that she needed an emotional response from the people around her. Her whole life had been built around emotional transactions such as these, and whilst my response was perhaps the right approach for longer-term reflective counselling, it seemed to 'miss' somewhat in the highly charged atmosphere in which we found ourselves.

Laura picked up the glass from her lap and passed it silently to Jas. She looked about six years old, regressed, child-like and hurt because her 'transitional object' was being taken away from her.

The TSG came about twenty minutes later with a couple of ambulance crew following them in. I told them what had happened and then went out to allow them to manage the situation. As I came out of the bedroom, I felt a tap on my shoulder. 'Nice place, Doc,' said one of the under-utilised TSG officers.

'Not mine,' I said and then I realised he called me Doc. 'Do we know each other?'

'It was a month ago, you know, up the tower block. He was going to jump. Is he OK?'

I looked around the room and there were still a few people there. I think most of them were Laura's friends, waiting to see that she got to hospital safely and now enjoying chatting to the other TSG crew, who found themselves having unexpected downtime.

The TSG, in fact all the police I have worked with in the field, have been brilliant. They have been unfailingly professional, courteous and supportive. The first time I worked with them properly, I was seeing a patient with a history of violence and knife crime at his home. He hadn't come to the door, so I bent down and peered through the letter box to see if my patient was in.

The sergeant immediately pushed me to one side. 'One of my colleagues got acid in his face doing that.' He then showed me how to do it safely.

The next time I used the services of the TSG, the patient had threatened to kill us if we came to his home again. We knew he was becoming ill – neighbours had been complaining about his threats and his shouting all through the night.

I was there first and used my new-found skills to look through the letter box safely. I held the metal doorknob so I could control the door if it was suddenly pulled open. As I peered in, I noticed some wiring coming to the front door from the fuse box in the hallway. I backed off and briefed the TSG when they arrived. After they smashed the door in, we discovered the patient had tried, unsuccessfully, to wire the metal doorknob to the electric mains. The patient's incompetence probably saved my life.

'Is he OK?' asked the TSG officer again, calling me back to the conversation. 'We only just got him in time.'

I remembered the case he was talking about. 'Clark, yes, he's doing well. Thanks.'

He seemed satisfied and then made eye contact with a woman on the far side of the room. 'Nice party,' he said as he wandered off.

We had planned Clark's home visit carefully and managed to find a secure bed, a social worker, a locksmith, a magistrates' court order and the support of the TSG all on the same morning. In fact, the only person who wasn't involved in the planning was Clark. In fairness, we had tried to involve him, and had called on him more than once, but he told us to 'go away', and sounded a lot like Laura discussing Rupert's sexual inadequacy.

He was living in a tower block. He was under section 37 of the Act, which is a treatment order made by a Crown court after a conviction for an imprisonable offence. The judge added a section 41 because of his dangerousness, which takes away the psychiatrist's power to discharge, so discharge or release from hospital falls to a tribunal or the Ministry of Justice.

When you are discharged under a 37/41 there are normally

conditions attached. It's a bit like a probation order, except if you breach the conditions you go back to hospital, not prison.

For Clark, the conditions of his release required him to see us for assessments, take his medication and not to use illicit drugs. He had refused to see us and we knew he was not taking his medication. Given his past history in such circumstances, it was quite likely that he was using illicit drugs.

I had been through his medical records. He had a severe mental illness, paranoid schizophrenia, and liked to use cannabis and crack. He didn't have a dissocial personality disorder, though when he was unwell or stoned, or both, one could be forgiven for thinking that he did. His convictions were for rape and GBH and after that he'd spent close on five years in a medium secure psychiatry unit.

He told us, when we had previously tried to visit him, that he would throw the first person who came into his flat off the balcony, and if that were not possible, he'd throw himself off. His apartment was on the tenth floor.

We assembled on the ground floor at 8 a.m. and I briefed the TSG.

'How dangerous is he?' asked the police officer in charge.

'GBH, rape. He threatened to throw the first person into his flat off the balcony, or himself.'

'Weapons?'

'Knives, no firearms we know about.'

'Anyone else live there?'

'Not that I know of. He might be under the influence of drugs and he's got a psychotic illness.'

I pressed the lift button, but the light didn't come on. I pressed again and there was an ominous silence as I looked up at the display showing the lift firmly stuck on floor 14.

'They're always fucking broken,' said a voice from the back.

We reassembled, slightly breathless and sweaty, outside

Clark's door and, because of his threats, the police decided that knocking on the door in the traditional sense wasn't a good idea. The door was opened about two seconds later with the help of a mini battering ram strategically aimed at the lock.

A stream of officers ran into the apartment and found their man getting out of bed. He didn't have time to even gather his thoughts, much less get to the balcony. They restrained him and then left, leaving just two officers with him in the apartment. At that point I then went in with the social worker and we conducted our interview. These days it's an AMHP – an approved mental health professional – who is approved by the local social services authority to carry out certain duties under the Mental Health Act.

He seemed unfocused, which was understandable given the circumstances, but there was drug paraphernalia all around. He told us that he had been offered free drugs soon after getting out of hospital. Once he was using regularly, the dealers started to charge and then he got into debt. It's a common story. Men in these situations often commit robberies, women sell their bodies. Crack is a cruel master, and we all do what we can.

Apart from the broken lift, it had all gone very smoothly, and the police took Clark down the stairs to the van waiting to convey him to hospital.

It was only then that I had a chance to look around the apartment, whilst the social worker was calling for a workman to repair the door. I went into the kitchen and found a woman there frying some eggs. I introduced myself and she told me her name was Gloria, Clark's girlfriend. Suddenly I felt like an intruder and I apologised for the inconvenience. She seemed pretty distant and said it was 'OK'. I asked her if she knew what had happened.

'Sure,' she replied. 'He's not been taking his medication and now he's going back to hospital.'

I asked her if he had any symptoms.

'The voices came back a week ago, but he's not really paranoid. That's when I leave.'

'Is it just cannabis and crack?'

'Yeah, sometimes benzos to help him come down.'

I nodded. Without perhaps realising it, she had identified his relapse indicators (first voices, then paranoia) and the cause of his relapse (non-compliance and illicit drugs). Whilst the voices were unpleasant, it was the paranoia that caused his violence. It was a very good risk analysis.

'Would you like an egg?' asked Gloria.

Normally I would never accept such an offer, but for some reason I liked her – she had a forthright quality. I surprised myself and accepted her offer.

We sat for ten minutes by the large picture window in the lounge and ate our breakfast together.

'How long will he be in for?' she asked.

I shrugged. 'Not sure, could be weeks.'

She nodded. 'You know he's OK when he's OK, don't you?'

I did, and I told her.

Some people like Clark only commit their offences when they are unwell. There are plenty of dangerous people out there, and at times, Clark was one of them. But, and it is a crucial distinction, he was not a psychopath – he had a mental illness that was complicated by illicit drugs.

I left Jas' party, made my way home and was called by the junior psychiatrist in A & E two hours later. They had just assessed Laura and I was on call.

'I've got a twenty-four-year-old woman with deliberate self-harm – she's cut her wrist and that's been sutured but she's made quite a few more superficial cuts . . .'

'Four-centimetre parallel cuts to her left forearm,' I said. 'Six of them.'

'Yes,' said the doctor, confused by my psychic powers.

'Talk to her about her self-worth. She's not suicidal but she does need to talk things through. Try to encourage her to get some counselling.'

Laura had cut herself because she had a low image of herself, was intoxicated with alcohol and was angry that her sense of security and love had been taken away. If she was to be categorised as having a disorder, it would be an acute stress reaction and harmful use of alcohol and some emotionally unstable personality traits. Jas told me later that she was already seeing a psychologist because a friend of the family used to touch her when she was a child. She coped by becoming obsessional and agoraphobic. She lost a year of schooling because of school phobia.

Clark was at risk of injuring other people because he had a mental illness and he tried to improve how he felt about himself by using stimulant drugs. He had a relapsing psychotic illness with harmful use of cannabis and crack and some antisocial personality traits. When I went back over the notes from his last admission, I saw that he was twenty-four years old, the same age as Laura. His father had been sent to prison when he was thirteen and he had been expelled from school a few months later. He ended up in a secure children's home where he made allegations that he had been sexually abused when he was a young boy.

There are many reasons why people develop different forms of mental illness but at the risk of generalising, there are some things that just seem obvious.

If I take a child and only give them love when it suits me, leave them yearning for attention and approbation, and discipline them inconsistently, and abuse them so they think it's their fault and then stop their education and make them mix with delinquent drug users with pro-criminal attitudes, I can introduce you to Clark.

Why Laura ended up different from Clark I can't say.

Maybe it was her sex and the hormonal differences, maybe a different genetic inheritance. Perhaps a different choice of drug or perhaps it was the way those around her responded to her distress or that she had more stable caregivers.

Whatever the differences, both of them had a mental disorder. Both of them were diminished from what they could have been, and both hurt themselves and those around them in different ways.

We don't have all the answers about the biological causes of mental illness, and in some ways we are still scratching at the surface, but we do know that social and environmental factors are at least as important, and never more so than in childhood.

The child really is the father of the man, and mother to us all.

A prayer for Timothy Rockall

Doctors like to think that medicine is a profession, but in reality, it is little more than a long apprenticeship. Sometimes we get things wrong and it is in these situations we should reflect on our mistakes and learn from the experience. That's the theory at least, but sadly, there are all too many instances when we have failed to reflect or have ignored our mistakes altogether.

That's what happened at the Bristol Royal Infirmary and it is why reflection isn't a choice any more, it's a requirement.

Between 1991 and 1995 as many as thirty-five children died at the Bristol Royal Infirmary, children who would have survived their heart surgery if they had been treated somewhere else. It took the newly appointed anaesthetist, Dr Stephen Bolsin, just a day to realise there was a problem with the cardiac surgery. The surgeons were poorly trained and just too slow. When you're operating on the heart, the longer the operation, the more complications you get.

Speed is of the essence.

Which is ironic, because Dr Bolsin was saying things were wrong for six years before anyone started to listen to him. By 1995 he had told everyone he could think of that there was a problem. He had hit a brick wall of indifference. Nobody wanted to acknowledge something was wrong.

Sadly, it is sometimes only a crisis that changes things for the better and in medicine, this usually translates as a patient dying. In this particular case, it was Joshua Loveday, a child aged sixteen months, who had heart surgery one day and died the next. After that came the public inquiry. I clearly recall reading the report and feeling more concerned with every page I turned: poor organisation, paternalism, a lack of leadership, poor communication and club culture. Put simply, services were dangerous, and the most troubling thing was, the doctors hadn't noticed.

I was appointed to St Jude's the year before the report came out. It was my first consultant interview, and I didn't know if I was in with a chance. St Jude's has a reputation for excellence, and I was worried that I might not be seen as St Jude's 'material'. If I am being honest, I had already unconsciously recognised the club culture and the paternalism of the organisation, but I hadn't yet given it a name.

It's worth mentioning that a consultant interview is quite a big thing. At St Jude's, the panel consisted of two professors, a representative of the chief executive, the medical director, two consultants, a Royal College representative and a lay member.

We've come a long way. At the last consultant panel I convened, I had a patient sitting by my side. Actually, he was a service user, and an 'expert by experience', and the best bit was that he was being paid for his time, just like me.

Having so far only been a junior doctor (in hospital, if you're not a consultant, then by definition you are a junior doctor) I was feeling decidedly nervous about the impending ordeal. That's when the phone went – it was 9.30 p.m., the night before my interview.

It was one of the professors who was going to be on the interview panel the next day. We exchanged pleasantries, in so far as you can exchange pleasantries with someone who holds your future in their hands, and I was waiting for the 'good luck' – preferably in a non-Gestapo way – but instead, she told me that my CV was 'pretty average', my research was 'inferior' and my publications 'sparse'.

'Anything positive you'd like to say?' I enquired, reeling from the blows.

There was a short pause. 'Not really,' said the professor, and then hung up.

I decided to call Anthony, who had managed to survive at St Jude's as a consultant for fifteen years. He listened to me – I think he listened to me, but I am pretty sure that I heard the gentle chink of ice thrown into a cut-glass tumbler in the background, and then the reassuring glug of what I assume was single malt poured to somewhere just over his second finger.

I guess that's what happens after fifteen years.

'Sounds like a normal Friday academic session,' he said, bluntly. 'Welcome to St Jude's.'

'But the Prof just said I was shit.'

After a short and considered pause, he said, 'Ben, in my experience, unless you have sexual congress with the lay member in front of the panel, I think the job is pretty much yours.'

The next day the interview seemed to be going well, the professor had either had a personality transplant overnight or had been replaced with a doppelgänger, and towards the end, the medical director introduced the lay member. She seemed lovely and was very charming. And then she asked her first question.

'Dr Cave, I'd be interested in your views about long-term patients in forensic services having conjugal visits.'

I tried not to corpse.

She went on. 'I just think we can be so terribly conservative when it comes to sex.'

I did briefly wonder if there was some grand conspiracy or secret initiation to consultancy at St Jude's but no one else was smiling, in fact by this point the panel looked slightly bored. I said something vaguely sensible about the right to a family life, risk considerations, safeguarding . . . and wondered whether it would be too early to go directly to the pub after the interview.

I got the job. I had passed the test and I put my junior doctor years behind me. Whatever mistakes I made from that point on belonged to me. I couldn't blame inexperience and I couldn't say that I hadn't received the correct supervision. Actually, it felt quite good. It felt like I had arrived and yet the journey was just beginning.

Some years later I summoned the courage to remind the professor about the phone call the night before my interview – we were both talking at the same conference. She remembered calling me but looked confused at my recollection of events. 'I was trying to be helpful,' she said.

It might sound a little odd coming from a psychiatrist, but people can be very strange.

The world I had just entered was about to change, and rightly so, and it's hard to describe just how massive the consequences of the Bristol inquiry were going to be. The next five years saw organisational changes the likes of which the NHS had never seen. Patients and patient safety were put at the heart of the reforms. There was a duty of candour when things went wrong, better recording of consent, and above all, professional regulation.

You may be wondering what happened to the doctors at the heart of the scandal. The General Medical Council (GMC) conducted the longest hearing in its history and found them all guilty of serious professional misconduct. In 1998, the head of the department was struck off, the chief executive was struck off (because he also happened to be a doctor – so they could) and the surgeon who did the operation on Joshua Loveday was suspended from operating on children for three years.

The whistle-blower, Dr Bolsin? Well, he applied for several jobs in England but back then nobody liked a whistle-blower, and he soon realised he wasn't being given any of the jobs he was applying for. He eventually exiled himself to Australia and seems to have done very well, very well indeed. And it's probably his legacy that means that if we make mistakes, we are now expected to consider what went wrong, why, and learn from the process. It's called 'reflective practice', and it is an integral part of our annual appraisals and, every five years, our revalidation. It's recorded, analysed, shared and filed. On one hand, some people don't think it goes far enough, and on the other, some doctors are quite suspicious about it. They're worried that if we record things that didn't go right, our mistakes could be used in litigation against us.

And things don't always go right in psychiatry. We are dealing with difficult, challenging and often unpredictable patients. Let me give you an example. If Purple Man was my first big 'win', this next patient was my first big 'loss'. I am still troubled about it, and although I believe I did everything I could, I still reflect on how I might have done things differently.

It was almost Timothy's birthday. He was going to be forty and his mother, Mrs Rockall, had come to Lakeview with presents for him. Even years later, I remember my meeting with her. Giving bad news is never easy.

He was a normal lad, good-looking and confident. At around sixteen, he started to behave strangely with his friends at school. He 'went in on himself' and started to play truant. His history teacher spoke to him and Timothy told him that one of the other pupils wanted to kill him. Sometimes he shouted at them angrily, and they complained to their teacher. Timothy was told off, but no one picked up on the fact he was developing the psychotic illness that would go on to define his life.

His behaviour got steadily worse and eventually when he was seventeen, he hit one of the other pupils and was suspended.

Back at school and seeing a counsellor, they were doing a PE class and Timothy said that he didn't feel too well. He went back to the changing room, went into one of the other boys' bags and took out a CD. He broke it in half and then used the jagged edge to cut his neck. The cut extended from just behind his left ear and stopped just past his windpipe.

He was found unconscious with significant blood loss when the PE teacher came to see how he was doing. An ambulance was called, and he was rushed off to A & E.

He needed a transfusion during surgery and then he was seen by a liaison psychiatrist. He spoke about people plotting against him which were taken to be persecutory delusions and his speech was very disorganised. He got very angry when he was asked about hearing voices.

He stayed in hospital whilst his physical injury was treated and then he was transferred to psychiatry services at St Jude's. He was discharged on medication which he promptly stopped and then he had a couple of longer admissions. He was eventually discharged on depot medication, but he always stopped it and then became unwell again, usually after three months.

The diagnosis after his first admission was an acute psychotic episode. By the time he was on depot medication, it was clear that he had schizophrenia. When I saw him, he had been detained in hospital under the Mental Health Act for over twenty years – continuously. He had a treatment-resistant schizophrenic illness, and pretty much all of the antipsychotic drugs that he had been given were ineffective.

Over that period, he had clocked up fifteen assaults on staff because he thought they were trying to attack him, and twelve assaults on other patients, two of which were serious. One woman on a mixed ward accused him of raping her, but she only told the ward staff about it two weeks later, and although he was questioned by the police, he was never charged or convicted.

Despite all the assaults, he had only ever been convicted twice: once for possession of cannabis and the other for a minor assault. It is notoriously difficult to get the police or CPS to investigate or charge psychiatry inpatients. 'They're in the right place already . . . it's not in the public interest,' they tell me.

When I interviewed him, he sounded suspicious, irritable and although he denied it, he was clearly hallucinating.

'Leave me alone,' he would shout at his imagined perse-cutor when he was in the privacy of his own bedroom.

After our third meeting, he hinted at a conspiracy theory and told me that he had lost control of his body when he first cut his throat all those years ago. 'It still happens sometimes,' he said.

One of the best things that happened in psychiatry was the invention of antipsychotic drugs in the 1950s. The first such drug was chlorpromazine – before that there was no effective treatment for schizophrenia. Antipsychotic drugs block receptors in the brain for various neurotransmitters. These neurotransmitters are chemicals that nerves use to communicate with each other. As you can imagine, there have been lots of new medicines since the 1950s, but still there are some patients who don't respond to them and remain stubbornly psychotic.

There is one drug called clozapine which is licensed for use in 'treatment-resistant schizophrenia'. It has a unique action in how it blocks serotonin and dopamine receptors. For a good number of patients with this condition, it is a lifesaver. I have had patients get better, go home and stay well for years with clozapine.

But for every patient who does well, there are those who don't – and the list of side effects is significant, whether it helps their mental state or not. One of the more serious side effects is something called agranulocytosis. People with this condition don't make enough of the white cells that fight infection, and that means that even a minor infection could kill them. Clozapine was taken off the market because of this side effect, but because of its remarkable effect for some patients, it was reintroduced in 1990. Since then, if the drug is prescribed, it is linked to automatic blood tests to monitor the white cell count, and if you have too few, a so-called 'red result', the drug is stopped. It's also stopped if you miss the blood test.

I saw that Tim had been tried on clozapine some years earlier, but he'd had a red result. The notes told me that in the two months that he had taken it, there had been a massive improvement in his condition, such that they had planned his discharge. After it was stopped, he started back on high doses of other antipsychotics, and predictably, they did no good at all. He just slid back into his paranoid and violent state that typified his every waking hour.

He was one of the most chronically unwell people I have ever treated. His illness was progressive, unremitting and severe. It had robbed him of his life. He had never worked and he had never lived independently.

I asked him about his sex life, and he told me about a brief fumble when he was fifteen. He then referred to the incident on the ward when he had gone into a female patient's bedroom. He thought they were 'an item' – she accused him of rape.

As a doctor, we have a duty of care to our patients and what we do must be in their best interests. '*Make the care of your patient your first concern*,' is how the GMC puts it.

Every time we treat someone, even with an aspirin, there is a cost–benefit analysis to be done. Will it help to reduce the risk of heart attack? Probably. Will it cause their stomach to bleed? Probably not.

Even in this simple scenario there is a complex decision to be made. How many of us would take aspirin if the risk of a stomach bleed were 50 per cent? Almost nobody I suspect. What if the risk were 1 per cent? Perhaps a few more might take it. One in a thousand or one in ten thousand? That's the sort of risk that most people might accept.

But whatever your personal risk barometer, we're not dealing with aspirin, and we're not dealing with choice.

The cardiology patient can be given the facts about aspirin, and they can go off and make their own choice about whether to take it. But many of my patients are not in a position to make a decision for themselves. Whilst it's always good to have the patient 'onside', if they are under the Mental Health Act, they can be treated against their wishes. So, it's not the patient's decision to take clozapine, it's my decision on their behalf.

With Tim there was another layer of complexity. Sure, part of the decision to give him clozapine is to act in his best interest (despite the known potentially serious side effects), but there is another reason to treat him, and that is to reduce his risk of violence against other people.

It might be difficult to acknowledge it, but forensic psychiatry sometimes acts in society's best interest. In Tim's case, it is fortunate that there was a confluence – it was, I thought, in his best interests to have clozapine, and it was probably the best drug to manage his risk to everyone around him – the nurses and the other patients.

My decision was made. I was going to start Tim on clozapine. I really didn't think that there was an ethical doubt about it.

I spoke to him and I spoke to his mother. They listened to the arguments and I talked about the risk of agranulocytosis and how we would manage it.

'We'll do regular blood tests. It won't be a problem,' I told them.

Tim looked troubled and was starting to respond to the voices. 'Fuck off,' he said under his breath. Whatever else, it was not going to be his decision whether or not to take clozapine, he just wasn't up to it.

His mother looked like she'd reached a decision. 'Dr Cave, he did get better with clozapine, but it almost killed him. If he takes it again, it will kill him.' It wasn't what I was expecting her to say.

I went away to consider the matter. I had another chat with Mrs Rockall on the phone. I spoke to the psychologist who had been working with him, and his lawyer, and advocate, and the nurse with whom he had a good relationship, and then I had another meeting with his mother and another with Tim and then he was seen by another doctor to examine and approve my treatment plan.

And with all that in place I got Mrs Rockall and Tim into an interview room off the ward and told him I was going to start him on clozapine.

That's when he hit me.

I now mentally associate the word *clozapine* with my left cheek being rapidly pushed between my teeth and falling off my chair.

It was on my short journey to the floor that I thought back with some fondness of the first time a patient took a right hook at me. My earlier assailant was a woman of eighty-seven. I never learnt her name and she lived for just half an hour after I met her. I had been called on to the psychogeriatric ward by a nurse to certify her as dead. Many of the patients there had end-stage dementia and unsurprisingly, a death on the ward was a weekly occurrence.

The nurse had obviously given the patient a cursory look and seen that she wasn't breathing. That's when she called me. I was nearby and arrived soon enough. Maybe I fell into the same trap and did not observe her for long enough, but the nurse seemed to be quite right – the patient had stopped breathing. I pulled down her bedclothes and proceeded to press on her sternum.

Doctors are taught how to confirm death, and one of the procedures is to watch the patient 'not breathe'. So the first box was ticked. Later in the checklist comes the bit that I was now engaged with, and that involves pressing on the sensitive bits of their anatomy such that if you were alive, it would hurt a lot and you would wake up and complain about it.

It seems a shame that it's not more technical than that. I know that it is a really lame excuse, but I was just doing what I had been taught. To avoid any doubt in the matter, if you are dead, it doesn't matter how much pain the doctor tries to inflict, nothing will happen, nothing at all. The dead do not wake up, they do not give you an indignant look and they most definitely do not give you a right hook that knocks you off your semi-perched position leaning over them.

I will never know how many times my patient had woken to find a semi-perched man next to her, but unfortunately, I was the last of them. As I pressed on her sternum, you will by now have gathered that she woke up, looked at me indignantly and swung a fist at my face that was not expected but was most definitely deserved.

I fell to the floor and had to suffer the indignity of the nurse's mirth as I was getting to my feet to apologise to my, most definitely alive, patient.

Having apologised, I am pleased that she seemed to forgive me and perhaps, thanks to her dementing state, seemed to forget about the whole unfortunate matter.

I then spent another thirty minutes with her. I watched her breathing wax and wane. Respiration often becomes irregular prior to death – it's called Cheyne-Stokes breathing, after the physicians who first described it.

And then slowly, almost fitfully, she just stopped breathing. And this time it didn't start again. Some years later, I had the privilege to do the same with my father, only he didn't hit me.

She had seemed comforted by my holding her hand, so I just carried on holding it. Nothing happened. There was no sudden change, no sudden discernible difference, just the quiet solace of death.

And after half an hour or so of thought and introspection on my part, I took my hand from hers, stood and listened to her chest. It was quite silent. No lub-dup, no breathing noises. And when I pressed my knuckle hard into her sternum, there was no response, just an unseeing stare right back at me. I pressed her eyelids down. I don't know why; it just seemed the right thing to do.

Rest well. Rest peacefully.

Timothy had just hit me. He was most definitely not dead – he had another four months before his birthday. I saw him standing there being restrained by nurses. He was then taken back to his room and given a sedative medication.

I wasn't injured and after about half an hour, I went back to see his mother again.

'Rest assured, Mrs Rockall, I will keep a very close eye on Timothy. He's not going to die.' I was confident and sure, and only wincing occasionally as I ran my tongue over my ulcerated inner cheek.

She looked at me and shook her head.

After various blood tests, I started the clozapine and despite some early problems with constipation, which is a well-recognised and sometimes serious side effect, he seemed to tolerate it really well. We did blood tests more often than we needed to, and his mental state started to pick up.

After about a month, it seemed that his condition was improving. He would talk to me about his illness and even started to talk to the psychologist about his violence and his sexual disinhibition when he got unwell. He became less hostile, less prickly, more relaxed and easier to be with.

After three months it was absolutely clear he was

responding so well to clozapine that he was a different man. He spoke about his illness in the past tense. He told me that much of the last two decades of his life seemed like a bad dream – he was now awake and back in reality.

Timothy was doing really well, and he was looking forward to his birthday in just a month's time.

I was first alerted to a problem when he came into a ward round and just looked off colour. He didn't look right. It took me about ten years of working as a doctor to get the 'something's not right about him' sign, and he had it in abundance.

His skin had lost its colour and there was a clamminess to him. An examination revealed a low-grade fever but his blood tests and his all-important white cell count were normal. Actually, it was a bit on the high side which meant, to a shrink like me, that his immune system was working just fine, fighting off an infection. We looked, we looked everywhere, but we couldn't find the source of infection.

I went back to my office after the ward round and looked up all the case reports and studies I could find about clozapine and infection. There was a lot of material, but none of it gave me any answers.

At this point there is another cost–benefit analysis to be done. So far, the benefits were clear – for the first time in many years, he had his life back. The illness was being treated successfully. The illness that had stolen his life and hurt others was on the retreat. He had developed insight and we could see the light at the end of the tunnel.

But there was still something not right about him. His blood work was OK, and his examination was unremarkable. The chest X-ray was normal.

'Dr Cave?' said the receptionist, calling me in my office. 'Mrs Rockall for you.'

'There's something not right about him, Doctor,' she

said. 'Have you seen him?'

We spoke for a bit and I agreed that he wasn't right. It was then I decided to take the first of my lifelines. I called a friend.

The friend in this instance was the medical registrar at a nearby hospital. I explained the situation and he agreed to see Tim in A & E. I wrote a letter and we sent him there by ambulance. He was poked and prodded by the doctors with white coats and they gave him some antibiotics and sent him back. 'We can't find the source of the infection either,' is what they told me.

About a week passed and I was seeing him daily. Every time I asked the nurses how he was doing, they invariably told me that he was stable, but not looking right.

I thought about stopping his clozapine. There had been some reports about increased likelihood of pneumonia with it, but he didn't seem to have pneumonia, and once again, I thought back to what he was like before we changed his medication.

'No change to his medication,' I announced at the end of each ward round, probably as much to reassure myself as the team. 'Check his white cell count again,' I would bark at my junior doctor and she would groan and remind me that she had done it the day before.

'Do it again,' I'd say, forcing a smile.

I sent Tim back to see the medical registrar a week later. He was pale and listless with a low-grade fever. He wasn't acutely unwell – he could get up, dress, go to therapy groups and even tried to kick a ball around in the recreation area. But he was listless, he had no energy, and then he started to have night sweats.

We took him back to the general hospital again and the medical registrar came to look at him. I suggested they admit him to give him a thorough work-up.

They did his bloods again. They did every test they could think of. Nothing was showing up, just the stubborn low-grade fever.

And then they did what all good medics do in such situations. They took a lifeline and asked the audience. In this case, the audience was a multi-disciplinary meeting where all the white coats meet up. It was an impressive line-up and there must have been 400 years of experience from all over the world. There was one diagnosis that kept being mentioned.

'Tuberculosis,' they said.

I nodded. It kind of made sense. 'No doubt about it,' they reassured me.

I saw Mrs Rockall and told her the good news. Don't get me wrong, tuberculosis is not a good diagnosis, but at least we knew what we were dealing with.

'He's going to die, Doctor. That clozapine isn't right for him.'

I knew better, thankfully, and reassured her that he would be fine. Notwithstanding, I spoke it through with my senior colleagues. The consensus was to continue with the clozapine.

But he got worse and when I went back to see him, he was deteriorating despite being on loads of antibiotics, many of which I hadn't even heard of. It was the medical equivalent of Domestos – *kills all known germs, dead.*

Mrs Rockall wrote to me again and then she called me. 'He's dying, Doctor.'

I talked to Tim and I was quite frank with him. 'I'm worried you're not getting better.'

He knew the score and by this point was keen to continue with the clozapine. 'I don't want to go back to that place,' he said earnestly. I pressed him on the matter, but it was clear he understood his decision, and the importance of it.

So, I went back to my office and took the phone off the hook. I read the literature again, I consulted widely and then I called my friend, the registrar.

'How's he doing?' I asked.

'It's fifty-fifty,' he said. He wasn't one to mince his words.

That's when I took the decision to stop his clozapine. It wasn't because Mrs Rockall asked me to, though that weighed heavily on me. It was ironic because Tim had hit me because I wanted to start him on clozapine and now we had swapped our positions. He pleaded with me. He knew the risks and he accepted them. 'They're treating me for TB. My white cells are fine. Stopping clozapine won't help. Anyway, they said the TB takes time to treat.'

Tim was trying to reassure me, but by this stage I had spoken to psychiatry colleagues, medics, an immunologist and a pharmacologist, and I knew there were concerns being voiced about clozapine and pneumonia and some worries about immunosuppression, not simply linked to the white cell count.

I still had a psychiatry nurse with him 24/7 to monitor his mental state and I knew what would happen when I stopped the clozapine. People can deteriorate quickly, even over a matter of days, and I knew from experience that if Tim became floridly psychotic again, we probably couldn't keep him in a general hospital and he'd probably be too paranoid to comply with the medication he was getting from the white coat doctors.

I took a decision. I stopped the clozapine on a Thursday. On Friday he was restless, despite being on a new cocktail of sedating antipsychotics. On Saturday, he started to get suspicious. By Monday, I was increasing his benzodiazepines just to reduce the distress he was experiencing. He'd taken to his bed, too weak to mobilise.

I went to see him again on Wednesday. He was in a side room with a nurse sitting outside, by the entrance. He was clammy and told me that the doctors were trying to kill him.

On Thursday the medics looking after him called to tell me that he had deteriorated a lot over the last twenty-four hours. They were doing everything they could for him.

I called his mother and we planned to meet the next day. It was his birthday that weekend and she was planning to bring in his presents. 'I'll drive you over to the hospital after we meet,' I said.

The call from the psychiatry nurse sitting with him came at 10 a.m. on Friday morning. 'There's nothing I can do here. The resus team were trying for over thirty minutes. I'll come back to the unit. Sorry, Ben,' he said.

I sat by myself for a few minutes to collect my thoughts. I stared down at the floor where I had lain after Tim hit me and rubbed my cheek absent-mindedly.

'Dr Cave,' said the receptionist on the phone. 'Mrs Rockall is here for you.'

I called Elaine and went to reception. Mrs Rockall had two 'bags for life' filled with presents. I walked her up to the interview room where Elaine was now waiting for us.

'I thought we were driving to the hospital to see him?' said Mrs Rockall. And then I think she saw my face and she stopped dead.

I didn't need to say anything, she knew what had happened. People always know, the telegram in wartime, the police officer at the door, the nurse taking you to a side room and the doctor's face.

'I am so . . .' I started, but I couldn't finish what I was trying to say. I forced back the emotions. She had to hear it. 'Mrs Rockall, Timothy died an hour ago. I am so sorry.'

I sat there. She looked at me for longer than I can say, and slowly her head bowed, and I could see the tears flowing freely down her cheeks.

'He was my only child.'

We sat with her and we cried together.

'Dr Cave, Nurse Elaine. Please would you pray with me.'

'Of course,' I said. It's not something I'd ever been asked to do before, but it felt entirely natural. It almost felt like coming home.

'Our Father,' she started, 'who art in heaven . . .'

Elaine and I joined in. 'Hallowed be thy name . . .'

It was an hour later when I drove her to the general hospital to collect his things and do the paperwork.

The post-mortem showed that Timothy had multiple abscesses on his lungs. It's likely the cause of death was sepsis arising from this. It turns out that he didn't have TB, at least no cultures ever gave a positive result.

Research papers and case reports published over the years since Timothy died have linked clozapine to pneumonia and an impaired immunological response. Now, I'd have stopped the clozapine much earlier, whether Timothy liked it or not.

Did I get it wrong? Was I blinded by the treatment being successful?

I don't know. You be my judge.

Mrs Rockall, I am truly sorry for your loss. I ignored your prophetic warnings. Please know that I always tried to act in Timothy's best interests.

I think that's all any doctor can do.

When the drugs work:
Ecstasy and bloody feet

I only agreed to accept Charlie to my ward because I thought he would be a challenge. He had already been in hospital for close to four years and over that period he hadn't improved at all. He was just as psychotic as the day he came in. He was still insightless, his self-care was appalling and he kept absconding from hospital. When he did the police invariably found him naked in the woods, usually after dog walkers phoned in complaints.

There was one other reason I was happy to take him under my care. I'd been to see him and spent an hour talking to him and by the end of it, I thought he had the most lovely spirit of anyone I had ever met.

I went back and told Elaine he'd be coming in and I told my ward doctor, Tayo.

'So, what's he coming in for?' asked Tayo, scanning the notes.

'He's in for treatment of his schizophrenia,' I replied.

'But he's got three convictions for public indecency. Won't he need to go on the sex offender programme?' He was a new breed of forensic psychiatrist where if you did anything wrong, it had to be explained through the prism of mental disorder or antisocial behaviour.

'They don't count,' I said. 'He's not a flasher.' Tayo did not look convinced. 'Come and meet him. I'll interview him. Let me show you how it's done.'

Tayo tried to raise a smile but still looked a little peeved. He had an MSc, a PhD and already had a string of research publications, but for now he needed to understand why people got into trouble, and that it wasn't always because they were 'bad'.

'How's it going?' I asked Charlie.

He shrugged. 'Don't want to be here.'

'I know, Charlie. You've left the three services that you were in before you came here.'

Charlie nodded.

'You absconded,' said Tayo and I shot him a glance.

'Why?' I asked.

He shrugged again and reached out to pluck at something from between our faces. He stared at something he imagined in his hand for a while and then seemed to lose interest.

'What was it?'

He looked back at me and put his finger to his lips. 'Sh.' Charlie then seemed to cup something from the air in his hands and stood and went to the window. He used his elbow to push the ventilation grill open. 'There's no window,' he said accusingly.

'Put it by the grill – it'll get through.'

Charlie nodded and seemed satisfied with the outcome and came to sit down again. As he did, he wafted some air over me, and I smelt his awful body odour.

'What did you catch?'

'A spirit.' There was no irony. It was as real to him as catching a daddy-long-legs and releasing it.

'Can you tell me about them?'

Charlie smiled a little. 'They're from the trees. Everything is alive, even the bed I am sitting on. They all have spirits.'

Charlie gazed round the room and his eyes fell on Tayo. 'Your spirit is a dark one.'

I suppressed a smile. 'How old were you when you started to see the spirits?'

Charlie shrugged again. 'Dunno, maybe twenty or so. I heard them first.'

'What did they say?'

'They called out to me – they called me to the woods.'

'Is that when you take your clothes off?'

Charlie nodded. 'It's to get close to them – to commune.'

'Is that when you were arrested?'

'I wasn't doing anything wrong. I was naked, but there was nothing dodgy about it.'

Privately, I was inclined to agree. Some people are easily offended by the sight of a naked man, but I kept my views to myself.

'Were you masturbating?' asked Tayo.

There are times when you want your colleagues to shut up, and this was one of those situations. Charlie had already said there was nothing dodgy about his communing with nature in the forest – he had, in my view, already answered the question. Tayo lacked tact and subtlety. There are occasions when you have to ask questions like this, but this wasn't one of them. Interviews are a *process,* not an event, and the information that the patient gives often ebbs and flows. I find it amazing how often people can hold mutually contradictory opinions and be quite comfortable with it – I'm starting to think that's the normal state of being, but it can give rise to some interesting exchanges with lawyers in court.

'Well, Doctor, does your patient have insight into their illness?'

'Well, it depends how you ask the question. If I ask them whether the voices they experience are real, they tell me they are. If they recognise that their experience is different from most other people, they tell me it is. If I ask them whether they will take medication, sometimes they tell me they will, and sometimes they will not. Do they think they have a genetic disorder causing abnormal dopamine transmission that causes perceptual abnormalities? They do not. Will they accept medication notwithstanding the side effects, just to avoid a prolonged admission? They will . . .'

'Doctor, a yes or no will suffice. Does he have insight into his illness?'

Normally at this stage, I capitulate, because the jury is finding it hard to follow and the barrister wants to get on to talk about issues of responsibility, so I turn to the judge, look a bit hurt, put on my best thoughtful voice and say, 'Partial, my Lady; in my opinion he has partial insight.'

Charlie wasn't a bad person, and he wasn't fazed by Tayo. He knew the questions that the police asked him, and after years of treatment, he knew all the questions that psychiatrists asked him too. He just sat there and shook his head, waiting for us to move on. I obliged him. 'Can I look at your feet?' I asked.

Charlie had come to us after absconding from his previous hospital again. He was barefoot at the time, and that was, in part, why the staff there were not expecting him to leave.

Now his feet were red raw, partly from the cold and partly from walking barefoot on roads and verges and in forests. Both his feet were swollen and had cuts, blisters and splinters all over. The wounds were infected and discharging pus.

'They're a bit of a mess,' I said, knowing that he'd need a trip to the local A & E to get some of the glass and wood splinters out of them. I took a swab from one of the wounds that looked infected and wrote him up for some antibiotics.

'I need to send you out to get your feet looked at. Please don't abscond.'

Charlie grinned. 'I won't need to, Doc – I saw the fence on the way in. I can leave whenever I want. I won't though,' he added, 'I'm too tired.'

Charlie called us back as we were leaving and looked at Tayo. 'You asked if I was masturbating.'

Tayo nodded.

'I didn't need to. I was in ecstasy.'

Ecstasy is a state of extreme happiness. It transcends the ordinary happiness that we hope for in our day-to-day lives, and implies an altered level of consciousness, sometimes a trance-like state in which you are separated from yourself. People often associate it with the euphoria of a religious experience. We have been interested in inducing ecstasy in ourselves for as long as we have existed. We use meditative practice, music, intercourse, fasting, religion, dance, cultural practices and psychotropic drugs to experience its wonders.

A person I was once treating for schizophrenia just occasionally had the experience of being possessed by God. When I asked her to describe it to me, she was at a loss for words. It transcended any other experience she had ever had, and she was quite without a vocabulary to describe her brief and intense euphoric experience. I have seen the same look of longing in the face of the problem gambler, trying against the odds to recreate the 'big win' that set them off on their dependence, and on the face of the degraded heroin user, still desperate for the comfort of the opiate fix.

I don't mind admitting it, as a non-drug-using agnostic who can't dance, only got to Grade 5 violin and finds it hard to miss a meal, I am a little envious and I think I might be missing out.

Tayo asked Charlie what he meant about being in ecstasy and we stood at the door waiting for an answer.

There was a faraway look on his face.

'Well, it was, I mean, it was really amazing. I think, no, it's more like, well, everything came together. I was the world, the whole world, it was all in me, it was, you know . . .'

He looked down at his feet and no doubt saw the bloody mess they had become. 'It was perfect,' he said quietly.

We waited a little longer, but Charlie remained silent, still looking down. I remember a handful of events in my life that have given me such joy that I well up with tears just thinking about them, but it has always been about me or those I love. Charlie, despite his illness, and probably because of it, had experienced the divine.

'Can you check his clozapine levels,' I asked Tayo, as we trundled back down the ward. 'I'd be surprised if he's been taking it. I reckon he's been covertly non-compliant at his previous hospital.'

He nodded. 'Seems a shame to treat him.'

Charlie's clozapine level came back as zero. He had been on loads of drugs for his illness and nothing had worked. That's why the clozapine was started. As far as I could work out Charlie had been carefully palming his medication for about a year.

He later admitted to me after we gave him liquid clozapine that he had been putting the tablets between his teeth and his cheek, and then spitting them out some time later. It is much more difficult to keep the liquid medication in your mouth and then hold a conversation with the nurse. Even then, in the early days of treatment, he tried to vomit the medicine back up after he got back to his room. We ended up giving it to him on an empty stomach and then the nurses would sit with him for two hours. It was a long, arduous and difficult process.

Charlie absconded twice more under my care, but they were more half-hearted attempts, and instead of retreating to woodland, he went to a local coffee shop and then came back to hospital under his own steam. I never admonished him for it, in fact I gave him more leave from the unit. I never gave him any form of sex offender therapy.

'You're not treating him like a forensic patient,' grumbled Tayo occasionally.

'That makes me very happy,' I would respond, and he just looked a little confused.

Charlie was eventually discharged from my ward eighteen months later. He did well on clozapine and was last seen talking at a national conference, teaching psychiatrists about what it is like from the service users' perspective. He was very impressive. We need more experts by experience.

Mrs Bainbridge's 'sleeping' tablets

It was back when I was working in prison that I first realised how much of a problem illicit drugs are.

'It wasn't my fault,' said the man in front of me, a thin man with straggly hair and fresh track marks up his arms. He'd come into Campsmoor the night before and had been sent to the health care centre where I was assessing him.

'It says in the notes that you don't use drugs, but what are you actually taking?' I asked. He was holding his abdomen, rocking back and forth and he had gooseflesh on his arms. I knew the answer already.

'Heroin.'

'How come you're here?' I expected him to say robbery, or theft, or burglary. Anything that would get him some money to buy his next fix.

'I nicked a car.'

I nodded.

'And dangerous driving.'

'What happened?'

'Well, I was late for my dealer, and I was going past the petrol station, you know, looking for anything on the seats, and I saw that one of the cars had the keys in the ignition. Twat. So, I got in and drove off and this bloke comes running out of the shop. I knew him – he was the copper who'd nicked me last time.' He paused for breath. 'So I put my foot down and spun into the side of another fucking police car.'

I tried to suppress a smile at the image. Substance use and dependency disorders are complex matters and don't fit comfortably into traditional concepts of mental disorder. It's probably just a consequence of my job, but the people I see with dependency have been very bad. Some of them have been very bad indeed.

In fact, substance use can cause psychosis and affective disorders, and people with psychosis and affective disorders are more likely than most to use substances, even if only to ameliorate their symptoms. So it's complex and it is never more true to say that dependency is a complex synthesis of biological, psychological and social factors.

If people use substances, a proportion of them will develop a dependency. I once went trekking for a few days in the Golden Triangle, where Thailand, Laos and Myanmar meet. It's one of the biggest producers of opium in the world. It's a dangerous place and our guide carried a rifle on his back to protect us. On the way into a village, he took us through a small chicken farm, and I saw his hand tighten over his gun as the chicken farmer approached us. He seemed pleasant enough. He smiled his welcome and I took out my camera to capture his weather-beaten face and two remaining black teeth. He put his hand out and I gave him 50p or so.

Our guide put his hand on my arm. 'No more.'

'What's the problem?' I asked.

'He an addict. Everyone use opium here. Some get addicted. He did. Then he steal from village.' The guide pointed to a small wooden shack built on the hillside on small stilts. 'He live there.' Then he pointed to the village, still half a mile down the valley. 'Keep him away. No more money.'

The only point I'd correct him on is using the word addict. It carries with it all sorts of preconceptions, and moralising is never far behind. Dependency is a better term, and it has clearly defined characteristics.

First, we use drugs for their psychoactive effect.

'Do you use drugs?'

'No, Doctor.'

'Do you use cannabis?'

'Yes.'

'Cannabis is a drug.'

'It's natural though, Doctor.'

I suspect every doctor has had this conversation with a patient at some point in their career. Deadly nightshade is natural, but you probably wouldn't give it to your friends.

After you have established the patient is using a psycho-active drug, it's worth finding out why they take it. The alcoholic's underlying condition might be a social anxiety; the person misusing codeine might have ongoing pain that could be treated better.

Then we ask about control. A person with a dependency uses more and more of the drug and finds it increasingly hard to cut down or stop using it.

Craving comes next and it really does focus the mind like nothing else. 'I don't go out any more,' they tell you. 'I used to go to the gym all the time, but I only leave the house to get the drugs now.'

Before you know it, you get tolerant. 'I used to get pissed so easily, but I never get drunk now. I drink a bottle of vodka, and I just feel normal.' *Drinking yourself sober* is the expression.

By this point, you might be getting withdrawal states. It could be mild shakes that vodka on the cornflakes sorts out, but it could be seizures or DTs (delirium tremens). People climb up the walls, they get paranoid and think insects are eating their legs. You never forget your first case of DTs.

Tolerance, or more particularly loss of tolerance, has its dark side. It's hardly surprising that prisoners who have, perhaps unwillingly, been detoxed from heroin, are at risk

of accidentally overdosing on their
their tolerance and what once would ι
them, is now a lethal respiratory depre.

Eventually, inevitably, the drug takes
fall apart, they can't work, their relationsι
then they reach rock bottom.

The physical burden of heroin dependency ᴠ
mous: HIV, hepatitis, abscesses, endocarditis,   ..onia,
kidney damage. The cost to society in terms of criminality
and delivery of health care is staggering. When the person
sitting in front of you has all of these conditions, when
they've been to prison for theft and violence, when they
can't hold down a job because they steal anything they can,
when they've been thrown out of their family home and
when there are three outstanding court cases and a warrant
for their arrest, that's what dependency looks like.

It's an incredibly destructive cycle.

If there is any good news about substance use, it is that
we can control it at a societal level. It is only a slight over-
simplification to say that there are three things that determine
how a society interacts with a psychoactive drug.

If it is *affordable*, we use it more. If it is readily *available*,
we use it more. And if using it is socially *acceptable*, we use
it more.

If it's all three, we use it a lot.

Just think about alcohol. Alcohol is affordable, available
and acceptable. In fact, it's so affordable, the minimum
pricing strategy is deliberately driving the cost upwards.

The state has, in effect, made a deliberate decision to
control the amount of alcohol and tobacco we use. Both
are incredibly bad for us and both, it has to be said, are
incredibly efficient at raising tax revenue.

Smoking tobacco used to be affordable, available and
acceptable. But now the price is deliberately high, it's hidden
from view and it's less acceptable than it ever was. So, people

...g less as a result. Simple really.

...re is an active debate about legalising cannabis in the ...K, but in reality, society could decide to legalise every drug going. When I worked in drug dependency services, people with a serious opiate dependency were thieving every day to finance their habit. I met one patient who liked to sleep in on Sunday mornings, so he did an extra session of shoplifting on Saturday. I asked him why he'd come to consult me, and he told me that there were two points when he knew he had a problem. The first was when he moved from smoking heroin to injecting it, just to get the same fix. The next was when he used Sunday's supply of heroin on Saturday night.

It's a beautiful description of dependency. And the debate about heroin is long overdue, which is why I need to tell you about Mrs Bainbridge, a single-minded and wonderful woman I was treating on a medical ward before I went into psychiatry. All doctors I know have given opiates to their dying patients, to ease the pain, knowing it would shorten their lives.

Mrs Bainbridge was lovely, the sort of stoic you'd be proud to have as a mother. We spoke together about her life. She'd travelled in northern Thailand, well before it was fashionable, and she had raised three children, one of them a nurse whom I got to know. Her husband was an accountant and then, approaching his seventieth birthday, was mugged in the street. About a month later he got motor neurone disease and Mrs Bainbridge watched him wither away, and then she buried him.

Six months later she was persuaded by her children to go on a round-the-world cruise. She enjoyed it but became unwell just as she got back to the UK. She went to her doctor who sent her to hospital. She had bowel cancer and it had already spread. Two years later she was dying from various complications of her illness. Even then, she didn't seem to worry about herself.

'He was mugged,' she told me. 'They took his phone. The person was a drug addict.' She looked off into the distance. 'What sort of person would steal an old man's phone? He got motor neurone disease after that. Do you think the stress might have caused it, Doctor?'

'I don't know,' I told her. 'Listen, we've got the scan results back. It's gone to your bones. I think that is why you're in so much pain at the moment. Your breathlessness, well, you've got fluid on the lung. I can drain that off, and it'll make you feel better, but it'll come back.'

'The pain, Doctor. I am not sure I can cope with the pain.'

'We can treat the pain,' I told her, with a confidence I didn't feel. I spoke to her family. Everyone knew what was happening. She was dying.

'Can I go home to die?' she asked.

'Let's get the pain under control.'

We increased her opiates to respond to her ever-increasing pain, but we were always playing catch-up. I drained her lung a couple of times to help her breathe, but eventually, enough was enough. It was difficult to see how we'd ever get her home.

She called me over after a ward round. I sat on the bed next to her and she held my hand. She told me that she had spoken to her children and told them to come and see her that evening. 'We're going to say our goodbyes,' she told me. 'Doctor, after they've gone, I was wondering if you could *increase* my medication.'

She paused just before she said 'increase', just to make sure the word was properly articulated, and that I heard it clearly.

'Are you in a lot of pain?' I asked her.

'Terrible, Doctor, terrible,' and then she winced a bit, to show just how terrible it all was. She was acting, and I knew she was acting, and she knew that I knew she was acting.

And the irony is that it was no act. Her pain was terrible.

'No one needs to die in pain,' was the mantra from the terminal care consultant I'd studied under, so I made the changes to the drug chart and showed it to the nurse in charge.

'Are you sure?' she checked. 'That much?'

'Definitely,' I nodded.

'Shall we start the new dose after her family have seen her? They called to say they're visiting tonight.'

I nodded again. 'Good idea.'

I happened to be called back to the ward later on to see another patient and I found myself leaving with Mrs Bainbridge's daughter – the nurse. 'How long has she got?' she asked.

She knew the answer already, but just wanted to talk it through. 'Not long,' I said. It was a lovely conversation about life and death and, more importantly, about how we die. I told her she would probably die very soon, 'but not in pain,' I added, certain in the knowledge that I was using enough opiates to supply a large part of South London.

I went home, called a friend to come round, drank more alcohol than doctors would recommend, and returned the next morning with something of a headache.

Sometimes, on wards like this, the kinder nurses took pity on the on-call doctor and did not wake them when someone died an expected death, which meant that the first job of the day was to go to the cubicles with the curtains closed round them and certify death.

'How many to certify?' I asked, looking round the ward.

'None,' said the nurse in charge. 'No deaths last night.'

'But Mrs Bainbridge, the woman in bed six. What about her?' I mumbled, immediately regretting my friend's suggestion to open a second bottle of wine.

She shook her head again.

'You did give her the prescribed medication?' I asked, accusingly.

She pointed to the bed where Mrs Bainbridge had been. 'Go and talk to her.'

I looked over and there was a tall woman in a floral dress standing by the bed. She looked a bit like Mrs Bainbridge's daughter, but older. Her face was relaxed and she was smiling at me.

I went over to introduce myself, and as I approached her, I stopped and put my hand up to my mouth. I'd never seen her standing before. 'I didn't recognise you,' I said.

'I wasn't expecting to see you either,' said Mrs Bainbridge, taking my hand again. 'Thank you for the *sleeping drug* you gave me last night. I've not slept so well in weeks.' Now she really did give me a knowing wink when she said sleeping drug. 'If I discharge myself, Doctor, could I carry on with the same medication at home?'

I laughed and looked at the tall, elegant and well-rested Mrs Bainbridge. 'You know that the sleeping drug is . . .' but Mrs Bainbridge gently tightened her grip on my hand, telling me it was time to stop talking.

'That *sleeping drug*, Doctor,' she said, and she used her words very precisely, 'will let me die at home.'

I discharged Mrs Bainbridge the next day and I watched her walk out of the hospital with her daughter holding a large bag of opiate drugs. Mrs Bainbridge died three weeks later. Her daughter phoned me and asked what to do with the leftover medication.

Sell the stuff outside the drug dependency service. It'll pay off your mortgage.

But I gave her the proper guidance and commiserated.

From the drug dependency service, it is just a short walk up the hill to the pharmacy where most of the patients take their prescriptions. Whether Adrian, a patient I treated several years later in the medium secure unit at St Jude's, had consciously noticed the post office next door to the pharmacy, I cannot say. Whether he thought to himself as he walked past it to get his methadone, 'One day, I will rob that post office,' in the same way I wondered if I'd ever work at St Jude's, I do not know, but what is incontrovertible is that he did rob the post office next door to the pharmacy. That fact alone would not normally trouble me. Drug users rob and steal all the time and robbing a post office is hardly national news. What troubled me was that he was under my care, and I had just given him leave, as it turns out, so he could go and rob the post office.

Psychiatrist helps robbery.

When a patient is detained in hospital, they don't spend all their time on the ward. Section 17 of the Mental Health Act allows me to give patients leave from hospital. It can be for a couple of hours to go to the barber, or for a full day to attend college. As discharge approaches, patients are often given a series of overnight leaves to their new accommodation. It's a way of testing things out, to make sure that the patient is ready for discharge and that the community services are ready to swing into action.

By the time Adrian robbed the post office, he had been in hospital for close to four years. He had become paranoid in his twenties and his compliance with medication was poor.

'I don't have schizophrenia,' he would protest at his tribunals. 'They're holding me here because of my drug use.'

The truth was that he had schizophrenia and he also had opiate dependence. That should mean you get more treatment, but sadly the opposite is sometimes true. The drug services don't feel able to treat you because of the schizophrenia and the community teams don't know how to treat the dependence, so you end up with no treatment at all.

Adrian started off using cannabis in his teens and quite quickly graduated to amphetamines and one day he tried some heroin. He smoked it initially. I remember his look as he described his first experience. 'It was just the best thing. I've never been more at peace.'

He started to inject about three months later and was soon spending close to £100 a day on drugs. There aren't many jobs that give you that sort of disposable income, so he did what everyone does – he turned to crime.

'I'd stop people on the street and pretend I had a gun. Then I'd take their wallet and their phone. I tried shoplifting but this was quicker. Mostly I did kids from the posh schools. Sometimes I did old people. I didn't want any trouble.'

But he was caught by the police as he was trying to rob a fourteen-year-old girl just outside her school and then he was taken to Campsmoor.

'I've been hearing voices for about two years now,' he told the nurse in reception. 'I went to the doctors, but they just said that I needed to go to the drug services. I tried but they said I had schizophrenia. I get paranoid about everything.'

After a month he wouldn't come out of his cell. He had stopped eating because he thought his food was poisoned and he thought that one of the prison officers was making him pull his hair out. When I first met him, he had large patches of alopecia. 'He makes me do it,' he said, before turning to the nurse working with me. 'Why are you looking at me like that?' Then he tried to turn the table over and then he spat at us.

We transferred him out to hospital at that point and after he was convicted, he stayed with me at St Jude's. So when the tribunal turned to me to find out why he was still being detained under the Mental Health Act, I said, 'It's quite clear that he has a relapsing and remitting illness characterised by hallucinations, passivity and paranoid delusions. He has schizophrenia complicated by drug use, not drug-induced psychosis. We're treating his mental illness, not just his dependency.'

Eventually, and it took close to four years, Adrian was ready to leave hospital. He was a little paranoid from time to time, but nothing that meant he needed inpatient care. He would need close follow-up by the community teams and even closer monitoring of his depot medication. The social worker had found him a specialist aftercare forensic hostel. It was a really good facility and far nicer than anything I had lived in whilst I was a medical student. If anything can be said to be routine in forensic psychiatry, it was Adrian's planned discharge.

Unfortunately, the only thing standing between Adrian and his hostel was Adrian himself. He seemed intent on messing it all up. Some patients are like that. I would give him leave under section 17 and he would come back late – just a few minutes to begin with.

'The bus was late,' he said.

Then it got progressively longer. 'He went to see his family,' Elaine would tell me, 'but he didn't come back. We've circulated him to the police when he was an hour late . . . yes, his mental state's fine.'

Sometimes the police brought him back – I think he was using them as a taxi service – and sometimes he'd come back by himself. This went on for a few months and each time he was back late, I stopped his leave for a while, all of which was delaying his eventual discharge.

Then he got on to a college course which the OT, the occupational therapist, had set up for him. It was about sound recording and it was something that he actually wanted to do. We gave him section 17 leave, we had confirmation that he had arrived there safely, but the college called us at 3 p.m. to say he had not attended his afternoon tutorials.

It got to 6 p.m. and there was no sign of him. The police were informed that he was AWOL and took a description of him and what he'd been wearing. I got home and spent an uneasy evening wondering what he was up to and waiting for my phone to ring. I went in the next day and found him in the entrance foyer waiting for a nurse from the ward to collect him.

'I'll take him back,' I told the receptionist and turned to Adrian. 'So, what happened?'

He shrugged. 'Just lost track of time, I suppose.'

I wasn't impressed and was quite curt with him when we reached the ward. 'You've lost your leave. We'll talk next week. You need to give the staff a witnessed urine sample.'

I was called later to be given the results. It was positive for opiates and cannabis.

I saw him as planned at the next ward round.

'It's not right, I didn't take anything,' he complained. 'I just went to see some friends, and they were smoking all sorts of stuff, so it was probably that.'

I tried to keep my voice level and not betray my irritation. 'Adrian, I can't give you any more leave. Not until you are able to use it without using drugs.'

It was several months later that we ventured down the same path. He had been to all the substance use groups. He had seen the psychologist for one-to-one sessions. His mental state was stable and his risk assessment was updated.

Then I was given a section 17 form to sign.

'You're not going to abscond, are you?' I asked.

'No, Doc, definitely not,' he said.

I silently went through the arguments as I reached for my pen. His schizophrenia was well treated. He was antisocial but he wasn't psychopathic. We knew he hadn't used drugs for months. He had done all the groups. If he did take something, it was his choice – he wasn't self-medicating his paranoia and it wasn't because he was withdrawing – and there was only so long that I could justify his ongoing detention when it was increasingly clear that we were only actively treating his dependency. Even the tribunal had told me they wanted him to have more leave so he could 'prove himself'. All in all, I thought his risk of serious offending was quite low, at least in the short term.

I signed my name and then turned to a pile of other forms: consent forms, leave forms, tribunal reports, court reports, discharge summaries, police reports. Sometimes it felt like I was being paid for my signature – someone to blame when it all went wrong.

And it was about to go wrong.

The day for his leave was set. He was to go to the hostel, meet his care worker, go to college, re-enrol, see his mother and then come back to the unit.

In fact, my phone went off at 10 a.m. whilst I was on the ward. 'He hasn't arrived at the hostel,' I repeated for Elaine, sitting next to me.

'He left two hours ago,' she said, taking out her mobile and calling the college and then his mother. 'He's not there either.'

We phoned the police and reported him missing.

'Him again,' said the person on the other end of the phone. 'Why do you keep letting him out?'

Because that's what we do in a free and fair society. We try to rehabilitate people. We respect their freedoms and their rights even when it's not convenient, even when there are risks and I am fed up with implied criticism from people – especially journalists – who are wise after the event and think that everyone should be locked up for ever . . .

'It was the doctor's idea,' I said, solemnly, winking at Elaine.

There was nothing else we could do, so I filed the problem away and got on with the ward round.

I got the next phone call three days later.

'Is that the forensic psychiatry consultant?'

'Yes,' I looked at the screen on my phone. 'Who is this?'

'I'm one of the A & E doctors. We've got your missing patient down here. He's broken his leg.'

'I'll ask our nurses to come down,' I said. 'Can you call the police to let them know he's with you.'

'Don't need to – they're with him now. About ten of them. He robbed the post office.'

Fuck. 'I'll be down in ten minutes.'

I got there in five and followed the nurse's directions to the side room. Adrian was lying centre stage, his left arm stretched out to an IV drip and his right, handcuffed to the bed frame. Given that his left leg was encased in a large plaster cast and he was surrounded by five police officers, the oldest of whom looked like an excited sixteen-year-old who had made their first arrest, it was clear he wasn't going anywhere.

'Hi, I'm the consultant,' said the voice behind me. 'My name's Nish.' I turned and there was the faintest hint of recognition.

'Have we worked together?' I asked.

He shook his head. 'Don't think so. We've plastered him up. He's had quite a lot of opiates for the pain. His mental state seems OK. You can have him whenever the police have finished with him.'

'So, after you left the post office, what happened next?' asked the officer closest to him.

'I heard the alarm go off and I jumped over the wall and missed my footing. I tried to get up, but I couldn't move so I threw the bag with the money in it as far as I could. Someone was just coming out of the chemists and he took it . . .'

The police officers were scribbling furiously. I'd never seen Adrian so forthcoming – the drugs he'd been given were clearly having an effect. No doubt he had lost his tolerance to opiates. He didn't seem bothered he had been caught. He didn't seem troubled he was surrounded by last year's new recruits and he was curiously indifferent to the absence of a solicitor.

That was it really. Adrian had been caught. He took it in his stride and whilst he was using opiates for his broken leg, he seemed happy enough. The police seemed happy and the next day I saw a picture of the post office manager who had been robbed and even he seemed quite happy. 'I raised the alarm, followed him out and wrestled him to the ground,' he was quoted, under a picture of him standing, arms crossed, outside his shop.

It took me a week or so to get to the bottom of things. Even after the years in hospital, Adrian was still indebted to his dealer. Debt is never a good thing, especially when you owe money to people who are quite happy to hurt you rather than send the bailiffs round.

After absconding he knocked around for a few days with some of his friends, smoked some cannabis and compounded his debt by using heroin. At this point, the dealers told him that it was time to settle his account with them, so he decided to rob the post office.

This part of his plan, he told me, went quite well. Admittedly, he seemed somewhat indifferent to the effect his crime had on the soon-to-be-traumatised postmaster, but consideration for the feelings of others was not one of his top ten character traits.

It's not a big character trait in many of the people I treat.

Adrian was leaving the post office with his 'ill-gotten gains', probably just an hour before I was called by Dr Nish. He heard the alarm go off and hastened his stride. The post office, being on a slight hill, has a low wall coming out from it which levels the forecourts. As he jumped over the two-foot wall, he failed to anticipate there was a four-foot drop on the other side.

It's not just consideration for others he lacked. It would be unfair to characterise all patients in medium secure units in the same way – some are very bright indeed – but some find opening a tin of beans quite challenging. The sad reality is that most have had very restricted schooling and even basic literacy can be a problem. They are impulsive by nature, and mostly, there is little forward planning in their crimes. Come to that, there is little forward planning to their lives in general. I have never been convinced that longer sentences would deter them.

Whatever the reason for Adrian's clumsiness, and the cannabis he used that morning and the opiate withdrawal can't have helped, he misjudged his footing, landed awkwardly, and broke his leg.

From a psychological perspective, he had so far demonstrated a propensity to mix with the wrong crowd, an inability to manage his finances, a pro-criminal attitude, impulsivity in his offence, and rapid reinstatement of drug use.

Next came his lack of adaptability. Not having a 'plan B', he told me, he just sat there with his 'bag of loot' and wondered what to do with it. Then he decided to 'throw it away' so he could deny having committed the robbery. I rather suspect he saw a friend leave the pharmacy and decided to be generous with his booty.

His arrest came pretty quickly. The police may not come to your home after a burglary, but they do come very quickly indeed to a post office with the alarm going, especially when the culprit is sitting ten yards from the front door with a broken leg, waiting to be arrested. Once the police came, the postmaster came out and 'wrestled him to the ground', presumably when no one was looking. Then he was taken to the local A & E, and you know the rest.

But, despite the happiness all round, there was a new decision to be made. Adrian had committed a new offence, and whilst the previous offence had resulted in a hospital order, there was no reason that this one needed to. I brought him back to Lakeview House in the short term, but I questioned the purpose of him staying there.

The next step was him going to magistrates' court, but because it was a serious offence, he was committed to Crown court. He pleaded guilty and then I had to do a report to discuss the sentencing options. I told the court that whilst he had schizophrenia, it wasn't sufficiently severe to need hospital treatment, and I didn't recommend another hospital disposal.

Then the court did what they do with people who rob post offices. They sent him to prison.

By this point, any happiness had entirely evaporated. Adrian was upset about going to prison. 'I'll stop taking the fucking medication.'

His lawyers seemed to imply that anyone with half a brain would not have given him leave as it was quite obvious that he was going to reoffend. Well, one of them said I was 'at best incautious and at worst foolhardy . . .' but they would say that wouldn't they.

What stung was my managers asking me to review all the section 17 leave decisions on my ward.

Who knows who he's letting out.

Even the postmaster was starting to get PTSD. 'I've just diagnosed him,' said Anthony at my office door. 'His solicitors asked me to do a report to examine the mental consequences of his ordeal.' He smiled. 'I think that it must have been the way that he held on to him until the police arrived. He's quite a hero you know.'

'Maybe I should have seen it coming.'

'Ben,' he responded. 'You know there is a way to stop all absconding and all reoffending.'

'Enlighten me, Anthony.'

'Don't ever give anyone leave, and never discharge anyone.' He winked at me. Sometimes he liked to pretend to be a columnist for the *Mail*, but it was a cover for his liberal values.

Adrian went to prison. About a month later he was as good as his word and he refused his depot. The Mental Health Act doesn't apply in prisons, just in hospitals, so he was quite within his rights to stop taking his medication, if he so wished.

Two weeks later he accused the prison officers of trying to poison his food, so he refused to eat. One of them sat down with him to find out what was going on and Adrian hit him over the head. He was taken to segregation and had pulled out most of his own hair by the time that I got to see him.

'He needs to be in hospital,' I told the prison doctor.

'If you want,' he replied, as if this thought had never occurred to him. So we did the paperwork to transfer him, but by this point we didn't have any beds available at St Jude's, so we sent him to a private service 140 miles away in the Midlands. They sell their beds to the NHS.

I called the week after he was admitted there. Adrian had managed to assault three members of staff. He'd been seen by the police and they didn't seem too interested in referring the case to the CPS. 'They won't do anything with it.'

'I like it here,' Adrian told me, his head bandaged to try to stop him pulling out his hair. 'I don't know anyone.'

What he meant was he didn't know any of the dealers and people didn't approach him all the time to either buy or sell drugs. I gave some advice about his treatment and then drove back to London.

I spoke to our management teams and then wrote to the local trust in the West Midlands. 'If we can get Adrian discharged into your area,' I suggested, 'he's more likely to be able to stay clear of drugs in the future.' I wondered if there were any chicken farms he could work on, and just for a moment wondered if he had mugged Mr Bainbridge all those years ago. 'Anyway, there must be someone in the West Midlands who wants to move to South London. We can do a swap.'

Actually, it's not as silly as it sounds. When someone like Adrian leaves prison or hospital, they may be a reformed character, but nobody else knows that. Their friends and associates are often linked into drug use or criminal enterprise, and I can see how difficult it must be to stay away. It's good that we are trying to treat people closer to home, but sometimes, just sometimes, the opposite is what we need to do.

Sadly, either there were no drug-using mentally ill criminals in the West Midlands, or if there were, they didn't want to come down to South London.

Not surprising really; the price of drugs in London is a scandal.

So, I went back to the unit in the West Midlands where Adrian was being treated, partly to plan for his return to Lakeview House, and partly to prepare a report trying to encourage the CPS to press charges on the, by now, five assaults against staff.

All in all, I went up to the West Midlands four times over six months. Eventually we got him back to Lakeview. It was clear that he was never going to get aftercare in the Midlands.

He never got charged for the further assaults. For some reason, it wasn't in the public interest. He came back, we stabilised his psychosis and then I sent him back to prison to complete his sentence.

Guess what? He stopped taking his medication six weeks later. 'I don't need it. I've got drug-induced psychosis, not schizophrenia,' he told the prison doctor.

There has got to be a better way of ensuring that prisoners with severe mental illness continue to get their medication, rather than watching them relapse after they decide not to comply with their treatment.

Adrian bounced between hospital and prison for the duration of his sentence and then he was released. He ended up on depot medication, a community treatment order and methadone. He still uses heroin occasionally, but he has not reoffended seriously since he has been taking the methadone. I wonder how many more people like Adrian could be kept away from a life of daily offending, thuggish dealers and dirty needles if we gave them the opiates that they crave.

Why not give them heroin?

The war on drugs can be fought on two fronts. Stopping the importation is important, but it's the end user who keeps the business model going. The sooner we give heroin to people who need to use it, the better. I'm not talking about 'drugs for all', but a targeted use of heroin for people with an established dependency.

I expected Mrs Bainbridge to die the night I 'upped' her opiates. I was treating her illness and I knew that the treatment might shorten her life.

Dependency is an illness and some people given heroin because of their illness will die. But most won't. They'll be fine. And the drug will be pure, and the needle will be clean. So they won't get HIV or hepatitis or abscesses and there won't be a debt to pay to a violent dealer, and Adrian won't need to rob a post office, and the post office manager won't get PTSD six months later, and the taxpayer won't have to spend money putting Adrian in hospital or prison or both.

And maybe, just maybe, Mrs Bainbridge could have gone on her round-the-world cruise with her husband.

Skiing with SpongeBob:
Roid rage

I love skiing. As a youngster, my brother bought me some plastic planks that screwed on to some old boots from the army surplus shop, and we learnt to ski on a hillside in Derbyshire. A local farmer had rigged his tractor to put a rope on to a loop system that we could use as a makeshift drag lift. You had to grab the rope and try not to dislocate your shoulders as it dragged you over stones, cowpats and occasionally, bits of snow.

We ended the days with sore arms, blistered hands, caked in frozen mud, and as happy as could be.

You can imagine my excitement years later, going up a glacier in the French Alps in a small bubble lift, just big enough for two average-sized people. There was no mud, my hands were blister-free, and a pair of very expensive Rossignol skis glinted in the sun, joggling reassuringly in their holder, as we trundled slowly, ever so slowly, up the mountain.

At this altitude, difficult patients, people shouting at you and violence in general, all seem a very long way away, which is one of the reasons why I love it. The man in the bubble with me, Evan, was staying in the same chalet hotel. I'd only met him the night before over dinner. The holiday was a bit like the *Big Brother* format where strangers are thrown together. The only difference is that no one got evicted – unfortunately.

I have mentioned already that I am quite tall. If I have 'altitude', then Evan was something of a wide plateau, a bit like SpongeBob SquarePants in human form, his thick arms poking out horizontally from somewhere I imagined his neck met his body.

We got talking – it's difficult to avoid talking to someone in a bubble lift when your legs are wrapped around each other, your body is hunched forwards and you are trying to coordinate your breathing so that you don't breathe in, as they breathe out. I think he'd overdone the Reblochon a bit.

'What do you do?' asked Evan.

I waited for the cheesy-alcohol fumes to dissipate and planned my answer. It is sometimes a dilemma what you say to such a question. 'Doctor,' works well, but it is invariably followed up by, 'What sort of doctor?', or if you are very unlucky, 'I have these boils in my groin. What do you think they are? Here, I can show you.'

I thought briefly about pretending I was a climatologist, or a used car salesman, but given that I had some patchy memory loss of the night before, I decided that honesty was the best policy, and I hoped that he wouldn't ask me if I was analysing him.

'I'm a psychiatrist,' I said, promising myself I wouldn't eat any more Camembert or drink red wine ever again.

Evan didn't say anything, which was a pleasant surprise, but he did look a bit shifty. It then occurred to me that it would be polite if I asked him what he did, besides pressing large amounts of weights up and down in the gym. Nobody gets to look like Evan without pushing a lot of weights up and down.

'I work in a gym,' he said.

'That explains your physique,' I said.

'Physique?' he replied, not so gently.

He later confided that he wondered if the word 'physique' had something to do with homosexuality. Not yet aware of

his very clear and not entirely positive views about homosexuality, I realise I went on to compound the problem.

'You've got really big muscles,' I explained.

He didn't answer, but his look was telling. I later learnt that
this particular facial expression, which Evan now displayed,
is often associated with imminent violence. Fortunately,
Evan was not a patient, not yet anyway, but he was the first
person to introduce me to the world of anabolic steroids.
Let me reassure you from the outset, the steroids you are
taking for your asthma are not the anabolic steroids beloved
of some bodybuilders.

Carry on with your inhalers.

I now smiled at him and tried to pull my glove off so I
could see how much of the seventeen minutes to the top
of the glacier were still remaining.

'What are you doing?' asked Evan suspiciously, evidently
unable to peer over his pectoral muscles.

'Ten minutes left,' I said, more to myself than to him,
and trying the complicated manoeuvre of putting my glove
back on. 'What do you do in the gym?' I asked, peering
out of the window at the yawning chasm beneath me.

'I coach people how to lift weights.'

I know I do all gym instructors a great disservice, but I
wondered how long it took to say, 'Push it up, lower it
gently and don't overdo it.' Maybe I was missing something and, as it turns out, I was. For the next five minutes,
Evan relaxed and didn't shut up. He gave me an in-depth
analysis of weight training, aerobic and anaerobic strategies,
physiology, nutritional supplements and then described his
own dietary requirements which seemed to involve a lot of
protein and not much else. He'd obviously forgotten about
last night's cheese and wine blowout.

I was really impressed with his knowledge, which was
the equal of any physiologist, and then he told me that he
had just started to 'stack the pyramid'.

'Stack the pyramid?' I ventured, cautiously, looking down again at the rocks beneath us.

'Stacking' referred to his use of anabolic steroids, more specifically the use of first one steroid preparation, then two, then three, over a period of four or five weeks. So, at the top of the pyramid, you are taking massive doses of several anabolic steroids to bulk you up, and then you reduce or taper them over the next four or five weeks, giving the body a chance to recover from the onslaught.

I had read some of the American literature describing what they term 'reverse anorexia' in bodybuilders. It's a type of dysmorphophobia where the individual feels they are scrawny and weak, and they often avoid social contact.

Unfortunately, steroids don't just cause muscles to grow, they rot your liver, shrink your testicles and, if you're a woman, cause a deepening voice, facial hair, male pattern baldness and clitoromegaly. I'll let you look that one up yourself, but if you don't want to mess up your browsing history, anything ending with '-megaly' is big.

That's just the physical stuff. Mentally, people get angry and hostile, even psychotic. The term for this is 'roid rage'.

'I get very twitchy when I'm on steroids,' said Evan.

I looked out of the window again, figured the slope was 30 metres beneath me and idly calculated it would take me just under two and a half seconds to reach it, by which point I would be going a shade over 50mph. It's always good to know your options and I found the risk assessment a welcome distraction.

'Like, when I get really paranoid,' he went on, 'that thing you were doing with your hand, that would mean you think I'm queer . . .'

Come to think of it, 50mph is not so fast, and if there's a snowdrift . . .

'. . . and I wouldn't like it if you said I was queer,' he added, just to complete the picture. 'I wouldn't like that, at all.'

At this point I stopped my mental calculations, and though work colleagues might dispute that I have ever analysed anyone, I confess that I came close to analysing Evan and his aversion to homosexuality.

I once looked after a 'straight man' convicted of murder. I know that he was straight because he told me repeatedly how straight he was. Thirty years earlier, he told me, he had been on a camping holiday with another man to whom he was definitely not attracted. They decided to look at some gay magazines together and then the other man had inexplicably made a sexual pass at him. My patient naturally took exception to this, because he was straight you understand, and then he killed the other man.

'Well, I'm straight,' he explained, just in case I had missed something. 'What else could I do?' as if murder was a perfectly reasonable response.

I looked over at Evan. Are you over-compensating your masculinity because of repressed homosexual urges?

Thankfully, I only thought this. I kept my mouth shut and probably because of my peerless skill in this regard, we both arrived at the top of the glacier safely. We untangled our limbs from each other, extricated ourselves from the bubble, and I pressed my expensive boots into my equally expensive Rossignols and skied off.

It was, by chance, a run that I had previously skied with Mike. You've met him before when our biology teacher told us we might need to reconsider our career options. He's now a GP and a frustrated ski champion, who also came to Derbyshire with me and destroyed more than one pair of gloves on the farmer's rope.

My skiing at the time wasn't great and I asked Mike for some advice.

He looked at me and then said, cautiously, 'It's a bit Zen.' Mike knows I don't 'do' Zen. Despite his initial caution, he then gave me some of the most important advice that I have ever received. 'Just pretend you're a good skier,' he said.

I tried to let it sink in but probably looked a bit vague.

'You know, bend your knees more, exaggerate your movement, make yourself look like Franz Klammer.'

I now glanced over my shoulder at Evan and saw him struggling. He could probably tear me apart, but his physiology was geared to moving heavy weights short distances, and his aerobic capacity was shot to pieces by his training regime.

I exaggerated my knee bend and relaxed my body forwards, channelling Franz's spirit through my hips and making the best turns of my life.

Mike was right. I could ski.

'Ben,' said Anthony, immediately making me think he wanted something. 'Can I have a word?' He came into my office and stood next to me, rather awkwardly. 'I've got this patient I'm worried about.' He sounded tentative, which wasn't like him at all. 'Well, he's made some threats to me, really quite specific threats, and I wonder if you could take over his care.'

Anthony was not one to shy away from a challenge. He was known for his no-nonsense approach and in the ten years we had been consultant colleagues, he'd never made a request like this.

'Sure,' I said, mentally checking if my home alarm had been serviced recently. 'Tell me about him.'

We discussed the case over the next week and I read up his notes. Simon, the patient, was thirty-five and worked as a doorman. He had tried to kill his wife, and after twenty stab wounds to her forearms, chest and her abdomen, she was lucky to be alive. He was in the secure unit at St Jude's to be assessed prior to sentencing.

I discussed his case with Elaine, got her agreement and then we moved him to our ward. I planned to meet him in the ward round.

Instead of going to the end of the patients' beds, psychiatrists get to sit down, and the patients come to us. At
Lakeview, we use a room just off the main ward corridor,
so you can see the ward and the patients can see you. It's
modern, functional and big enough for about fourteen people
to sit round a large table in the middle. It's soundproofed
with two thick layers of glass and a venetian blind for privacy.
About twice a year, someone reminds us how strong the glass
is. Sometimes they punch it. Last week it was a cup of tea.

I found myself distracted during the first part of the ward
round, peering out from my fishbowl, looking at Simon. I
was looking at how he was moving, his activity levels, the
way he carried himself and how he was interacting with
staff and the other patients.

Then Elaine went to get him. First, he turned to the
window behind him as if to check his hair and then he
reached down into his trousers and spent rather longer rear-
ranging himself than seemed entirely necessary.

I didn't shake his hand when he came in.

'Finally, I have someone I can trust. I don't think Dr
Franklin really understood me.'

Image and charm. Flattery and splitting.

He went on and told me that he didn't want to talk about
the alleged offence. 'It's difficult. I don't want to go over
all that again. It's very difficult for me.'

Victimhood and deflection. Control.

'Tell me about Dr Franklin,' I asked. 'Why did you get
so angry at him?'

'I wasn't angry, he was just asking stupid questions.'

Minimisation, external blame attribution.

'You jumped over the desk in the ward round and had
to be restrained by three nurses. One of them broke her
arm in the restraint.'

He shrugged. 'I didn't break it. It was her being clumsy.'

Bastard.

'It sounds like the questions got to you in some way.'

Simon bared his teeth and sucked in a lungful of air and then breathed out slowly. He was making us wait for his next pronouncement. He scratched his chin and looked out of the window. I thought that he was probably psychopathic. Everything seemed to be about control.

'I don't want him in the room,' said Simon, pointing at the nurse next to me.

'Why?' I asked.

'Ask him. He's just like Dr Franklin.' Simon got up, pushed his chair back under the table and left.

I turned to the nurse next to me, who seemed surprised at this turn of events.

'I was with Dr Franklin when Simon jumped over the table, but he's never had a problem with me.'

'What were you talking about when he got angry?'

'Dr Franklin was asking him about his sex life. It's weird. He always seems to be checking himself, you know like he did before he came in here.' He pointed to his flies. 'Sometimes, at night, we can hear him through the door. He's shouting for us to *shut up*, but the ward's really quiet. Listen, Doc, we're doing a collection for Grace – there's a card to sign in the nursing office.'

I went and put some money in the collection pot. Her colleagues didn't know it yet, but Grace, the nurse who had 'clumsily' broken her arm, had decided to resign. 'I'm going back to secretarial work,' she had told me just the day before. 'I'll get almost the same, and it's the second time I've been injured . . . I've never seen anyone look so angry.'

My next meeting with Simon was three days later. I'd compiled a summary by then. There were a few antisocial markers in the past, but nothing serious. He had anger management problems in his teens, but that hardly explained his offence or his recent behaviour on the ward. He came into the ward round and sat down opposite me. He was angry from the outset.

'So, you been speaking to him, then?'

'What do you mean?'

'You know what I mean; you've been speaking to him, that Dr Anthony Franklin.'

'I spoke to him a week ago,' I answered, truthfully.

'Don't give me that, I heard what you were saying.'

'What was I saying?'

'Same as my wife said, same as Dr Franklin said.'

For a moment, he looked like Evan in the bubble lift, and I started to do my risk calculations.

Simon was a doorman, which is a euphemism for a bouncer. He had tried to kill his wife. He had made threats and had tried to assault a colleague; a nurse had broken her arm in the ensuing melee and had resigned from her profession. There were some psychological traits suggestive of an antisocial personality and it seemed quite possible from the nurse's account that he was hallucinating.

And why was he 'checking himself' all the time, whatever that meant?

I ended the meeting as quickly as I could and made sure that the C & R team were on standby for my next meeting with him. We decided to take the precaution of using a different room for the interview, a room with furniture so heavy it couldn't be thrown at you.

The meeting didn't start well. He sat there and put his hand down his trousers and glowered at me.

'Stop changing me. I'll fucking sue you all. Why are you all doing this to me? Dr Cave, make no mistake, I will get out of here and I will find you. I will kill you and your family.'

Just pretend you're a good psychiatrist, I thought to myself. *Don't respond to the threat. Channel it away.*

Simon got up and went to pick up the chair next to him. I think I knew what was going to happen and, possibly due to my obsessional nature, I mentally went through all the items that have been thrown at me over the years: a Dictaphone, one pen, a few sets of medical records, two jugs of hot water, part of a door, a snooker cue and two balls (a red one and a blue one), a pot plant . . .

It was like the end of *The Generation Game* with things you've never wanted going past you on the conveyor belt.

'Do you think I can't find out where you live?' Simon was now balancing the chair, the chair that was designed to be unthrowable, on his overinflated chest.

And now for your Brucie bonus.

Simon threw the unthrowable chair at me like a shot-putter putting their shot.

I thought back to when the hospital director had come into my office to ask my artistic advice about which upholstery pattern we should order. 'Tartan check or purple white chevrons?' she said, holding up the swatches.

'The chevrons look like my migraine,' I concluded. 'Anyway, I'm colour-blind, and I've got no taste.'

We got the tartan check, that according to the sales blurb was meant to 'meet all the needs of your secure environment'. It was supposed to be rip-proof, stain-proof and throw-proof.

Unfortunately, Simon was clearly much stronger than the designer of this particular throw-proof chair had anticipated when he sketched it out in his Hoxton studio over a small quiche and a glass of Sauvignon.

The tartan check pattern now spread alarmingly as it took over most of my visual field. My retina duly reported the incursion to my occipital lobe which fired off some warning messages and my temporal lobe threw in some uncomfortable associations with a severed tongue which was entirely unhelpful, and really just confused matters. Fortunately, my motor cortex was quick off the mark and sent a *'tartan threat'* warning notice to pretty much every muscle in my body which made me first crouch like Franz Klammer on the Zielschuss compression and then jump . . .

There was a disappointingly anticlimactic thud as the 75kg tartan chair landed where I had been standing just a moment before, followed closely by another thud and a grunt as I landed on the other side of the room.

Didn't he do well.

The C & R team sprang into life and Simon found himself on the floor with nurses holding on to his limbs, one looking after his breathing and airway and a hypodermic going into the upper outer quadrant of his buttock.

His cries of 'I'll fucking kill you all' gradually abated as the combination of sedating and antipsychotic medication had their desired effect. It was the first time he'd been treated. I wrote him up for regular antipsychotic drugs after that. I checked on one of the nurses who had been injured in the restraint. 'I don't think you've broken anything,' I reassured her, 'but best to go to A & E. You're going to have one hell of a shiner.'

The next interview with Simon took place the following day. He was lying flat on the bed, still in seclusion.

'Please don't do it; please don't do it to me.'

'Do what, Simon?'

It might sound odd, but probably two or three times a year, you get a moment like this that makes everything explicable. The moment that everything falls into place. I was about to have another Columbo moment. I do love Columbo moments.

'You're working with her,' he said.

'What do you mean?' I asked.

'You're turning me into a woman,' he said.

I looked at the four staff in the room and saw another four outside. I went down on my haunches so that my eyes were on his level.

'Tell me about it,' I instructed, and he did.

It had started about six months earlier when he had first used anabolic steroids. He had come off second best in a brawl outside a nightclub and decided that he needed to bulk up. He changed his diet, put himself on a strict training regime and bought a variety of oral and IM steroids. The results were impressive, and he put on large amounts of muscle bulk.

'I've never pressed so much,' he told me. 'I loved it. I kind of fell in love with myself.'

But, as he came off the first cycle of steroids, he got depressed and felt out of sorts. 'I couldn't perform properly,' he confided.

He got angry about it, and by the third cycle of stacking the pyramid he was effectively impotent. 'My balls started to get smaller,' he said. 'She was taking my manhood.'

He started to question his wife about what she was doing to him and then heard her discussing his impotence with one of her friends.

'I couldn't stand that,' he said, sitting up on his bed. He told me that one of his mates down the gym suggested he try some cocaine. 'It'll help you keep your pecker up.'

By his fourth pyramid he'd put on about 15kg and started to develop testicular atrophy. He had rendered himself impotent and was self-medicating with cocaine.

The voices started as he began to taper the dose of steroids. The hallucinations told him that he was changing sex; his reducing chest size and his shrinking testicles simply confirmed what the voices said.

He felt more and more depressed, so he used ever higher doses of cocaine.

We got Simon out of seclusion after forty-eight hours. He started to accept antipsychotic medication and he made good progress. Once he was sufficiently stable, he started talking to the psychologist. It was almost predictable. He was unsure about his sexuality and admitted to bisexual feelings.

By the time he went back to court, he'd been on medication for three months and was doing well. There was a court report to write. I spent ages on it. I argued that he had a drug-induced psychosis. Whilst he was clearly psychotic when he tried to kill his wife, he wasn't legally insane. He knew what he was doing and he knew it was wrong.

The court heard all the evidence and gave him a sentence that reflected the severity of the crime – it was attempted murder after all. He went to prison, but my report probably meant that his sentence was less severe than it would have been – several years less, if I were to guess.

Once he was off the drugs, and once his psychosis was under control, he was a fairly decent bloke. 'Doc, that stuff I said about wanting to kill you. I'm sorry, I didn't mean it you know.'

'I know,' I said. 'You were ill.'

I can ski quite well now – and just for a fraction of a second as the chair was coming towards me, I had imagined how Franz Klammer might feel soaring his way to victory. Just for a fleeting moment I jumped high enough to see what genius looked like – I was Klammer winning the Hahnenkamm. Then, it was back to earth with a thud and now it feels like I'm pretending again. We all pretend things to ourselves, but I wonder if Evan sometimes feels that he is pretending more than most.

Evan, if you are reading this, perhaps it's time to accept the person you are.

And go easy on the steroids.

Two Jesuses and Mohammed

When I was working in the drug dependency service, just down the hill from the post office, I had two clients, partners, both of whom were using heroin. It was an NHS facility providing outpatient treatment for people with drug or alcohol problems. This particular couple were always well turned out – that was part of their business model. I use the term 'business model' loosely. They would go into high-end stores and walk out with fur coats, sunglasses, fine wines – in short, any designer goods that have a high resale value in the market.

'What's the biggest thing you've ever stolen?' I asked.

'Ah,' said the man, fondly, as if talking about the day he became a partner in his law firm. 'That was the day I walked out of Harrods with a whole rack of Versace.' He paused to reminisce. 'One of the shop attendants held the door open for me – I told them it had been recalled because of a manufacturing problem.'

Then, after a moment's reflection, he told me that he had 'gone straight'. I must have smiled or something, because he told me quite insistently that he really had gone straight.

'We've been going to church. I'd like to be baptised. You know, repent all my sins.'

His partner took off her 'top of the range' Berghaus ski jacket – the one I wanted but couldn't afford – and reached over to hold his hand. I saw the old scars from where she had injected up her arm.

'Listen,' I said, 'you both need to do witnessed specimens, and then I can issue your scripts. I'm keeping you on daily collection until I'm back from leave.'

'Skiing?' asked the man. It was January.

'Yes,' I replied, already regretting being drawn into conversation and wondering if they might find my address and burgle me whilst I was away.

The man looked at the woman, who nodded back to him. 'Listen, Doctor, would you be interested in one of these jackets?' He picked up his partner's Berghaus. 'Your one . . .' he pointed to the back of the door, '. . . well, it seems a little tired.'

I looked him up and down. His shoes were more expensive than mine, his trousers were made by Armani, his shirt was Boss, and his leather jacket, well it would be several years before I bought one that expensive.

I signed their scripts and, standing to leave, reached out and threw on my old ski jacket – £45 from TK Maxx. It was sort of a drab olive-brown colour like you've just rolled down a muddy bank. You don't see many like it.

'I know what you're thinking,' said the man. I waited and he expanded soon enough. 'If you took the Berghaus, you think we'd hold it over you, you know, blackmail you. We wouldn't do that, not now we've discovered God.'

'Actually, I'm very fond of my . . .' I looked down for the name of the make, but it just had a squiggle, '. . . I'm very fond of my anorak.'

The first gift I ever received from a patient was a bottle of wine. He was a blind man with a deep vein thrombosis. I orientated him to the ward, told him what the view looked like through the window – a busy roundabout unfortunately – and got him to hold the pump dispenser containing his anticoagulants and fiddle with the buttons to learn how to use them.

It was the best bottle of wine I have ever had.

Now, I'm not saying that everyone using heroin has an agenda . . . *actually, that is exactly what I am saying* . . . but I do think that the GMC need a rule that the only gifts doctors should accept come from lovely people who have been treated for DVTs.

In the interest of complete transparency, I need to disclose that I once accepted a bottle of whisky from a drug-using patient whom I treated in the low secure unit at St Jude's. He'd had a terrible time. He had a childhood like most of my patients and then he got into trouble, was sent down for robbery, developed schizophrenia, was sent to hospital and got cancer. He was still only twenty-two.

I referred him to the oncologists after he had a fit on the ward. That was the first time anyone realised there was a problem. He had some treatment, but it was too late to do anything to stop the disease. It had already spread to his brain, and the tumours kept growing.

He had nowhere to go, no family, no loved ones, so we had a meeting with him and he asked to be allowed to die on the ward. We would be his family.

A week before he died, we ran out of one of his medicines. He was on a cocktail of drugs by this point, to reduce his pain and suffering. One of them was ketamine, which was ironic, because it was one of the drugs he used when he was well and robbing people. The first time I heard about the medical uses of ketamine was from a doctor friend who used it in her work with a helicopter rescue service.

'Do you need a flying psychiatrist?' I asked her during the dinner party. It turns out they didn't.

When she landed at the scene of a major car crash or train wreck or underground disaster, her job was to identify whom they could save, stabilise them and work with the fire crews to extricate them from the wreckage. 'That's when we use ketamine,' she told me.

'I thought it was a party drug. A hallucinogen, a psychedelic.'

'It is, but with ketamine inside you, I can do things to get you out of the wreck and you wouldn't mind.' Everyone seemed to be listening to us by this point. 'It's a really good dissociative anaesthetic,' she went on, getting a bit technical for a psychiatrist, 'and it doesn't depress your breathing, which is good when you're hypotensive and I'm amputating your . . .'

Fortunately, the main course arrived at this point. It was leg of lamb. Never have I felt such solidarity with vegetarians.

So, realising the ward was out of ketamine, the nurse in charge called me up and asked me what to do. 'I'll call the pharmacy,' I said.

Just so you are fully in the picture, I was out shopping at the time with Libby, my second wife. We were in Bluewater, a '. . . benchmark for the ultimate shopping and leisure experience' with 'striking architecture . . . the perfect place for the whole family to enjoy'.

Like most men, I have certain characteristics. Besides having hairy ears and not being able to pee straight, I also don't like shopping, which is why my wife was in John Lewis and, in the absence of any readily available dissociative anaesthetic, I was in Caffè Nero, having my second flat white.

'So, I need some ketamine . . .' I said to my very helpful pharmacy supplier on the phone, probably like someone talking too loudly on the train on the morning commute.

'. . . Two weeks' supply I reckon. I'm not sure he'll last more than that . . .'

'. . . Yes, I'm OK for morphine, we've got plenty of that.'

Then Libby came back, dumped her shopping and went to get a mint tea. I watched her go to the counter and then glanced around the shop. Everyone was looking at me.

Most of them were looking quite angry, but the young man in the corner looked like he was about to come over for a chat.

I picked up Libby's shopping and went to the counter. 'Better get a takeaway,' I said. 'I think I've been mistaken for a drug dealer.'

The patient with the brain tumour died a week later. I saw him every day.

'I've never done anything good with my life, Doc. What's the point of it all?'

I was at a loss. I went through his life's story with him and I tried to find something that he had done that was good. When he was seven he had made a birthday card for his mother. 'I decorated it. I was really proud of it.'

He won the 100 metres sprint at a school sports day when he was twelve. When he was seventeen, he had a child. He knew the mother for just a week and he saw his son once a year – literally a handful of times.

'He's great,' he told me, 'he's with his mother. At least I haven't had a chance to fuck him up.'

I nodded. That was it really. A nice card, a short sprint and a quick fuck. There wasn't much else to say. He needed a priest, not a psychiatrist. I suggested it on one occasion, but he didn't want to. 'You know me as well as anyone,' he said, and he wasn't wrong.

The day before he died, he asked to go out. One of the nurses pushed him round the grounds and took him across the road to McDonald's. He came back with a dozen big Macs and gave them to the other patients. He gave me a bottle of Bell's he'd bought from the corner shop.

Then he went into a decline and died early the next morning. The last entry from the nurse sitting with him read, 'patient reassured'.

I took the Bell's to Elaine and she put it in her drawer to be saved for the staff Christmas party. The ashes came back to the ward and the hospital chaplain, himself a Muslim, planned a small memorial service the following week, where patients and staff could say their goodbyes and then scatter his ashes in the grounds. 'Will you say a few words, Ben?' he asked.

A few days later, Mohammed, a patient with a psychosis and a mild learning disability, asked where his friend was.

'Your friend?' I asked. He had just come back to my ward from the PICU, the psychiatric intensive care service.

'He died,' answered the nurse, sitting with me. 'I'm sorry. We told you when you were in seclusion; you probably don't remember. You went to seclusion the day he died.'

Mohammed sat still for a minute trying to take it in. 'He bought me a Big Mac.' The nurse passed him a tissue. 'He was always kind to me.'

And that is what I said at the memorial service. He was a kind man. That was it really. Nothing else seemed to matter that much.

It was a month later that Keith Thomson was admitted to the same ward. He was twenty-seven, worked in the building trade and was a skilled plasterer. He liked to go fishing at the weekend. He had been arrested at a petrol station throwing matches at a driver filling up. He tried to start a fire when the police came.

He had used a variety of street drugs over the years. He'd started with cannabis and then through his teens had tried MDMA and LSD, before settling on amphetamines as his drug of choice. The problem was his drug psychosis hadn't remitted, even after two months, and by that point we were effectively treating him for a schizoaffective disorder. He had hallucinations he ascribed to God and a variety of grandiose religious delusions.

'It was like I was coming home,' he explained to me, 'the first time I took crystal meth – I couldn't believe how great it felt.' Crystal meth is the smokable crystal form of methamphetamine. 'I like it more than crack. It's more predictable and anyway, it lasts longer.'

'So, Keith, I asked him, 'what was going on when you were at the petrol station?'

'Jesus,' he said, but he didn't sound angry or distressed.

'Sorry, Keith, I'm not sure what I said that upset you.'

'I'm not upset,' said Keith. 'My name's Jesus.'

'Jesus?' I said, trying to process things.

'Yes,' he said. 'Jesus.'

'Jesus?' said the scowling nurse next to him, the one wearing a crucifix.

'Yes, Jesus,' affirmed 'Jesus'. 'J-E-S-U-S.'

'Jesus,' confirmed the psychologist. 'You want us to call you Jesus?'

'Yes,' said 'Jesus', nodding beatifically.

We spoke for another ten minutes or so before I called it a day. 'I'm not sure that setting fire to a petrol station forecourt is the same as turning over the tables in the temple,' I concluded, 'but let's plan to talk some more next week.'

'Jesus' nodded serenely as he left the room.

'I'm not calling him Jesus,' said the nurse with the crucifix round his neck. 'It's blasphemous.'

'Well, for now, let's accept his wishes,' I said. 'He's very unwell. Let's get a drug test done. Who's next?'

'We've got to see Alberto,' said the nurse. Alberto was in hospital for dragging his neighbour out of his flat and then stabbing him in the arm. He'd been under my care for a while and had started on medication. He was doing quite well, and his persecutory delusions were starting to recede.

'How are you?' I enquired.

'Tired,' he replied. 'I was up all night with "Jesus" preaching at us. He never stopped.'

Ah, I thought. *It's not just a name – he's acting on his beliefs.*

The nurse read some of the medical records from the night before. 'It says here that you got into a fight with him.' He waited for an answer.

'It's true. I told him that my name was Jesús and he just went for me.'

'Is your name Jesus?' I asked, looking down at his notes.

'Alberto Jesús – I call myself Alberto here. It's easier.'

I nodded in agreement.

What we call ourselves seems to matter. I once treated a person who wanted to be known as 'Warrior Overlord'. The nurses dutifully called him Mr Overlord. We knew he was better when he asked us to call him Stephen again.

You seem a little upset, Mr Overlord. Would you like a night-time sedative?

Some of the nurses in this situation though had a real problem calling Keith anything other than Keith. It offended them.

'It's just his psychosis talking. Why does it matter?' I challenged. But they weren't persuaded, and they carried on calling him Keith, and every time they called him Keith, he got angry at them.

Unfortunately for everyone, Alberto, at this point, decided to display a side of his character that we had not previously recognised. If I was being charitable, I would describe his decision as mischievous, but given he was a serious offender with a mental illness and a high psychopathy score, it was probably a little more psychopathic in reality. When Alberto next came into the ward round, no doubt having seen the nurses' disquiet at being asked to call 'Jesus' (formerly known as Keith) Jesus, he decided that he too wanted to be called Jesús. 'So, I don't want to be called Alberto any more. I want to be called Jesús,' he announced.

I groaned to myself.

'It is my name,' he said breezily.

I looked at the nurses. 'How about Jesus 1 and Jesús 2?' but they just looked stony-faced, especially the one with the crucifix. I'd noticed more staff wearing them recently.

'Well, what about South London Jesus and South American Jesús?' I ventured, but I just got more angry looks.

Jesús (fka Alberto) was insistent, and his request quickly changed into a demand, and then a solicitor's letter turned it into a requirement.

Actually, looking back, the nurses were not too bothered about his request, even though arguably it was made to upset them, even to poke fun at their beliefs and to upset a man with a serious illness. 'It is his name,' they rationalised. 'It's just a cultural difference between us.'

'So why the objection to Keith wanting to be called Jesus?' I asked. 'It's a choice, and a psychotic choice at that. If he wanted to be called Mary, we'd respect it.'

Through it all, no one seemed that bothered about having a patient called Mohammed on the ward, the man who had helped me with the eulogy.

I spoke to the chaplain.

'It's a difficult one,' he acknowledged, but I noticed that he had been calling both of them Jesus, even affecting what might have been a Spanish or Portuguese accent for Jesús fka Alberto. 'Whatever they want, really,' he told me, handing me a cup of coffee. He was a thoughtful man and I respected his counsel. 'I mean, I wouldn't want to use a name that's negative. I heard you say names aren't important – I know you didn't mean it like that, but names are important. We inhabit them and we become what we are called. Jesus, peace be upon him, was a good man. How could I object to people from a Christian background taking his name? Let it bring him joy.'

Eventually I started 'Jesus' fka Keith on clozapine, the other medication just wasn't touching him, and thankfully he got better, and one day he decided his name was Keith again.

Jesús fka Alberto was more stubborn, because whilst his illness was easier to treat with antipsychotic drugs, he was also an antisocial man, and treating his psychosis didn't do much to improve his relations with the nursing staff. He stayed in the system longer than he otherwise might have and was eventually discharged by a tribunal.

Whilst they were together on the ward, 'Jesus' and Jesús had a few fights and I think Jesús was winding up 'Jesus'. We have a duty to protect our patients under the Care Act of 2014, so several reports went off to safeguarding about 'Jesus' on Jesús violence, which led to several questioning phone calls.

I brought 'Jesus' into the ward round to discuss his progress soon after starting him on clozapine. He still had grandiose beliefs and tended to start his preaching when others wanted to go to sleep. I asked him about Jesús fka Alberto. He leaned forward and shook his head. 'That man who thinks he's Jesus, he's completely mad.'

Later, during the same ward round, the chaplain came to see me. 'I'm worried about Mohammed,' he said.

I looked at him and waited for the punchline, but none was forthcoming. 'What's happened?'

'Well, he told me that Jesús was pestering him for money. He can't really look after himself.'

'Just for clarity, you mean Jesús fka Alberto?' I asked.

'The real one,' he replied.

I found myself caught in a *Life of Brian* moment. *Are you laughing, Centurion?*

As I recovered myself, I turned it over in my mind. 'So, the real Jesús is persecuting Mohammed?' I reflected back to him.

'Yes,' he said, with just a flicker of a smile. 'I think it's a safeguarding issue.' And just before he lost it completely, he managed to say, 'Peace be upon them both.'

Capacity and death:

There was a crooked man

The first term you learn in forensic psychiatry is MDO. It stands for Mentally Disordered Offender, and there are a lot of them about. In the interests of fairness, there are a lot more offenders who don't have a mental disorder, and it's my job to tell them apart.

People who are bad are meant to go to prison or be punished in some way. People who are 'mad' need to be treated in hospital. That's the polarised option, but in truth it's mostly shades of grey.

Part III of the Mental Health Act is all about the interface between crime and mental illness and allows us to section people from the magistrates' court, the Crown court and to transfer prisoners to hospital for treatment. But the Mental Health Act only applies to hospitals, so you can't use it to treat someone against their wishes in a prison. Prisoners who retain capacity can't be treated against their wishes.

It's worth pointing out that the Act is mostly silent on matters of capacity – your understanding of your condition doesn't come into it. In some ways, this is just as well. If you have appendicitis, such that you have a pain in your abdomen and feel rubbish, then most people go and see a doctor and have the thing cut out.

But if you are hearing voices telling you that the doctor has put a listening device in your brain and it is controlling your actions, then you are unlikely to want to see a doctor, much less take their advice.

One of my patients at St Jude's, a chef called Adam, used to shout at me during my ward round, complaining about exactly this issue. He believed a listening device was surgically implanted when he was a child. 'They did it whilst I was having my tonsils out.' He didn't wake up from the operation as a little boy believing this; it came to him years later – it was a delusional memory.

The listening device made him hit his mother and then it made him walk down the M1, jumping occasionally into the traffic. Eventually, he threw a paving slab off a motorway bridge and it nearly hit the car beneath. The driver had to swerve on to the hard shoulder. Fortunately, no one was injured but it could have killed someone.

'Does it control what you do?' I asked.

'Are you taking the piss? You know it does, you're a doctor, you're fucking part of it.'

It also caused him to have headaches and unusual sensations in his head. Sometimes he could hear the people who were operating the machine talk about him.

His family reported him being a lovely young man until about six months earlier when he got jealous about his girlfriend and thought that she was trying to kill him in his sleep. He came round to their home one night having had too much to drink and told them he had found an empty syringe his girlfriend was using to inject him.

His parents thought he was drunk, which was uncharacteristic, but then he took a screwdriver from his father's garage and tried to push it into his scalp to remove the listening device.

Adam had all the blood tests and I gave him a brain scan too. There was nothing wrong. He asked to see the scan and I showed him.

'They've made it invisible,' he said, sighing deeply. 'We'll never be able to get it out now.'

He wasn't a drug user and he hadn't been taking medication that can cause psychosis. Unfortunately, in the absence of any other identifiable cause, it was clear that he had schizophrenia, and it was a textbook example of schizophrenia at that.

'Adam,' I said during the ward round, 'I'd like you to have some medication.'

He shook his head. 'I had hoped you weren't part of it. There is no fucking way that I'm having your mind control shit. And if you try to inject me, I'll sue you.'

He said much the same thing the next day, and the next. The nurses had done their best to persuade and cajole him to take his medication – *we'll get a pizza takeaway* – but he was having none of it.

If it wasn't for the Mental Health Act, it is possible, perhaps even likely, that he would lead a life of chronic mental illness and in his case, doing bad things to others. He wasn't a bad man – he was a decent person and there was a clear functional link between his illness and almost killing a driver on the M1. Some of my other patients are the opposite. They don't have much of a start in life and for many of them, their 'bad' behaviour starts well before their illness.

The upshot of Adam's repeated refusal to accept medication was that I had to give it to him forcibly. I asked my nursing team to restrain him, hold him down, and then injected him with antipsychotic drugs.

I am the first to acknowledge that intramuscular (IM) medication without the patient's consent is an unpleasant thing, something that should only be used as a last resort when powers of persuasion have failed. I keep a painting by Henry Cockburn on my study wall. It's entitled *Sedated* and he depicts himself on the floor of a seclusion room being given IM medication. It's a brutal picture and a reminder to me that forced treatment should only be used when all other options have failed. I also know that such medication needs to be undertaken carefully using approved techniques. But I do get troubled when the ill-informed TV presenter views it as inherently wrong.

They held me down and injected me with something. It's not right. It was abuse.

Patients' rights are important, vitally important, but so is their right to be treated. Gentle persuasion and education about the need for medication doesn't always work and that's when an assertive approach is needed.

The hospital said that treatment was carried out in accordance with the Mental Health Act.

It's the Mental Health Act that allows me to treat people regardless of their capacity, and they get better, most of them, anyway.

You will gather by now that psychiatry is quite different from other branches of medicine. If, for instance, you have a heart problem, it's up to you whether you consult a cardiologist, and it is up to you whether you choose to take their advice.

If you understand the issues, are able to remember them long enough to weigh the issues in the balance, and then reach and communicate your decision, then you have capacity.

All you have to say is, 'No, I don't want this treatment,' and the cardiologist will leave you alone. He or she might think you're an idiot, and you may have a heart attack and even die, but they will leave you alone.

I experienced this as a house officer in my first surgical job. I received a letter of complaint from Simon Hughes, then the MP for Bermondsey. I was very excited to get a letter from the House of Commons. One of his constituents had been admitted under my care for a TURP, a transurethral resection of the prostate. It's a procedure where the surgeon cores out the prostate gland through a long tube up the urethra, which runs down the middle of the penis. I had clerked him in, explained the procedure and invited him to sign the consent form.

He looked at me in disbelief. 'You're going to do what?' he exclaimed, listening to how the urologist would remove his prostate. 'I thought I was coming in for my cataracts. Couldn't you do them instead?'

'I am afraid the urologist made a bit of a hash of the last eye surgery he did,' I explained. 'Best leave your eyes to the ophthalmologist.'

It turns out that he had seen a urologist for some problems with his waterworks at about the same time that he saw someone about his cataracts. When he was invited for surgery, he wrongly assumed it was about his eyes – he had decided that his waterworks weren't bad enough for an operation.

Once we worked out the problem, he seemed to see the funny side of it, and I discharged him from the ward and took him off that day's surgical list.

The letter from Simon Hughes said that my 'patient was bitterly disappointed that his 'cataract surgery' was cancelled at the last moment. I felt rather irritated and sent back my best indignant letter explaining the situation. The concept of what constitutes capacity wasn't so well articulated back then, but in essence I covered all of the salient points.

The patient had misunderstood the letter inviting him for a TURP and thought he was coming in for his cataracts. I told him what the surgery was actually for and he seemed to be able to understand – in short, he wasn't demented. And he certainly seemed able to consider or weigh the information and communicate his wishes quite clearly.

'You can stick your TURP up your arsehole,' he told me, once he'd got his dentures in.

I held back from correcting his anatomy and wrote back to the Rt Hon Simon Hughes and got a nice letter back from his office thanking me for the clarification. He got my vote after that.

So the man who turned down the TURP had capacity. He understood the issue, retained it long enough to make a decision, weighed it in the balance and communicated that decision. If you are unable to do any one of these tasks, you lack capacity. You are incapacitated. At this point and contrary to what many people think, doctors don't get another person to consent for you – you can't do that for an adult. If you don't know the patient's wishes, and if there's no lasting power of attorney, the doctor acts in your best interest.

If you're unconscious in hospital with a head injury, and there is no one around to give a history, the assessment of capacity might take in the region of five milliseconds before you're wheeled off to the operating theatre. If, however, you're in a vegetative state with little or no prospect of recovery, the assessment of capacity might be far more involved. Naturally, things are never that simple, and complexity is never far away.

Mental illness can affect your ability to understand issues. Dementia, for instance, might affect your ability to retain information, catatonia might stop you communicating, and delusions might stop you being able to weigh the information in the balance.

If you are mentally unwell and think yourself the world's best surgeon upon whom the medical fraternity has heaped honours and prizes, when in fact you are a retired park attendant, albeit a perfectly good one, the doctors and the courts may take an interest in your refusal to have surgery on your gangrenous leg because of your grandiose delusions, when the real doctors think that you are going to die as a result of your decision.

This scenario is pretty much the way our current concept of capacity came about in the case of 'C' at Broadmoor Hospital.

One person I remember treating, well, more rugby tackling, was a patient with a broken leg. He was literally hopping out of the hospital emergency room. I could see his femur protruding through his jeans. Such was the severity of his drug-induced manic state – he had taken PCP or angel dust – he had no sense of injury, no perception of pain and took exception to anyone trying to get him back to hospital to see the orthopaedic surgeon.

In this case, the Mental Health Act might allow us to detain him in hospital and treat his mental disorder, but it's the Mental Capacity Act (MCA) that allows us to act in his best interests and give him the operation on his leg that he so desperately needs. And it was a first for me – giving an injection of haloperidol in the middle of the road outside A & E.

Another patient who concerned me was a man with schizophrenia and diabetes who persistently refused to take his diabetic medication. His blood sugars were very high and he was rapidly developing eye problems and kidney problems from his raised blood sugars. He ended up being treated under the MHA for his schizophrenia and under the MCA for his diabetes. We held him down and injected him with insulin, because he wasn't able to believe he was diabetic. In his mind he thought that drinking apple vinegar twice a day was enough to make him live forever.

All of which brings me to Terry Rodgers. You've had the appetisers and now it's time for the main course. Actually, that was the problem. Terry had stopped eating. He was starving himself to death and his legal team wanted me to say it was OK.

No one really knew why he wanted to die, but it was common ground that he had shot his daughter, Chanel, four times with a shotgun.

'It's a fascinating situation,' said his barrister. 'You might recall the police hunt for him.'

After killing his daughter, Terry had 'gone on the run'. There was a massive police hunt involving hundreds of officers searching the local woods, and then a police officer spotted him near a roadside and recognised him.

'We need you to look at his capacity,' said his barrister. 'I expect it's something you do all the time.'

'Yes,' I said, 'definitely,' trying to convince myself that sending a patient home who didn't want a TURP, injecting a person with a broken leg on the street and requiring a diabetic to have insulin qualified me for this. 'All the time. When do you want me to see him?'

If you stop drinking fluids, you last about three days. If you stop eating food, you last a lot longer, probably in the region of a month or two – it's not an exact science. I've lost count of the number of patients I've interviewed who have told me they are going on hunger strike. My complete indifference to them missing breakfast and sometimes lunch has saved many lives.

'Is Monday next week any good?' I offered.

Well, at least it gave me some time to read up on it. Hunger strikes aren't new, but growing up in the 1970s, I mentally associate it with the IRA, so that's where I started. Dolours and Marian Price were imprisoned in 1973 for the London bombing campaign. They didn't want to be in prison in England, they wanted to be back in Northern Ireland, so they went on hunger strike.

They lost weight, and eventually the doctors said, 'Enough is enough,' and Dolours and Marian were force-fed. I suspect no one could have anticipated the furious debate that followed.

Force-feeding is a very unpleasant business. To get food into the stomach, you need to pass a tube up through the nose, around the bend and then down into the oesophagus – the food pipe. You can imagine how difficult this might be if the person is anything less than willing and it is particularly in these situations where there is an increased risk of accidentally putting the tube down the trachea. Lungs really don't like food in them and the oesophagus and the trachea live next door to each other. Every time we swallow, we need to move the food over the top of our airway to reach the oesophagus. It's a really bad design error. God messed up on that one.

Eventually, in response to the outcry over the treatment of the Price sisters, Roy Jenkins, the British Home Secretary, announced in June 1974 that hunger strikers would no longer be force-fed.

There was one important caveat – they had to be of 'sound mind'.

In March 1975, the Ethics Committee of the World Medical Association agreed with the position Roy Jenkins had taken and declared that force-feeding was unethical. This influential judgement became known as the 'Declaration of Tokyo' and explains why in 1980, and again in 1981, members of the Provisional IRA in the Maze prison were not force-fed during their hunger strikes, whilst demanding to be treated as political prisoners – Margaret Thatcher wanted them treated as criminals.

Bobby Sands was the first of ten Irish republican paramilitary prisoners to die.

We now find ourselves in a strange situation. If I am in the health care centre of a prison and see an inmate take a rope and try to hang themselves, I would intervene. I wouldn't think about it, I'd just get stuck in. If needs be, I'd hold up their body to help them breathe. I'd call for help and, if I could, I'd cut the rope off their neck. I've done it twice and both men survived.

I think any reasonable person would do the same. If a person is standing over a railway line looking like they are about to jump, decent people get involved. We don't stop to think about their capacity or whether they are of sound mind to make a decision to end their life, we just 'do the right thing'.

But feeding yourself, or not feeding yourself in this case, is different, and whilst hanging and trains can cause death instantly, when Terry Rodgers decided to stop eating, there was time to consider the situation – plenty of time in fact.

We could talk to him and we could try to take a view on why he was trying to starve himself to death. We could try to work out whether he was of 'sound mind'.

If he wasn't of sound mind, we would need to treat him. If he was of sound mind, then all we could do was watch him die.

Slowly.

It's an odd one for a doctor watching a slow-motion suicide, and, having witnessed it, I can empathise with doctors who have wanted to forcibly treat hunger strikers under their care.

But if you take away a political motive, and there was no such motive in this case, I think it comes down to whether you believe there can ever be a 'rational' suicide.

From the outset, Terry was not a sympathetic char-acter. His first wife, Theresa, was sixteen when they married and soon after he had broken her nose and kicked her in the stomach when she was heavily pregnant. After she fled their home, he lay in wait for her in her grandparents' house and attacked her with a claw hammer, fracturing her skull, wrist and fingers in the assault, beating her unconscious. He was convicted of GBH and sentenced to eighteen months in prison.

He then married his second wife, Anne, Chanel's mother. She's since described how he had beaten her senseless and threatened her with knives and a hammer and had tried to throttle her.

Why he was so violent we will never know for sure, but members of his own family have talked about how he was rejected by both his birth mother and adoptive mother, how he was abused in Borstal as a teenager and how he grew up to hate women.

He didn't talk about any of this to me in prison. When I first went to see him, he was perfectly polite, but he really didn't want to talk at all. I asked him about his hunger strike, but he didn't want to engage with me. I tried to talk to him for what seemed like ages. Even his lawyers couldn't persuade him to talk or engage meaningfully with me.

I couldn't assess him adequately in prison, so he was sent to a nearby medium secure unit. He tried to kill himself whilst he was there, but despite this, there was no clear evidence of him being mentally ill. He was quite open with staff that he just wanted to return to prison with the express intention of going on hunger strike so he could join his daughter, the one he had brutally killed. He held off going on hunger strike whilst he was in hospital for fear it would have been interpreted as a mental illness or unsound mind. He was as good as his word, and when it was decided that he wasn't mentally ill and that he could return to prison with a 'sound mind', he went on hunger strike again, almost immediately.

By now he was only drinking orange juice. It was enough to keep his bowels working, but he wasn't eating anything.

Slowly, inexorably, the weight just dropped off him.

I went back to see him again, lest there was any doubt about his 'sound mind', but nothing had changed. He still wanted to starve himself to death. In my capacity report, I said I couldn't pick up on any depressive symptoms, and he wasn't psychotic in any way. In relation to capacity, he understood what he was doing. He was clear that when he entered the terminal stages of his hunger strike, when he was likely to lose his mental faculties, even then, he didn't want any intervention.

The last time I saw him, close to the end, he had really gone off – he was confused and he didn't know who I was. He could barely sit up from the bed and was clearly very weak and feeble. It was the only time in my professional career where I could have stopped someone dying and didn't. He didn't look like the 'monster' who had shot his daughter twice in her home, reloaded the gun and shot her twice again. He just looked like a starving man who had sentenced himself to death. His weight had dropped to around 7 stone. I wrote to the court saying that even if the trial did go ahead, he wouldn't be fit to attend. I said he was going to die, probably in a week or so.

I was right. He had a cardiac arrest a few days later. He was never tried for his crime. Society never had its retribution.

As I've said, it's difficult to stand by and watch someone die from starvation. If he had been mentally ill, I'd have stopped him. If he had lacked capacity, I'd have stopped him.

Just as the doctors didn't expect such a reaction from force-feeding the Price sisters, I didn't expect such a tide of criticism from being involved in not force-feeding Terry Rodgers. He 'cheated the hangman,' said one commentator. The Sunday papers characterised it in mostly negative terms. One of the red tops said that I might as well have given him a gun to shoot himself, that I 'let him die'. Others said I should have kept him alive to face trial. It felt a little ironic because if he had been convicted, I suspect the same newspaper would have been calling for the return of the death penalty.

At his inquest, the prison governor said Rodgers told her, 'I don't deserve not to be in pain.' The inquest jury was told of the words he had written in Lincoln jail: 'I am resolute in my determination to die. My intention is to be with my daughter.' The jury took less than half an hour to return a verdict that he had taken his own life.

Perhaps the most heartfelt comments have been from those who had been closest to him. Theresa, his first wife, has expressed her anger that he was allowed to call the shots by going on hunger strike. In a TV programme, *Married to a Murderer* (Wag TV / Crime Investigation Network), she said he should have lost his rights when he killed Chanel and should have been force-fed, if only to make him live with what he'd done.

In a statement after the inquest, Chanel's mother, Anne, said, 'My feelings for him are hate – pure unadulterated hate.' She later told the TV programme, *Married to a Murderer*, 'I am a great believer in an eye for an eye. Revenge. And it eats me like a cancer.'

Perhaps more than anyone, she felt robbed of answers as to why Terry had killed Chanel.

I wish I had an answer for her.

I can understand the public outrage, but I really don't think there was much more that I could or should have done to stop him dying.

It was his choice.

I can see that it would have been desirable for him to go on trial. I understand that evidence needs to be tested and guilt established, but the only way to have kept him alive would have been to take away his autonomy over his body, and that was a legal fight hard fought and hard won.

There is a principle at stake here and it's bigger than one man's life or death or an individual's or society's need for revenge. I didn't like the outcome, but it seems to me that we depart from principles at our peril. Allowing Terry Rodgers to die sickened me, but we need to hold on to what freedoms we have, and the freedom to choose how we treat our bodies is the most fundamental principle of all.

Disclosure:

The best curry in the world

There are limits about what you can tell your doctor. If you come along to the Tuesday afternoon surgery about a nasty tickle in your throat and then have a chat about jihad and your intended suicide mission, don't be surprised when Special Branch comes calling.

The doctor has to disclose this due to terrorist legislation.

Child abuse is another area where there is no discretion in the matter. Doctors have a duty to disclose, and this overrides the duty of confidentiality.

It's a bit of a dilemma for doctors when patients confess things they really shouldn't. Before I start an interview when I'm doing a medico-legal report, I usually spend a few minutes discussing issues of confidentiality. It's good to have some ground rules. If a patient wants to talk about their recreational use of cannabis, you're hardly going to phone the police about it, but if they tell you they're planning a murder, things might be a little different, even if you accept the importance of medical confidentiality. I had a patient admitted under my care at St Jude's. The doctors in A & E said he had an acute stress reaction, and they were worried about his suicide risk. An acute stress reaction is the sort of thing that happens after a bad car accident or when something threatening befalls us.

'So, tell me what's troubling you,' I asked the man, now safely admitted to the ward.

308

'Well, Doctor, it's nothing, really. Just a little sexual peccadillo.'

I wasn't expecting this response. I have always used the term 'peccadillo' to mean a small failing, a minor wrong or a personal indulgence.

'Well, my godson, he's ten, and he came to stay last week. And, well . . .' he seemed to squirm, 'you know how it is.'

'No,' I said. 'No, I don't know how it is.' He didn't seem that interested in my 'limits of confidentiality' speech and proceeded to tell me how depressed he was.

'Well, I've been ever so depressed recently, Doctor. I've not been sleeping, and I've lost weight, and I can't concentrate, I'm so forgetful, and my sex drive has gone to nothing.'

I've not looked at the Wikipedia entry for depression, but I imagine it is very similar.

'It sounds like a description of depression,' I said, carefully.

He looked relieved. 'Oh, do you think so, Doctor?'

'Definitely,' I said. 'Do I take it you've been feeling like this since your godson came to stay?'

He squirmed a bit again, but squirming is normally part of a guilty conscience rather than a symptom of depression.

'What did you do?'

'Well, in some cultures, it's completely normal . . .' he started.

I gave him my best Paddington stare and then he told me what had happened. It was quite clear he had sexually abused his godson.

I called the police and they were quite happy to hear he was with us. 'The boy told his dad about it and there's a warrant for his arrest – he must have been staying in hotels the last few days.'

He was arrested the next day. He seemed surprised when the police came on to the ward. At this point, my patient experienced what an acute stress reaction actually feels like, which in fairness I think I would too, if I was about to go to prison for the next fifteen years.

'But I'm ill,' he exclaimed, as if that exonerated his actions. 'Did you tell them I was here?' he asked, accusingly. 'You had no right.'

If you look at the Google ratings for any forensic psychiatrist who does adversarial reports for the court, do bear in mind that a one-star rating does not always mean they are bad at what they do.

Just saying.

I imagine that he'll be up for parole in ten years or so. And at that point, they might want a psychiatrist to see him.

I was depressed. It didn't happen. I never had the love I needed. I'm the victim here . . .

That's how the system works. There is some legislation that requires doctors to divulge information given to them, but beyond that, it's a complicated ethical and professional decision, when and if to breach confidentiality.

The case that set it all off happened in the United States in 1968. A graduate student at the University of California called Prosenjit Poddar met a young woman named Tatiana Tarasoff. They dated, but ultimately Tatiana called time on their relationship. Poddar became depressed, resentful and stalked her. He went to see a psychologist at the university counselling centre and said that he intended to kill Tatiana.

In fairness to the psychologist, he got in touch with the campus police and asked that he be detained. They did so, but he seemed rational, hadn't acted on his threats and was quickly released.

In October the following year, Prosenjit stabbed and killed Tatiana. At this point, the only people who didn't know about his threats were Tatiana and her family.

Perhaps unsurprisingly, Tatiana's parents then sued the psychologist and other employees of the university. The case initially faltered, but in 1976, the California Supreme Court ruled that mental health professionals have a duty to protect the intended victim. This decision put public safety above personal confidentiality.

Legally, none of the Tarasoff case applies in the UK, but things have gone in the same direction. Medical confidentiality remains important, but sometimes there will be exceptional cases where disclosure without the consent of the patient may be justified in the public interest. The hurdle for disclosure without consent is a high one – as a rule of thumb, if you are sitting on information that, if you don't share, might put someone at risk of death or serious harm, then it's time to call the police.

All of which brings me to Mr Smith, and the letter that I received from his solicitors.

> *Dear Dr Cave*
>
> *Please would you assess Mr V. Smith who is going to the parole board early next year. He was convicted eleven years ago after a series of violent attacks on a near neighbour, thought to be racially motivated. He has undertaken all the work required of him in prison and has attended a managing anger workshop, a thinking skills course, and has attended groups on substance misuse.*
>
> *Please comment on whether he has a mental disorder and his risk of recidivism; in short, whether he presents a significant risk to the public if he is released.*

Eventually, even quite dangerous people like Mr Smith come up for parole, and sometimes, a psychiatric opinion makes the difference whether they are released or not. About half are and half aren't. The key issue is whether they continue to represent a significant risk to the public.

What's significant?

I don't want to trivialise the answer, but I think that the legal instruction should always be premised on Mr Smith living next door to the expert following release. What is significant takes on a new dimension if the offender lives next door.

I once went out to see a film with Jo at a local cinema. Just before it started, I felt a tap on my shoulder, and I turned round.

'It is him. I told you it was him.'

I recognised the voice. I peered at them through the gloom, saw two of my patients from the secure unit, waved to them and turned back to the film.

'Who's that?' asked Jo.

'Well, the chap on the left served five years for rape,' I whispered, 'and then developed a psychotic illness. I'm planning his discharge next month. The one who recognised me, he's with me for GBH. He's got schizophrenia and I gave him unescorted leave last week.'

'Shall we move seats?' asked Jo.

'Nah,' I shook my head. I was going to have to live with my risk assessments for the rest of my life, not just for two hours.

The parole boards have been a political hot potato in recent years with the Worboys case. John Worboys was convicted of attacking several women and became known as the Black Cab Rapist. He received an indeterminate sentence, but after ten years, the parole board decided to approve his release, albeit with strict licence conditions. The decision to release him was then quashed after a legal challenge and further charges were levelled against him after more women came forward.

He was convicted and got two life sentences.

Society doesn't always approve of decisions to release serious offenders (or let them starve themselves to death, come to that), especially when the decisions are based on the testimony of experts. Even though it was the parole board that took the decision, it was the expert who was publicly criticised in the Worboys case. It's the expert who puts their professional reputation on the line every time they take a decision or make a recommendation that goes against societal expectation.

When I met Mr Smith, he looked older than his sixty years – most prisoners look older than they actually are. We found ourselves in a glass-walled cubicle by the side of a corridor. If there had been a lattice between us, it could have been a confessional booth.

'Sorry, Doc, I just need to calm myself down. One of the screws stopped my visit this morning because she thought I was getting drugs in. What a bitch. I mean, I wasn't going to give a sample when she was so fucking disrespectful, was I?'

It's always difficult to counter an opening comment like that, so I tried to put it to one side.

'You do know why I'm here, don't you?' I asked, wondering if I'd got the wrong Mr Smith, the slightly paranoid one with anger management problems and active drug use.

'Yeah, you're the doctor who's going to do a report that'll get me out of this fucking dump so I can go back to the missus, if she hasn't already fucked off.'

For the briefest of moments, I had a horrible thought that he was the right prisoner, but I was the wrong expert witness.

Mr Smith is a much-misunderstood man of advancing years. He values his privacy and has done much to enhance his cognitive flexibility over the long years of his incarceration. He values family life and looks forward to returning to his wife . . .

I looked at Mr Smith and the prominent Union flag on his right forearm. 'The conviction was thought to be racially aggravated?'

Smith laughed. 'Sure, he was a Paki, but that wasn't anything to do with it.' He swore a bit, told me that he was a reformed character and asked if we were finished because he was teaching a young lad how to box. 'I mean you've got to look after yourself these days; there's so many fucking immigrants, and that's not being racist.'

'No,' I said. He took it for an agreement, which didn't please me, but when you are in a small glass confessional booth, with a violent, racist, misogynistic pugilist, my best advice is to accept what they say, uncritically.

Whilst Mr Smith still holds legitimate concerns about the level of immigration, he assures me that his historic violence had nothing to do with the racial characteristics of the victim. I am pleased to report that he is actively engaged in helping young vulnerable prisoners in their sporting endeavours . . .

But I couldn't help myself. Instead of uncritical acceptance, I persisted. 'Mr Smith, it's my job to understand why you attacked Mr Patel all those years ago. I need to know why you did it and I need to tell the parole board if you're going to do it again.'

Mr Smith looked over at me with a degree of contempt. 'It's not right is it. You're an educated man, Doctor; you must see it.'

'See what?'

'They're taking over. We're giving away our country to them. Look at some of the scum in here. I shouldn't be here. It's my fucking country.'

'What happened between you and Mr Patel?' I asked.

'Nothing,' said Mr Smith.

'The notes say you broke his cheekbone with a baseball bat, and then you poured petrol over him.'

Smith shrugged.

'Why did you do that?'

There was a pause that lasted a lifetime. 'Teach him a lesson.'

'A lesson?'

'A fucking lesson,' said Smith, his voice steadily rising. 'A fucking lesson he'll never forget.'

People were hovering in the corridor near us.

Finish the interview Ben, you've got enough.

But I ignored myself again and carried on. 'The impact statement said that Mr Patel thought you were going to burn him to death.'

Smith smiled and seemed less aroused, more focused, and the effect was chilling. 'I wish I fucking had. He shouldn't have married her.'

'Did you know Mr Patel's wife?' I asked, surprised by this new turn of events.

Smith nodded. 'We went to school together.'

Go gently.

'You liked her?'

'Yes.'

'You think she shouldn't have married him?'

Smith was quiet, and there was perhaps a brief moment when I think he had a choice to be someone different. He could have reflected. He could have considered what he had done. He could have renounced his white supremacist beliefs that were papering over his own jealousy and insecurities.

I'd love to say that he fell into my arms and begged forgiveness.

But he didn't.

He was too far down his chosen path to turn back. There was no going back, not now. He had invested too much time and too much of himself in his perverted philosophy.

It was an afterthought really. I wondered if Mr Smith had been attracted to Mr Patel's future wife. 'Were you jealous?' I asked.

It was a badly judged question. No, let me be honest, it was a perfectly judged question. It was so loaded that it required him to make a choice. I had given him a loaded gun and he could either point it back at me and be a violent angry racist, or put it to his own temple and be an insecure young man who didn't get the girl.

'Jealous,' he started, his voice quiet to begin with and then he repeated *jealous*, reaching a crescendo, turning it into a question.

'JEALOUS?' he shouted. People in the corridor were now openly staring at us.

'JEALOUS OF A FUCKING PAKI. Don't be so fucking stupid. He's a piece of scum. They all are. I should have finished the fucking job. He married a white girl. He married my girl. I'LL FUCKING KILL HIM,' he screamed.

Funnily enough, I didn't feel threatened. Not in the slightest. But I did stop the interview – it had gone its course.

I called over one of the onlookers. Smith was taken back to the cells and one of the officers came to take me back to the prison reception.

'What did you say to him?' she asked. She was Muslim. I wanted to ask her things. I wanted to know how she dealt with racism. I wanted to know how she coped working in a prison. I wanted to know if she felt British, whether she felt betrayed by her own country and why people used race to stoke anger.

'I asked him about his offence,' I replied.

'What did he do?' she asked. For some reason I had assumed she would have known.

'He attacked a man, many years ago.' We reached reception and I thanked her for walking me back.

'Is he mad? Is that why he's seeing a psychiatrist?'

'No, he's not mad,' I said. 'I'm sorry; I wish he was.'

I got home late that night and went straight into my study. Libby, the girls' stepmother, or belle-mère as we prefer to call her, came in.

'You're quiet.'

'I can't write it,' I complained. 'He was so . . . .' I found it impossible to articulate my feelings. I wanted her to tell me that I was so full of anger to Mr Smith that I couldn't be involved any further, and that I'd have to recuse myself. I wanted her to press the silent alarm and take me off the case, but she didn't.

'Write it,' she said. 'Keep it factual. No emotion. Whatsoever.'

I spent that Saturday afternoon at the keyboard, only grumbling occasionally to myself. I found myself reflecting on my two mixed-race children, an earlier Hindu marriage ceremony to Jo, and my former in-laws who had adopted every good British value there is.

The girls came over from their mother's that evening and barged into my study. They asked what I'd been doing.

'A report,' I said, slightly tersely, trying to save and close the document on the screen as quickly as possible.

'You spelt misogynist wrong, Dad,' said the older one, too young I thought to know what it meant.

'You can't say "Paki", Dad,' contributed the younger one, unhelpfully.

I protested my innocence, that it was a direct quotation.

'Have you ever been subject to racism?' I asked as I shooed them out of the study.

They both paused at the door. 'No,' said the older one, simply.

The younger one shook her head. 'Me neither. We went to Nanny Rice yesterday and we've got you some curry. Do you want some?'

I opened up the report later that evening after the best lamb curry in the world. Before sending it, I amended one or two of my opinions, but at its heart, it remained a negative report and I knew it would be unhelpful from the solicitor's point of view. Needless to say, I was not supporting his application for release to the parole board.

A few days later the solicitor phoned me just after I'd got home from work. 'Yes, I got your report, Dr Cave.' I waited for the punchline. 'I don't think it's an accurate appraisal of Mr Smith's evident progress. Did you read the work he's done on anger management?'

'Anger management?' I spluttered, wondering if I needed the same course. 'Evident progress? You've got to be . . .'

I went on to point out that the reports that bore witness to his progress were little more than certificates of attendance and self-evidently hadn't worked. I mentioned Mr Smith's racist views, and his active and ongoing threats to Mr Patel, but the solicitor was not swayed.

Then the penny dropped. 'You're not going to submit my report, are you?'

'That's a matter for Mr Smith, Doctor, but I wouldn't advise it – it's not in his best interest.'

Some years ago, a psychiatrist called Dr Egdell had found himself in a similar position. He had been asked to see a patient, W, in a secure hospital and report whether he could be discharged or at least treated somewhere less secure. The patient, some ten years earlier, had shot four members of a neighbouring family, shot another neighbour who had come to investigate, and then shot another two strangers later the same day. Five of his victims died.

Dr Egdell took a careful history and found that W, even as a child, had made home-made explosives by packing chemicals into a pipe and then using a fuse to light them. He was insightless into his illness and disclosed that he always carried some bombs in his car, which he referred to as 'fireworks'.

Not surprisingly, Dr Egdell was worried about the diagnostic work-up, how dangerous W might be, and recommended that he was not ready for a step down to a lower level of security.

Sounds about right to me.

The solicitors withdrew the application to the tribunal but didn't tell Dr Egdell who, being a diligent type, phoned the tribunal office to ensure that his report had been received safely.

'What report?' came the reply.

Dr Egdell then phoned the hospital, who hadn't seen his report either, and they said that they would welcome any new information. He then called the solicitors to seek permission to send on his report, but the solicitor said 'No.'

At which point I'd like to think that Dr Egdell said: 'Fuck it.' If he didn't, I apologise, but he did send his report to the hospital and the hospital sent it on to the Home Office and then, when W's case did eventually come before a tribunal, it became clear to W and his solicitor that just about everyone had seen Dr Egdell's report.

That's when the proverbial fireworks went off. W decided to sue everyone within a Catherine wheel's radius of him, and it all went to the Court of Appeal.

It seemed clear from the outset that Dr Egdell had breached confidentiality by sharing the report, but the question was whether this was legally wrong.

Much like the Tarasoff case, the judge concluded that Dr Egdell not only owed a duty to his patient, but also to the public.

W lost his appeal. Dr Egdell was found to have acted within the law. His actions were '. . . necessary in the interests of public safety and the prevention of crime,' said the court.

A week later, having read up on the Egdell case, I phoned back the solicitor who was acting for Mr Smith.

'Listen,' I said, 'I've been thinking about things and I've discussed it with a couple of colleagues. I really think that my report needs to be heard by the parole board.'

Once again, the solicitor insisted I respect my duty of confidentiality.

'It seems to me that there are a lot of similarities with the Egdell case,' I started, putting my cards on the table, 'and that Mr Smith is in prison for a violent offence. My report touches on the reasons for his offence. The parole board needs to make an informed judgement about his risk, and they won't be able to do that without my report.'

Well, that's how I'd like to remember it, but under oath I'd say that the conversation went on for about an hour, was thoroughly ill-tempered and I was left with the word 'litigation' ringing in my ears.

My next call was to Milton.

'Egdell,' he said, before I'd finished telling him the story. 'That's what I said.'

'Well, you're right,' he said, 'that was easy,' and being only marginally better than him at small talk, the conversation lapsed soon after we had planned our next cycle route.

I phoned back the solicitor. 'I just thought I'd let you know that I'm sending my report to the parole board.' Just for good measure, I sent it to the prison too.

I saw the solicitor about a year later when he was representing a patient of mine who I thought was too dangerous to release.

'How's Mr Smith?' I asked.

'He's still in prison,' he said neutrally.

I looked to him for more – he knew what I was after and he shrugged. 'I don't always like what I do. You, you can act in the patient's best interests. I have to act on their instructions.'

'Mmm, that must be tough . . .'

The solicitor looked down and a little troubled.

'What is it?' I asked.

'Where do you think I'm from?'

'I don't know,' I said. 'Greece?'

'Everyone thinks that. My mum's from Gujarat. She's a Patel – it's a common name. It's as common as Smith is here.'

Hamsters and homicide

If I become unwell and feel the 'madness hamsters' are stealing my brain (thanks Edward Monkton), I will go to an acute ward in a general psychiatry unit. It might have a locked door, but the level of security is little more than most people's homes.

If I hit a nurse on this ward because I think they are a giant hamster, I will be sent to a PICU, a psychiatric intensive care unit, where they will give me lots of drugs until I admit that the hamsters are not real, or if they are, I am not too bothered about them any more.

If I break into a local pet store and try to kill the offending hamster, the one trying to steal my brain, and get myself arrested by the police, I might find myself in a low secure forensic psychiatry unit.

If in the process I hit the owner of the pet store and cause a head injury as he tries to stop me, I will go to a medium secure unit, and if I kill him, I will go to a high secure hospital, one like Bramworth.

Actually, that's not strictly true. It's getting harder and harder to get into high secure accommodation, and medium secure units deal with very dangerous people these days. You'd be more likely to go to a high secure hospital if the hamster you were trying to kill was a well-known celebrity, or you were politically or religiously motivated.

For the last twenty years, there have been an average of 672 homicides each year in England and Wales. Scotland adds around sixty and Northern Ireland about twenty-five or so. It could be worse. The South Africans have 20,000 homicides each year and the Mexicans a staggering 35,000.

Of the homicides in England and Wales, about 11 per cent of them are committed by people with mental disorders. I need to repeat that with emphasis.

Just 11 per cent of homicides in England and Wales are committed by people with a mental disorder. That means the overwhelming majority of people who kill someone *do not* have a mental disorder.

If you decide to murder your husband because he forgot your anniversary – I am sorry, Libby – then most reasonable-thinking people might believe that prison is the right place for you. You'll get a life sentence and the judge will set a tariff you have to serve before going to the parole board.

If, however, you kill your husband after years of brutal domestic violence, then the situation might not be so clear-cut. And if you are so deluded when you kill your husband that you thought he was an alien, intent on the destruction of mankind, then most people might think that prison would be entirely the wrong place to send you.

In these situations, you might reasonably say your responsibility was diminished – that's when abnormal mental functioning affects your understanding, judgement or self-control.

Peter Sutcliffe (the Yorkshire Ripper) was charged with murder but denied this saying he was guilty of manslaughter on the grounds of diminished responsibility. Four psychiatrists had said he had schizophrenia. But the judge wasn't having any of it. He rejected the plea of diminished responsibility and the trial went ahead. He was eventually found guilty of murder and given twenty life sentences. Three years into his prison sentence, he was transferred to Broadmoor

Hospital, spent the next thirty-two years there, only being sent back to prison in 2016. He died there four years later.

So, if the hamsters come calling during a prison sentence, it's perfectly possible to be transferred to hospital for treatment.

If Sutcliffe had been successful in claiming the hamsters made him do it, he would probably have been found guilty of manslaughter on the grounds of diminished responsibility. In this situation the judge could have put him on a hospital order with a restriction order (section 37/41) and then he'd have gone to Broadmoor from the outset.

But it is a one-way process. It would also mean that he couldn't be sent back to prison when the psychiatrists felt he was better. The only thing they could do would be to support his discharge, even if that was just a year or two later. You can see the dilemma. It's the forced dichotomy between being responsible for your actions and being sent to prison, and not being responsible for your actions and being sent to hospital.

There is now a third way and unfortunately psychiatrists have been slow to latch on to it. It's called a hybrid order and it allows the judge to send someone to hospital for treatment, whilst still imposing a prison sentence. It's a tacit recognition that even if you have a mental disorder, you might still have a degree of responsibility for your offence.

Jarvis would have been perfect for a hybrid order if it had been available to him back then. The psychiatrists in his case, twenty-five years earlier, had diagnosed him with schizophrenia and, unlike the case of Sutcliffe, had convinced the court that his responsibility was diminished when he tried to kill his wife and killed her friend. He was put on a section 37/41 and then he was sent to Bramworth Hospital. When you hear on the news that a person has been 'sent to a high secure mental hospital without limit of time', that's what we're talking about with Jarvis. The section 37 is the hospital order and the section 41 takes away my power (as the responsible clinician) to discharge the patient – only a mental health tribunal or the Secretary of State for Justice can do that.

After about twenty-two years in Bramworth, the consultant there felt that Jarvis was ready to go to a lower level of security. I went to see him, agreed with her appraisal and supported his move down a level of security to me at St Jude's.

My job was to treat him, see how he did, and if all went well, gradually make plans for him to live in the community.

He came to St Jude's with two filing cabinets of notes. I got a letter a year later from one of the administrators at Bramworth asking for the cabinets back, but they stayed with me. After I'd read their contents, I felt like I'd earned them.

It's not a psychiatric term, but Jarvis was a 'wayward' child. There was no particular reason for it – by all accounts his early life had been normal enough. His parents were happy to indulge an early interest in zoology and only mildly perturbed that most of the specimens he brought home ended up being cremated on the log-burning stove. They were a little more concerned by his behaviour at school. It started with biting other children at primary school and moved on to hitting them just as he got to secondary school.

His teachers knew he was a difficult child; they always do. 'Jarvis is a bright child but he does not apply himself. I am worried about his disruptive influence on other children and his marked sensitivity to any negative comment. I hope the school counsellor can help him with his anger issues.'

Unfortunately, the school counsellor could not help, and he was expelled from three schools before he left full-time education.

By this point he was appearing regularly in the courts for shoplifting and TWOC-ing – that's 'taking without consent', in his case stealing cars for a joyride before leaving them burnt out on a quiet road.

The school system effectively washed their hands of him after he took a chair leg to a teacher who had tried to stop him fighting a classmate. He was a bully, he was impulsive and he was angry. It's not a good combination.

It's odd. I've met quite a few psychopaths, real psychopaths who don't give a damn about other people, and I have never met a single one of them who thought they were themselves a bully.

'You fell into the wrong crowd?' I repeated back, incredulously, at our first meeting.

'Yes,' he said earnestly, 'they bullied me from the age of ten. I just had to stand up for myself.'

Flirtations with glue and solvents whilst at school were soon replaced by cannabis and MDMA, and by fifteen he was using cocaine and heroin.

Convictions and community-based sentences followed, but his offences were getting more and more serious. He progressed from cannabis to class A drugs – indecent assault became a rape charge (not guilty) and ABH became GBH (victim did not attend court).

'I wasn't guilty of any of it,' he told me. He sounded very convincing, and I imagine he would have passed any lie detector test.

His marriage was a difficult one. He met his wife in his solicitor's office and convinced her that he worked for a rival firm – their relationship was based on a lie from the start.

She left him for a while when she discovered that he was in prison, and not conducting a financial audit in Manchester, but he weaselled his way back into her life.

That's when he started to hit her. He said he suspected her of having affairs. It wasn't much at first, but it became more and more serious. He controlled her, he monitored whom she could see and told her what she could do. He coerced her, but through it all they had two children together and she raised them pretty much on her own.

After several years, and with his suspicions growing and the beatings getting worse, she'd had enough. Remarkably, she had the wherewithal to talk to a counsellor without him finding out, and was given the option of going to a refuge.

A week later, after hitting her across the face with a belt, he stormed out and didn't come back that night. She woke early, gathered a few possessions, packed some clothes and toys for the children and walked them out of the house. Her youngest was five years old.

Respect.

She went to the refuge, got herself together, found a new home on the other side of town, consulted a lawyer about a divorce and got on with her life. She was a survivor.

When I went through Jarvis' records, it became clear that he had been seen by the psychiatry services before the index offence. He had been assessed by the Child and Adolescent Mental Health Services, CAMHS, but the records could never be traced. What I could find were medical records relating to three short admissions to an acute psychiatry ward. Each was quite similar in that he presented highly aroused, angry and shouting at members of the public. He said that fire would consume the conspirators and his persecutors.

Reading the notes, it was clear that he was psychotic, but the episodes were short-lived and either responded to the medication he was given or simply to the passage of time. One or two doctors questioned if his problems were drug-induced, but there was no evidence either way – he always refused drug tests. You can't force someone to provide a urine drugs test and anyway, there are all sorts of ways to fake one. If you are being watched as you pee into the bottle, then it can be difficult to switch or adulterate the sample you've been asked to provide. One way to overcome the witnessed test, for a man at least, is a product called a Whizzinator. It is a fake penis supplied with 'one vial of the highest quality synthetic urine'.

Really, I'm not making it up.

One of the ways to detect whether a sample of urine is genuine is simply to feel how warm it is. I have been given cold urine to test more than once and it is fascinating to hear the explanations.

'I was outside in the cold all morning . . . It's always like that . . . I drank some cold water to help me pee.'

At the risk of encouraging sales, those clever people at Whizzinator have thought of everything – their product has built-in heat pads that warm the synthetic urine on the way out. My favourite bit is that the plastic prosthetic penis comes in different colours: white, tan, brown and black.

So, Jarvis had a track record of lies and deceit, violence and psychosis, and the psychosis might have been related to drugs – we didn't know either way.

One week before the offence, all those years ago, he 'happened' to see his son going into his new school, the one his mother had put him in after she left. Jarvis said he had been working on a nearby building site, but the suspicion was that he had been searching for them. He waited around, watched his former wife collect both children and followed them back to their new home.

He bided his time until Saturday evening and then he knocked on her door at 7 p.m., carrying a bag over his shoulder. When she answered, he bundled her inside, knocked her unconscious, and then went into the lounge where he found a man he wrongly assumed to be her new partner watching TV.

He took the hammer from his bag and beat him repeatedly around the head. The blows didn't kill him. He went upstairs and locked his children in their rooms. They had heard the screams from downstairs, could see the state he was in and had nightmares about it for years afterwards.

After locking the children away, he dragged the semi-conscious bodies into the cellar, took a 5-litre jerry can from his bag and poured petrol over the man and set fire to him.

I hope he was unconscious until he died.

CCTV images then show him walking, jerry can in hand, into the nearest petrol station.

'What were you doing?' I asked.

'I needed more petrol,' he said.

The attendant refused to serve him and called the police because of his appearance. 'He looked like he was covered in blood.'

He was arrested as he returned to the house, empty jerry can in hand. The neighbours by this point had noticed smoke from the cellar window at the front of the house and called the fire brigade. They had broken in and found his children in a state of shock in their bedrooms, physically unharmed. His former wife was taken to hospital suffering the effect of smoke inhalation and head injuries. The notes I read never really spoke about her mental state.

The transcripts of the police interview were revealing. He reported when he was interviewed that he had heard the voice of the Devil telling him what he had to do.

He went on trial for murder and pleaded guilty to manslaughter on the grounds of diminished responsibility. The evidence about his mental state was divided, but because of his previous contact with psychiatry services, he ended up being described as schizophrenic and was successful in his plea. The court accepted his responsibility was diminished.

He was sent to Bramworth and after over two decades they decided he didn't need to be in high security any more. He was on medication, he was 'well', he had done loads of group work and he'd had extensive individual therapy.

It's true – he had.

When I first met him, I asked him why he had killed the man at his ex-wife's home.

'I was hearing voices, Doctor.'

'Really?' I asked. It was his first explanation to the police. It hadn't changed over all that time. He was blaming his illness for his offence. It was as if his own personality counted for nothing. 'So, it's all down to your illness, your schizophrenia?'

'Yes,' he said, 'the voices, they told me what to do.'

I went back to my office and looked at the filing cabinets standing in front of my desk. Jarvis had asked me for copies of all of his medical records, and I knew from the first time I went through them that his ex-wife's and children's latest address was included in many of the records. I had to remove any link to them, and there was no room for error.

I looked at my watch and phoned Jo to say I was going to be home late. She didn't seem that interested and, in fairness, we were both consumed by our careers and we were often back late.

In the early years we were happy. I remember coming back from a weekend away in Brighton and being stopped at a police cordon at the end of our street. It was late, about midnight, and an officer peered into the car and asked where we lived. I told him and he asked if we had seen anything. 'Sorry, we've been away for the weekend.' He nodded, a little disappointed.

'What's happened?' I asked.

'There's been a murder,' he said, and waved us through.

I got into my room and looked out and could see an arc light illuminating the front of the house about six doors down. I didn't know it at the time, but it was where Jarvis had committed his crime.

I wasn't sure how much I could believe Jarvis. You can never be sure that someone is lying to you, but there are clues. Sometimes the person can appear evasive or unclear in their detail. 'No, I was away for the weekend, well, I was out for the day, we went to Brighton. No, sorry, it was Cambridge . . .' and you see their hand go up to their mouth as they look away.

As you get more confident in your ability to lie, the details become easier to master, but the price you pay is the story sounding rigid or inflexible. Lies don't change and they can't adapt. The truth is paradoxically more flexible, it bends to accommodate new information, but it still all fits together like a flexing jigsaw.

People sometimes get angry at you for asking a question when it exposes their lies. 'What does it matter if it was Brighton or Cambridge? Why are you even asking?' And sometimes they keep talking, if only to stop you asking another question.

I opened the top drawer of the filing cabinet and decided that Jarvis needed the 'full works'. I had five formal interviews with him, each one lasting close to two hours. In the first he blamed his illness for everything. 'But I'm on medication now, so it's fine,' he tried to reassure me.

In the second I talked to him about his personality. 'I don't think this is relevant. I've done the therapy. I'm here to rehabilitate to the community.'

Before the third meeting, another patient complained that 'someone' had been threatening him for money.

The third meeting itself was characterised by Jarvis getting quite angry with me whenever I asked him something difficult. 'It's all in the past. I've done my time.'

Later two other patients on the ward started to stay in their rooms – they just wouldn't come out, even at mealtimes.

'What's wrong?' I asked.

'Nothing,' they said, unconvincingly.

At the fourth meeting, Jarvis asked if permission had been given by the Ministry of Justice to give him leave. 'Not yet,' I answered. 'Can you give me a urine specimen please.'

'I gave you one yesterday,' he answered, indignantly. 'And it was negative.'

'It was negative,' I agreed, 'but it wasn't a proper specimen.'

He looked at me. 'It wasn't fucking cold. The nurse is lying to you. It was definitely my piss.'

'I didn't say it was cold, Jarvis.'

'What was wrong with it, then?'

'It wasn't urine.'

Then I turned the screw a little more. 'By the way, you've got diabetes.'

Jarvis stared at me.

'There's sugar in your urine,' I explained, 'a lot of it.' I looked pointedly at the carton of apple juice by the coffee machine. Jarvis stormed out and went back to his room. I went back to my office and carried on redacting his notes and then on impulse went to the clinical room and collected a urine pot, put his name on it and placed a little yellow sticker on the side so that I'd know if he switched tubes. It was time to give Jarvis one more chance to provide a urine specimen.

One of the night staff stopped me halfway. 'I'm worried that Jarvis is threatening some of the other patients, Doctor,' she said, whispering her concerns.

I looked down the corridor at Jarvis' room, six doors down, the light shining out from the inset window.

'Well, let's go and ask him.'

I didn't knock. I opened the door and saw Jarvis with another patient, who I knew had a drug problem. An improvised foil crack pipe fell out of Jarvis' hand and on to the floor. He had a lighter in his other hand.

When his room was searched, the nurses found £350 hidden behind the sink and he had no way to account for it. He blamed the other person for supplying him drugs.

'When did you start to use drugs again, Jarvis?' I asked him at our fifth meeting.

'I don't use drugs, Doctor; it was the first time I'd done it.'

I tried to look hurt and disappointed, but I think it was lost on him.

'Are you sending me back to Bramworth?'

I didn't answer him. I was worried that if he knew that, he'd have nothing to lose, and I needed to keep the ward and the other patients safe.

The problem with Jarvis was that he had two different problems. Sure, he had a psychotic illness, and it might very well have been schizophrenia, but he also had an anti-social personality, and it was sufficiently bad to be termed psychopathic. His illness was well treated − by and large the medications we use are pretty good for that − but after his illness got better, we were still left with his callous and self-serving personality.

He was transferred back to Bramworth the following week. We told him on Wednesday morning he was going and then we had two nurses stay with him until the secure transport arrived at lunchtime. It was just enough time to pack.

As it turned out, he took the whole thing on his psycho-pathic chin and the transfer went without incident.

I was called by the psychiatrist at Bramworth a month later. 'I just wanted to make sure about one or two things. He said that some of the patients on the ward were taking advantage of him financially and made him bring drugs on to the ward.'

Jarvis was making his own narrative real for himself. He was the person who was misunderstood, the innocent dupe, the victim, and it was his misfortune to have been sent back to Bramworth.

I've got no real concerns about Jarvis spending more time in Bramworth. Being in hospital after so long is probably the only reality he has. But if anyone exemplifies the need for flexibility in the system, it's Jarvis.

We need to acknowledge that the offenders we see have varying levels of culpability and move away from the 'mad or bad' paradigm. The courts might not like it, but most of the people I have seen in forensic psychiatry are psychotic offenders. Sometimes the psychosis explains their actions and sometimes it doesn't.

We need high-quality hospitals and we also need properly funded psychiatry services in our prisons with the ability for them to work seamlessly together.

A love letter to nurses

Every few years when the politicians are standing for re-election, or when we have a pandemic, we seem to wake up to the brilliant and indispensable job that nurses do. We make promises to get more of them into the NHS and to pay them more, and then after the election or when the crisis is over, we promptly forget about them until the next time.

If you ask me to make a prediction, I would say that the future of health care will be a nurse-led service. Doctors, whilst highly trained, are becoming unaffordable and in truth most of the *needs* in health care involves health education, screening, prevention and large-scale treatment programmes. We will still need doctors, but so much more could be done by nurses.

If I haven't articulated it clearly enough already, let me say it now – nurses are brilliant. The work that nurses do is indispensable. Their spirit is indefatigable. They work in the most difficult environments with the most challenging patients and their commitment, and their compassion, is unparalleled.

It's no accident that there's a nurse in pretty much every story I have told you. If I didn't mention them specifically, they were there in the background, dealing with another patient, writing an account of the patient's behaviour in the notes, taking the troubled patient to one side to see how they were feeling, dispensing medication or, as a staff nurse on my ward did yesterday, driving out to the local shop in his break to buy his patient some hibiscus tea – the only thing she wanted to eat or drink.

Let me tell you something else about nurses. Sure, they sometimes laugh at junior doctors messing up ECT or not diagnosing death properly, but they guide us, they focus our work, they correct our errors, and generally just get on with things.

There's more – they're brave too. Maybe this whole book is my love note to nurses.

★

I am coming to the last few case files in my office – I've almost finished.

'Bye, Ben,' shouts Anthony, from outside the window, peering through the gap-tooth blind. 'Almost done?'

I nod back at him and smile. 'Almost there, just one more drawer to go.' I pick up my summary of Sean's notes. It was only two months ago since I wrote them.

I was on my ward at St Jude's when the alarm went off. Sean, a patient with schizophrenia who had a conviction for manslaughter was standing in the middle of the corridor. 'I'll fucking kill him. And I'm going to fucking kill Elaine too.'

I'd poked my head out of the side room.

'You, I'm talking to you, Dr Cave. I don't want to be here. I'm not fucking mad.'

The other patients had scurried back to their rooms leaving Linda, the cleaner who had been helping with lunch, standing in the dining area next to him. She looked petrified.

The first of the wall-mounted kitchen furniture he had ripped off flew past me and hit the window to the ward round room opposite me. I saw Elaine on the other side of the corridor.

'It's because the tribunal yesterday didn't discharge him,' said Elaine.

I nodded.

'Ben, why don't you wait here, I've got a good relation-ship with him.' She was calm and sounded like she was in a ward round with me, updating me about routine events. Part of a cupboard door hit the door frame on my right which gave me a chance to consider the situation. Elaine was probably right. I had spent about three hours the day before explaining to the tribunal why I thought Sean was too dangerous to be discharged. I wasn't his favourite person at that moment.

I stayed sheltered behind the door, using it as a protec-tive shield, poking my head round to watch Elaine advance towards him. Sean pulled his arm back to fire off another missile in my direction, but Elaine put her arm up as if she were stopping traffic.

'That's quite enough of that, Sean!' She articulated herself clearly, but she didn't shout. She was calm but commanding. 'I'll make you a cup of tea, and let's have a chat about it.'

Sean didn't respond, but he didn't fire off any more missiles either.

'Two sugars, isn't it?'

And then he said, 'Yes,' meekly almost, perhaps taken by surprise at the normality of the conversation.

They went off to the kitchen and Elaine told Linda to go and join me. She hurried off in my direction, dived behind me, sat down and started to sob. The emergency team then arrived, and I asked them to hold back with me and Linda.

Elaine made the tea and took Sean to a side room, guiding him gently by the elbow. Two of her ward staff joined her, one taking up station at the door and the other in the room with her. The emergency team stayed with me, at a distance.

Elaine and Sean emerged twenty minutes later and she asked me to write him up for some Lorazepam. 'It might just help him settle down a bit.'

And that was it. For about thirty seconds, Linda had been terribly frightened. Some furniture had been smashed.

Medication had been given with the patient's consent. Nobody had been restrained. Nobody went to seclusion. Nobody was injured and nobody went to A & E. The emergency team were unused, went back to their wards and we all got on with the day.

Now that's what I call nursing.

Elaine caught up with me later, in my office. 'You OK?' she asked.

'Yeah,' I replied. 'What you did back there . . .'

She smiled briefly. 'It needed to be done. Maybe I should have waited for the emergency team, it's just that he'd have ended up in the PICU, and generally he's doing OK.'

I smiled. 'That's not what I meant.'

She looked a little confused.

'You never make me tea.'

She guffawed and then looked down at the ground and it was hard to read her. I thought she had started to laugh and then it sounded more like sobs. Her hand came up to her eyes and I knew she was crying. I put my hand on her back and held it there for several minutes.

Then she sat up and ran her fingers carefully under her eyes.

'I'm OK,' she said. 'Am I smudged?'

'No,' I said. 'Do you want some tea?'

She left the room indicating I should stay there and came back five minutes later with two steaming mugs.

'I put sugar in both of them.'

We didn't talk after that. We just sat there together and drank our tea in silence, a very gentle silence, and then she went off to do the rotas, and I got on writing a report.

All in all, it was an uneventful day.

Throwing in the towel

It's very difficult to be sure when I decided to leave forensic psychiatry. The process of disillusionment has been a gradual one, like a river slowly eroding its own riverbed, entrenching itself in a certain path. I had grown tired of violence. I'd had enough of dangerous young men continuing down their self-destructive paths despite our best efforts.

If wearing my white coat and carrying my stethoscope had been a phase I went through many years ago, it turns out that forensic psychiatry was just the same.

If you pushed me for a single incident that focused my thoughts, something that distilled the steady drip of disquiet, it involves a naked masturbating arsonist and a barrister.

Try not to get them mixed up.

I had been treating Guy for three years at Lakeview. He'd been doing pretty well but occasionally relapsed into florid psychosis. He had failed a trial of clozapine and by this point he was on two antipsychotic drugs, two mood stabilisers and large amounts of benzodiazepines. Though his relapses were unpredictable, it was becoming increasingly clear that he had very poor tolerance to any sort of stress. Unfortunately, when he was under stress, he tried to use illicit substances. It didn't matter what it was – he'd use it.

He was a prolific offender and had multiple convictions for drugs, violence and acquisitive offending. One newspaper described him as a 'one-man crime wave' early on in his offending history. Later, and probably as his illness grew, he diversified into arson and this got him into forensic psychiatry. He'd set fire to his hostel as a result of his paranoia.

Then his mother died. With the benefit of hindsight, I really should have given him larger amounts of Valium to help him cope with the stress, but in fairness, we were trying to stop his reliance on addictive drugs, and anyway, he seemed to be making progress with the psychologist.

I was then perhaps only a little surprised when Elaine called me to the ward 'quite urgently'. I got there minutes later and saw him standing on the pool table in the middle of the ward, masturbating. A two-metre wooden strip, broken off from the side of his bed, lay beside him looking something like a medieval club. I approached him with Elaine's deputy, Robin, by my side. I wanted to have a chat with him and then, all being well, escort him back to his room to take some sedative medication.

'Guy, can we help you down. Let's have a chat.'

But he didn't want to come down from the pool table and he didn't want to talk. I could see why. He seemed to be enjoying himself, a lot.

Robin and I looked at each other wondering what to do next. Just then he broke off his onanistic pursuits, declaiming, 'It's not natural,' and then proceeded to tell us that he was the Dalai Lama.

What he actually said was, 'I am the Dalai Lama, and you can suck my cock.'

Then, presumably in the spirit of peace and harmony, he distracted himself with a little chanting and then returned his attentions to his still protuberant member. Robin was reaching for his radio to find out what had happened to the C & R team just as another patient decided to come out of his bedroom to have a game of pool. I knew that he didn't get on with Robin, so I walked over to him.

'What the fuck . . .' he said as he saw Guy on the pool table.

'Can I get you to go back into your room for a few minutes . . .'

I turned back to the pool table just as Guy reached down, picked up the club and without warning swung it down on to Robin.

'Watch out,' I shouted, a fraction too late.

Robin was able to take half a step back before the club hit him. It missed his head and landed on the top of his shoulder with a sickening crack. I winced at the sound and knew immediately that his clavicle had broken. Robin went to the ground and by this point the C & R team were arriving. Guy was restrained, forcibly medicated and whilst I was dealing with all that, Robin was taken off to hospital.

We transferred Guy to our PICU ward, and he was put into a seclusion room to stop him assaulting anyone else.

I saw him the next day. First the nurses went in and he allowed them to hold his arms, one of them sitting on either side of him. Three other nurses were in the room and another two were outside. That's when I went in and crouched down in front of him, sufficiently far away for him not to be able to kick me. He was a bit slurred from the medication, but he was still coherent.

He had already spoken through the intercom to his advocate who had left me an email asking how we were going to accommodate his Buddhist practice whilst he was in seclusion.

'You're discriminating against me. All I was doing was showing my love for the world. You don't understand me, and you don't understand my culture.'

I bit my lip.

Culture is important. I love culture and I love learning about other cultures. So being told that I don't understand someone's culture was a bit below the belt. I mentally reframed his comment.

I realise that there are complex issues in society, but I am sufficiently egocentric and narcissistic to exploit these tensions to justify my resolute denial of having an illness, my continued use of recreational drugs, and my indiscriminate use of violence to those who challenge my uneducated world view.

'Did you use spice?' I asked him, but he just laughed. Spice is a synthetic cannabis product, and Guy wasn't the first person I'd seen profoundly aroused and sexually disinhibited after using it. 'Listen, Guy, I'd like to get you back on to the ward, but I need to know that you're going to be safe there. I can't let anyone else get assaulted.' I could see the nurses tighten their grip on his arms as he struggled against them.

'Your society is so fucking shallow,' he snarled at me. 'You persecute anyone who challenges it.'

Maybe I was just looking for a way out of forensic psychiatry, but by the time a person has clocked up fifty convictions and fifteen prison sentences, I reserve the right to question their life choices. I called time on the meeting, left the room and then we went back to the nursing office to decide what to do.

'I don't think we can let him out of seclusion. He's still very hostile and angry,' I started. The team were in general agreement. One of them was going to call Robin to find out how he was doing, and we decided to carry on with the same medication. He would have it intramuscularly if he refused the tablets.

'Will you be doing the tribunal, Ben?' asked one of the nurses.

I'd forgotten about it, but Guy had appealed against his detention two months earlier and that meant his case was going to be heard by the mental health tribunal.

'When is it?'

'Monday.'

'Yes, let's hope he's out of seclusion by then. I'll write to let them know what's happening.'

Guy, perhaps because of his prolific offending, and perhaps because his father was fabulously wealthy, had very good solicitors and they had employed the services of a barrister to represent him at the tribunal. It happens sometimes.

Normally the doctor gives evidence first, so I told the tribunal about his illness, a chronic treatment-resistant schizophrenia, his personality (narcissistic and antisocial) and his use of drugs, all of which resulted in violence and arson.

Then it was his barrister's turn to question me and the evidence I'd just given. Over the years I have got to meet a lot of barristers. They're all bright, some of them are exceptionally bright, and they're all good with words. You are probably familiar with some of their techniques, like not asking a question if they don't already know the answer, but they have other tricks too.

'Is your name Ben Cave?' he asked me.

Well of course it bloody is. You can see my ID badge with my photo on it and I've already introduced myself to the tribunal.

'Yes, my name is Ben Cave.'

And he smiled and nodded as if I had made some sort of concession.

Then they ask the next question that they know the answer to. 'And you saw my client on Tuesday of last week.' It's only a statement so far, so they throw in a quick, 'Isn't that right, Doctor?'

'Yes, I did.'

Before long, they've got you saying *yes* to their questions. They're leading your response. They're conditioning your behaviour.

'And Doctor, am I right in saying that when you spoke to my client last Tuesday, there was no evidence of him having religious delusions?'

And the word 'Doctor' isn't a term of respect as you might expect, it has a vinegary taste to it, as if they've just discovered their Château Lafite Rothschild is corked.

'Yes,' I agreed, 'but when I saw him on Friday . . .'

'Doctor, a simple yes or no will suffice. If you could just answer the question.'

'Yes,' I say. They close down your answers.

You get the idea. They lead you. They condition your responses. They control the interview, and that's how they try to control your answer too.

'And, Doctor, am I right in saying that my client had no clear evidence of delusions or hallucinations when it is alleged he assaulted a member of the nursing staff?'

Alleged?

I thought back to the episode.

'There was no evidence of delusions or hallucinations, but he was very disinhib—'

'Doctor, just the question please,' he said, putting his hand up as if I were an overexcited puppy. 'And you'd agree that despite the large amount of medication he was forced to take, there was no evidence of thought disorder.'

'Yes.'

'So Doctor, if I understand it correctly, delusions and hallucinations and thought disorder are the cardinal features of psychosis and you are saying he had none of them?'

Yes but no but yes but no. Shouldn't I have a barrister shouting 'OBJECTION'?

'Well I can see that Dr Cave has no answer for me. Let us turn to whether my client was using illicit substances as has been asserted. There is no actual evidence that my client was using drugs is there, Doctor?'

'No, that's because he . . .'

'Doctor, is there objective evidence of drug use or not?'

'No . . .'

But when someone is having IM medication and has six nurses restraining them by the side of a pool table and then carrying them into a seclusion room, and your deputy ward manager has just been taken to A & E, a urine drug test is not the first thing you think about.

'No, there was no drug test undertaken,' he got me to admit, like a recalcitrant ten-year-old being forced to apologise for smashing your neighbour's window with a golf ball, again.

Sorry Mr and Mrs Blackwell. It's probably a good moment to confess to scrumping your apples too.

'Dr Cave, perhaps you could let the tribunal know when my client last had any psychotic symptoms.'

I thought back and I confess I found it hard to remember the last time that Guy had been clearly paranoid or halluci- nated. Thought disorder was never a feature of his illness. He was on close to twice the normal maximum dose of antipsychotics and in fairness it was probably his personality keeping him in hospital at this point.

'But he was profoundly disinhibited just last week, and if we exclude the possibility of illicit drug use, then we have to consider the possibility of a relapsing mental state,' I ventured.

I felt like a boxer coming off the ropes.

The barrister looked like he'd just necked a pint of the corked wine. I think that's when we really started to slug it out with each other – a drunken bar room brawl in a courtroom – the gloves had come off.

'Doctor, would you agree that medium secure units are highly abnormal places for patients to live for protracted periods of time?'

'Yes,' I answered hesitantly, wondering where he was going to land his next blow.

'Is it likely that my client was simply acting out his frus- tration at being detained unjustifiably in hospital, in what you accept is a pathological environment?'

He was wanking on the pool table.

'No,' I said through gritted teeth, 'I don't think this accounts for his behaviour. It's like concluding a prisoner should be released because they protest violently about being in prison.'

He didn't like the left jab I'd just given him.

But barristers train for events like this, and it's best not to jab them too much. This one feinted to the left . . .

'Maybe we can agree, Doctor, that one might become frustrated if unjustly detained in hospital.'

. . . and then went to work on me with a combination.

'Turning to your diagnosis, Doctor . . .'

At this point some of the merely bright barristers get out their book on diagnosis and use a checklist to try to say that the relevant criteria are not made out, but this one was very bright and he was going for the knockout blow.

'Is it possible that your diagnosis is wrong?'

It hit me in the side of the head. I hadn't seen it coming.

And Cave's on the ropes again.

You have a choice at this point. Either you can say 'yes', it might be wrong and then have that possibility thrown back at you for the rest of the hearing, or you can say 'no', and sound like an arrogant prick who lacks any ability to reflect on matters.

He needs a standing count.

Neither is great, so you try to steer a middle path that implies you, like any good doctor, can both introspect and make a good diagnosis, in a humble and confident sort of way.

. . . Six, Seven. The judge is looking at me for an answer.

'I have considered all the possibilities, but he fulfils the criteria for paranoid schizophrenia, and he has a pre-existing antisocial personality disorder. I think that accounts for the changing pattern of his offending history.'

It seems to work, so the barrister drops back and starts to dance around like Muhammad Ali.

'Are you accommodating my client's Buddhist practice?'

Sting like a bee.

I was slightly concussed by this point and I wanted to say that Buddhist practice did not normally, in my evidently narrow cultural world view, involve makeshift weapons, stimulant drugs, public masturbation or fractured collarbones.

But what I actually said was, 'We try to respect all religious belief and practice.'

Naturally, as it was a court of law, I kept my fingers crossed inside my boxing gloves, because privately I knew that the multi-faith room had been used to store another patient's shoplifted clothes before we could return them to the store.

'Doctor, what plans have you made if the tribunal are minded to discharge my client?'

'We can't plan realistically for an eventuality I am not supporting. He will leave the ward and use large amounts of stimulant drugs and be in police custody by morning.'

And Cave's off the ropes . . .

'So, you reported the alleged offence, but the police didn't attend. Isn't that right, Doctor?'

And this time the word 'Doctor' wasn't just given a vinegary taste, it was dipped in anthrax and served in a bitter shell of sarcasm. Thankfully, the very bright barrister was relatively junior – just imagine the damage a senior QC could do with a sharply pointed two-syllable title.

'The police didn't attend,' I confirmed. And that was the beginning of the end.

I wasn't given the opportunity to say that the police should have attended but didn't bother because, from their point of view, a nurse 'getting whacked' in the local mental hospital was no more than an occupational hazard and one the police have to put up with every day. I'd agree with them too, up to a point, if there was consistency in their decisions, but I had one patient who regularly assaulted the nursing staff. We finally got the police to visit and just as she was giving him an informal caution (i.e. not doing anything very much), the patient spat in her face. That seemed to do the trick and he was frogmarched off to the station to be charged with ABH.

'And you never actually saw the nurse's "alleged" injury?'

'No.'

And once again I didn't get the opportunity to say that I have seen countless fractured collarbones and that once upon a time could have given a full pathological description of what happens to the surrounding nerves and vasculature when it is broken into tiny bits by a large club.

'No, I didn't see the report from A & E after Robin received treatment.'

. . . 'No, I accept that technically I'm not sure if he received any treatment.'

. . . 'Yes, he could be off work for any number of reasons, but I don't think . . .'

. . . 'No, I haven't spoken to him. I tried but . . .'

Cave's on the ropes again. I think he's going down.

There wasn't much fight left in me and I think my opponent knew that.

Things went on like this for the remainder of the round and as I put my arms up to protect my head, with me saying 'yes' or 'no' to closed questions, I started to realise what had actually happened. It is remarkable how poorly we tend to remember things until we are helped to do so by a skilled interrogator.

My patient, a victim of society, was cruelly deceived by a bad person that we knowingly let him mix with, and became unintentionally intoxicated with spice, at the time a legal substance, and when interrupted during his meditation, he became frightened for his own safety and reacted in a way that all reasonable people might in the same situation.

I start to wonder if my name really is Ben and whether I should turn myself in for stealing the apples from my neighbour. I go on my knees and look up at the giant sensory homunculus tongue presiding over the court. My blood is on the canvas and I can't

347

wash it off. A tartan sofa that looks like Daksha is laughing at my divorce and in the front row, Dr Scott, grand-old chest physician, looks disappointed. Mr Tomkins, my biology teacher, is counting me out.

The barrister was standing over me, his right hand ready to finish me off, but he pulled his punch. He stopped short of accusing Robin of maliciously breaking his own collarbone – but once it had all been explained to me, I did in my concussed state start to actually remember that his client, Guy, had simply invited me for a game of pool, shortly after I had offered him some amphetamines.

And then I got up from my knees, and with the last of my strength pulled my right hand back and mumbled something about Robin having been assaulted.

Please referee, you've got to stop the fight.

My guard was down, and the barrister was floating like a butterfly.

'What assault?' he asked with his left, and finding no answer, pressed forwards and turned to the referee. 'My client denies the account given by the doctor. No evidence has been presented about the nature or severity of the injury. He hasn't been interviewed under caution. He hasn't been charged. He hasn't been convicted of any offence. He doesn't have any psychotic symptoms and he is not a drug user. We dispute the evidence of personality disorder and invite the tribunal to consider an absolute discharge.'

The clock on the wall started to melt and the barrister's face morphed into something altogether more sinister. I was in a Dali picture again but screaming like the Munch icon.

Thereafter, the barrister's words wafted over me, but I had long since retreated into my concussed two-syllable title. It was pretty much the only reality I had left and even that was starting to turn into a lobster-shaped telephone.

It took me a few days to recover and when I could remember things clearly again, I was pleased that the tribunal had not discharged the patient. Fortunately, the doctor on the panel was a forensic psychiatrist and didn't like some of the rabbit punches. But they did compliment the patient on the 'good progress' he was evidently making.

So, Dr Shipman, perhaps we'll start with a phased return – just three days a week, and see how it goes . . .

I came home the night of the tribunal and sat in front of an unplugged TV. I summoned what little cognitive facility I had left and called Robin to ask how he was getting on. He seemed quite relaxed, and his collarbone was improving each day, but he wasn't ready to come back to work just yet. I asked him if the police had taken a statement from him.

'Tomorrow,' he responded. 'But I don't think there's much point me pressing charges.'

I disagreed with him and told him so.

Bloody nurses.

Guy? He's still in hospital, but so far, he's doing well.

Robin did go and see the police to make a complaint.

They took a statement.

They referred the case to the Crown Prosecution Service.

The CPS didn't speak to Robin.

They didn't speak to me.

Apparently, it wasn't in the public interest to prosecute.

Robin got a letter stating that he was a victim of crime, but I think he knew that already.

He was eventually offered some counselling, but by then he was back at work and didn't want to take any more time off.

Bloody brilliant nurses.

Reminiscence therapy

Last night I finished packing my boxes at Lakeview. My room was tidy and my work was done. I came home but felt unsettled as if there was unfinished business.

Now it's early in the morning – I can't sleep and I have crept out of bed and made myself a coffee. I'm sitting outside on Dad's old garden bench, waiting for the sun to come up.

I look at my mobile phone, vibrating silently next to me. It's Elaine. 'I'm sorry to call you so early. But you said it'd be OK if I needed to, and I know you get up early.'

'It's OK.'

She paused. 'I couldn't sleep. Actually, I'm finding it very tough going. I can't go back. I just keep seeing him stab me.' She stopped for the best part of a minute and I just waited for her.

'It was *my* fault,' she said finally. I hold the phone to my ear, but I don't say anything. 'I was short with him. I was angry. He got to me. I think I made him do it.'

'It wasn't your fault.'

I hear myself. I'm talking to my daughters. I'm talking to Sam Nelson's little sister, nestled on her mother's bosom. I'm speaking to the dying man with the cheekbones wondering if he could have made his son better. I'm talking to Celia and Daksha. I'm talking to almost all of my patients who have acted out of character through illness. I'm talking to those who have experienced the suicide of a loved one.

I'm talking to Mum. *It wasn't your fault.*

I think back to Mrs Rockall and wonder if she still blames me for the death of her son. *It wasn't your fault, Ben.* But I'm not ready for that absolution. Not yet. Perhaps not ever. I'm not sure Elaine is either.

'It'd be a shame if the nursing profession lost you. We all do what we can, and you do more than most.'

'Do you think so?'

'You do more than anyone I know.'

I hear her take a sip of tea and look down at my coffee, steaming in the cold of the morning. 'Elaine,' I say.

'Yes.'

'It wasn't your fault.'

'Can we talk again later?' she says.

'Sure, Elaine.'

My coffee is lukewarm by the time I drink it. The first signs of dawn are the purple streaks touching the high clouds far away in the east. The birds chirp occasionally but there is no consensus, and the dawn chorus is still an hour away.

Mum used to love the birdsong. She was always up at this time. I look at my watch, notice the date and smile to myself.

Mum's birthday.

I was nine years old when I first made her a birthday cake. I had found her cookbook and it fell open at the right page. There were only two types of cake that she made, Christmas cake and chocolate cake, and they worked for all occasions. I followed the mixing instructions meticulously, baked it, decorated it with chocolate melted in a bain-marie and left it hidden under a tea towel overnight. The next morning at dawn, I stuck a candle in it, woke up big brother and together we burst into her bedroom singing 'Happy birthday to you . . .'

She was sitting on the side of the bed when we came in and I assumed back then that she had heard our preparations outside, but she hadn't. I realise now that she was lost in her own world, just staring into the distance. It looked like an effort of will before she gathered herself.

'Ben, Philip, what a wonderful cake.'

What's wrong, Mum?

Some years ago, when she could still understand things, I was talking to Mum about my work and she asked me about Mrs Johnson – Nerissa, the woman I tried and failed to give ECT. I told her she got better. She had known I was holding back; she knew I was trying to protect her.

I take a sip of coffee and I look at the sky again. The purple streaks have turned maroon. One or two more birds have joined the song, but it's still half-hearted.

Nerissa wrote to me after I left the job. I replied, more out of a sense of duty than to keep the correspondence going, and each time I got a letter, I'd call Aaron, the ward consultant, to tell him what she'd told me. 'I feel so awful . . . I want to die.'

That sort of thing.

A few years after the ECT 'incident', which by then had become folklore, Nerissa wrote to me again to invite me to the ward Christmas party.

'So, nothing bad in the letter,' I told Aaron. 'But what do you think, should I come?'

'It'd be great to see you.'

I met him on the way in and we had an awkward hug. It was like one of the prototype hugs with Dad. It had taken a while to perfect, a bit like his woodwork, but we had got there, he'd got there. Dad made the bench I'm sitting on. He loved being in the garage making things. I wish I made things. The last time I drove him home from hospital, we were talking about his death. We both knew it was a matter of days. To cheer him up, I told him that I wanted a new table for the dining room. For a little while his eyes brightened, and he asked me what sort of dimensions I was thinking about.

'Large, Dad, a really large refectory table.' And then I blurted out, 'Did I make you proud?'

'Yes,' he answered. And then he went quiet. 'Ben, you know the table you want?'

'Yes,' I answered cautiously.

'It'll need to be a small one.'

I pulled over and we hugged each other for the last time before the morphine drip went up. We were good at hugging by then.

I walked on to the ward for the Christmas party and said hello to the nurses I knew, but mostly they were new faces. 'Is that him?' I heard whispered. 'Buzzzz.'

I knew only two of the patients from my time there. Some had done well and been discharged, others had been transferred, one had died from a heart attack, and another was in prison.

'Guess who?' said Nerissa, coming up behind me and putting her hands over my eyes. I turned and we hugged. It was like seeing an old friend and I had to remind myself that she was a patient on the ward. We found two cans of Coke and a corner to sit together.

'How are you?' she asked.

'That's my line. I'm good, thanks. How's the writing?'

'Not really doing much. Can't focus. Can't get it together.' She looked around her. 'But that's why I'm here.'

She sounded worn out. There was a resignation in her voice that I hadn't heard before, a tiredness. Sometimes she simply stared into the distance.

Ben, tell Aaron to help her. She's given up. She's not going to make it.

She was on two antidepressants, an antipsychotic, a mood stabiliser, and she was seeing a therapist.

'I may have another course of ECT, but it's not worked as well as it used to. The days go on for ever. I'm not sure I can go on like this,' she confided. She caught my look. 'Yes, Aaron knows all about it. He keeps me on special obs when it's really bad.'

And then someone turned the music up. 'Nothing compares to you', she exclaimed. 'I've always loved Sinéad O'Connor.' She got up, took my hand, and dragged me, protesting, to the dining area where all the tables had been pushed to one side.

'I don't dance,' I cried, but she was having none of it.

I caught Aaron's eye for his approval, and he smiled at us. *It's OK*, he mouthed.

She put her head on my chest and we rocked back and forth, listening to one of the best songs ever written. When it ended, she asked me if I was happier than I had been. I must have looked surprised. 'One of the nurses said you were having problems.'

'Yes,' I answered. 'I'm fine, thanks.'

She looked at me carefully and it reminded me of Mum.

I take the last sip of coffee, taste the bitter grounds and stretch my arm out over the back of the bench. The wood has become smooth over the years; Dad used to sit in the same place. The sky moves from crimson to red with streaks of yellow.

'Can I join you?' says Libby, standing at the front door. I smile and nod and she sits and leans back on me. 'I woke up and you weren't there. I wondered if it was a black dog day?'

The first rays of light are just hitting the chimney pots on the house in front of us. 'No, actually, I'm happy.'

Libby turns, leans towards me and kisses me. 'You know today would have been your mother's birthday?'

I nod.

'Another coffee?'

'I'd love one.' I watch her go back in and push the door to.

Nerissa had snatched a kiss on my cheek and told me that she was going back to her room. 'I'm tired,' she explained. 'I get so exhausted.'

I watched her walk off and saw the door close behind her.

'Mum, I didn't see her again,' I say out loud. I'm sitting alone on Dad's bench. My bench now. 'They found her clothes on a beach two months later. There was no note. She'd just gone. You were right, it's not a laughing matter.'

I like to think she hears me, but by now the birds are singing so loudly. They're telling each other they are alive and they are celebrating life.

Deciding to be a doctor, part 2

My eldest daughter announced last year she is going to be a teacher and has just started a training programme. I am proud beyond belief of her achievements. She was always going to be a teacher. It's in our genes.

The youngest one announced last week that she wanted to be a doctor. I suppressed a smile. 'Really?' I said. 'You don't want to go into business?'

'No,' she said.

'What about law?'

'No,' she said again, slightly more emphatically.

'Military? They could sponsor you through medical school.'

'Interesting,' she said.

'Anyway, what sort of doctor are you going to be?' I asked.

'A trauma surgeon,' she announced.

I don't think I looked pained, I tried not to, anyway. 'Well, there's always time to think about it,' I heard myself saying.

'I have thought about it,' she retorted, and then she looked up at me and seemed to see me for the first time. 'You sound just like Gramps.'

Acknowledgements

Looking back, I realise the first draft of this book betrayed my elliptical style of communication. Fortunately my agent Mark Lucas, at the Soho Agency, was able to see something of value and nudged me to rewrite it. Thankfully, he also gave me a crash course on writing, and after he had inspired me, challenged me, beaten me into shape and gone through the first two drafts with a big red pen, he smiled a bit under his big moustache and sent it off to the publishers.

Just as well that Vicky Eribo, the publisher at Seven Dials, did not see the Post-it notes on every window, the scrunched-up paper in the bin, or the discarded Sharpies scattered on the desk. All she saw was a story with a message, and perhaps like the Eric Morecambe punchline, it had all the right notes, but not necessarily in the right order. She helped fix that.

I thank Mark and Vicky for their considerable support, skill and tutelage, and to their brilliant teams.

I am grateful to Kate Harrison for introducing me to the publishing world, and David Sillito and Sarah Bishop for their brilliant advice with the early narrative. You each helped me more than you can imagine. Thanks to my brother 'Phil', Simon Wilson and Mike Richardson who read early drafts and were kind enough to refrain from saying, 'Don't give up the day job.' And then there is 'Milton' – the shrinks' shrink, and one of life's good people.

I am indebted to Dave Emson for letting me reproduce Daksha's final note. I hope this book continues to 'fly the flag' for mental health and mental health workers. I like to think Daksha would approve.

If writing is a solitary occupation, psychiatry is the very antithesis. I have been blessed working with superb multi-disciplinary teams throughout my career. It's been a privilege to work with you all.

Of all the talented colleagues I have worked with, there are three consultant psychiatrists in particular who have shaped my professional life: Andrew Johns, Bernie Rosen and Janet Parrott. Thank you. Naturally, all the characters in the book are composites of people, but look carefully and you might just spot them.

Some years ago, I was walking with my wife, Libby, by Lake Annecy. She told me to write about my job and my experiences with the patients. The idea didn't germinate immediately, but she persevered and eventually the idea took hold and I put pen to paper. She read it, encouraged me and kept my medical humour in check. She has read the book out loud to me numerous times, supported me and generally brought her English degree and journalistic standards to the schoolboy who got a grade C in English and was so disappointed, he took it again, only to get another C.

This book is for Libby and my patients. It is as much your book as mine.